CAMBRIDGE
UNIVERSITY PRESS

CAMBRIDGE
Global English

for Cambridge Primary English as a Second Language

Teacher's Resource 3

Annie Altamirano, Helen Tiliouine,

Nicola Mabbott, Paul Drury & Bob Hubbard

Series Editor: Kathryn Harper

Shaftesbury Road, Cambridge CB2 8EA, United Kingdom

One Liberty Plaza, 20th Floor, New York, NY 10006, USA

477 Williamstown Road, Port Melbourne, VIC 3207, Australia

314–321, 3rd Floor, Plot 3, Splendor Forum, Jasola District Centre, New Delhi – 110025, India

103 Penang Road, #05–06/07, Visioncrest Commercial, Singapore 238467

Cambridge University Press & Assessment is a department of the University of Cambridge.

We share the University's mission to contribute to society through the pursuit of education, learning and research at the highest international levels of excellence.

www.cambridge.org
Information on this title: www.cambridge.org/9781108921657

First published 2014
Second edition 2021

20 19 18 17 16 15 14 13 12 11 10 9 8 7 6 5 4

Printed in Great Britain by Ashford Colour Press Ltd.

A catalogue record for this publication is available from the British Library

ISBN 978-1-108-92165-7 Paperback with Digital Access

Additional resources for this publication at www.cambridge.org/9781108921657

....

....

〉Contents

Digital resources

The following items are available on Cambridge GO. For more information on how to access and use your digital resource, please see inside front cover.

Active learning

Assessment for Learning

Developing learner language skills

Differentiation

Improving learning through questioning

Language awareness

Metacognition

Skills for Life

Letter for parents

Lesson plan template

Curriculum framework correlation

Scheme of work

Audio files and audioscripts

Progress tests 1–3 and answers

Progress report

Learner's Book answers

Workbook answers

Wordlist

You can download the following resources for each unit:

Differentiated worksheets and answers

Photocopiables

Sample answers

End-of-unit tests and answers

> Introduction

Welcome to the new edition of our Cambridge Global English series.

Since its launch, the series has been used by teachers and learners in over 100 countries for teaching the Cambridge Primary English as a Second Language curriculum framework.

This exciting new edition has been designed by talking to Global English teachers all over the world. We have worked hard to understand your needs and challenges, and then carefully designed and tested the best ways of meeting them.

As a result of this research, we've made some important changes to the series, whilst retaining the international and cross-curricular elements which you told us you valued. This Teacher's Resource has been carefully redesigned to make it easier for you to plan and teach the course. It is available in print for all Stages.

The series still has extensive digital and online support, including Digital Classroom which lets you share books with your class and play videos and audio. This Teacher's Resource also offers additional materials, including tests, available to download from Cambridge GO. (For more information on how to access and use your digital resource, please see inside front cover.)

The series uses successful teaching approaches like active learning and metacognition and takes a 21st-century Skills approach, with a focus on developing critical thinking skills. This Teacher's Resource gives you full guidance on how to integrate them into your classroom.

Formative assessment opportunities help you to get to know your learners better, with clear learning intentions and success criteria as well as an array of assessment techniques, including advice on self and peer assessment. This Teacher's Resource also includes sample answers to writing tasks, together with author comments to help you and your learners understand what 'good' looks like.

Clear, consistent differentiation ensures that all learners are able to progress in the course with tiered activities, differentiated worksheets, open-ended project tasks and advice about supporting learners' different needs.

All our resources are written for teachers and learners who use English as a second or additional language. In this edition of Global English we focus on four aspects of language:

• there is more grammar presentation and practice in the Workbook and on the Digital Classroom

• we have introduced scaffolded writing lessons with models of a range of text types

• we have included a range of literature

• and we have worked to ease the transition between stages, especially between primary and secondary.

We hope you enjoy using this course.

Eddie Rippeth

Head of Primary and Lower Secondary Publishing, Cambridge University Press

About the authors

Elly Schottman

Elly Schottman is a former elementary teacher, reading specialist and curriculum developer. She has worked for a range of publishers creating English language learning programmes for young learners. She also works for the children's division of US public television, creating early literacy, science, maths and global awareness materials for children, families and teachers. Elly particularly enjoys creating curriculum for young learners that encourages curiosity, creativity, collaboration and problem solving. *Cambridge Global English* has provided her a wonderful opportunity to help children develop English language skills while actively exploring science, maths and geography in the world around them.

Kathryn Harper

Kathryn Harper is a freelance writer, publisher and consultant. Early on in her career, she worked as an English Language teacher in France and Canada. As an international publisher at Macmillan and Oxford University Press, she published teaching materials for Europe, the Middle East, Africa, Pakistan and Latin America. Her freelance work includes publishing reading schemes, writing electronic materials, language courses and stories for markets around the world. Her primary French whiteboard course for Nelson Thornes, *Rigolo*, won the 2008 BETT award. She also volunteers as an English teacher for child refugees and a mentor for young African writers.

Paul Drury

Paul Drury is a freelance writer and consultant. He spent nearly 10 years teaching a wide range of levels and ages in Spain, Venezuela and the UK. After that he entered the world of publishing where he commissioned and worked on several best-selling preschool and primary titles. He has visited hundreds of classrooms and spoken to hundreds of teachers. He now spends his time writing materials and speaking on his special area of interest: Creativity. Please visit his website to find out more: www.nurturingcreativity.org

Annie Altamirano

Annie Altamirano holds an MA in ELT and Applied Linguistics, (University of London). She has over 30 years' experience as a teacher and teacher trainer. She has given teacher-training workshops in Europe, Asia and Latin America and has served as an examiner. She has worked with a wide range of publishers and written materials for children and adolescents. Her latest published work includes Cambridge Global English Teacher's Resource and Cambridge Grammar & Writing skills Levels 7 – 9 Teacher's Resource published by Cambridge University Press. She has visited schools in Colombia, Argentina, Brazil, Turkey, Indonesia and China to learn more about teachers' needs and expectations. Since her early years as a teacher, Annie has integrated the use of film, art, poetry and diverse visual elements in her classes and materials as a way of helping students develop their linguistic skills as well as their creativity. She shares her ideas in her workshops and on the posts on her website Blogging Crazy http://bloggingcrazy-annie.blogspot.com.es/.

Helen Tiliouine

Helen Tiliouine is an experienced teacher and writer of test materials. She has been involved in writing a range of ESL and ELT test materials, including *Cambridge Global English Teacher's Resource tests, Cambridge English Prepare! Test generator*, and *Complete First for Schools*. She is an experienced examiner.

Nicola Mabbott

Nicola Mabbott is a linguist who began her teaching career in Nottingham, England in 1998, teaching English as a Foreign Language to young adults. Since then, she has taught learners of all abilities and ages (from kindergarten age to retired adults) in Italy. She also regularly works as a Tutor in English for Academic Purposes.

Nicola has been writing for a variety publishers in the UK and Italy – mostly resources for teachers of EFL to young learners and adolescents - for over 10 years. These resources include games, quizzes, communicative activities, worksheets, self-study resources, short stories and reading and listening activities for school course books.

Nicola has a passion for language and languages and also works as a translator.

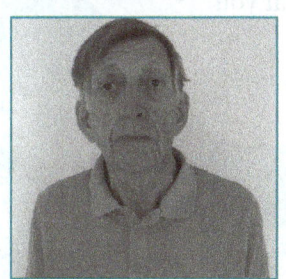

Bob Hubbard

Bob Hubbard's first teaching job was in a primary school in Dagenham, teaching a mixed ability/mixed age/mixed ethnicity group. Subsequently he became a teacher trainer at Hilderstone College, before teaching abroad in the Middle East.

He then worked for the British Council in Yemen and Somalia, writing English language textbooks for the host governments, and training their teachers to implement them.

Bob has worked as an examiner and item writer for over 30 years.

At Anglia Ruskin University, he taught graduate students, specialising in speaking and listening.

Alison Sharpe

Alison Sharpe is a freelance teacher, writer and publisher. She started her career teaching English in Japan, Taiwan and the UK. She then worked for many years at Cambridge University Press and Oxford University Press publishing learning, teaching, exams and assessment materials for teachers and students all around the world. As a freelancer, she has been involved in a wide range of projects, including developing online teacher training materials, the assessment of children's writing and editing language learning materials for young learners and adults. She is also currently a part time tutor of academic literacy at Oxford University's Department of Continuing Education.

Caroline Linse

Caroline Linse is a senior lecturer in Teaching English to Speakers of Other Languages at Queen's University, Belfast. Caroline has been a teacher, teacher educator, materials developer, researcher and language advocate for many years. She began her career as a kindergarten teacher in Mexico City and since then has been fortunate to have worked with learners and teachers in the USA (including rural Alaska), American Samoa, the Baltic Republics, Belarus, Korea and Northern Ireland. In addition, she has given workshops in many other countries including Bahrain, Oman, Taiwan, China, Ukraine, Peru, Guatemala, and Tunisia. Her academic publications draw upon her experience and research and are intended to advance the use of contextually embedded language rich instruction. She received her doctorate in education from the Harvard Graduate School of Education.

> How to use this series

All of the components in the series are designed to work together.

The Learner's Book is designed for learners to use in class with guidance from the teacher. It offers full coverage of the curriculum framework. The cross-curricular content supports success across the curriculum, with an international outlook. There is a focus on critical thinking, reading and writing skills with a literature section in every unit and a scaffolded approach to the development of written skills, with model texts. End-of-unit projects provide opportunities for formative assessment and differentiation so that you can support each individual learners' needs.

Digital Access with all the material from the book in digital form, is available via Cambridge GO.

The write-in Workbook offers opportunities to help learners consolidate what they have learned in the Learner's Book and is ideal for use in class or as homework. It provides plenty of differentiated grammar practice at three tiers so that learners have choice and can support or extend their learning, as required. Activities based on Cambridge Learner Corpus data give unique insight into common errors made by learners.

Digital Access with all the material from the book in digital form, is available via Cambridge GO.

In the print Teacher's Resource you'll find everything you need to deliver the course, including teaching ideas, answers and differentiation and formative assessment support. Each Teacher's Resource includes:

- a print book with detailed teaching notes for each topic

- a digital edition with all the material from the book plus editable unit and progress tests, differentiated worksheets and communicative games.

The Digital Classroom is for teachers to use at the front of the class. It includes digital versions of the Learner's Book and Workbook, complete with pop-up answers, helping you give instructions easily and check answers. Zoom in, highlight and annotate text, and support better learning with videos, grammar slideshows and interactive activities.

A letter to parents, explaining the course, is available to download from Cambridge GO (as part of this Teacher's Resource).

> How to use this Teacher's Resource

This Teacher's Resource contains both general guidance and teaching notes that help you to deliver the content in our Cambridge Global English resources. Some of the material is provided as downloadable files, available on **Cambridge GO**. (For more information about how to access and use your digital resource, please see inside front cover.) See the Contents page for details of all the material available to you, both in this book and through Cambridge GO.

Teaching notes

This book provides **teaching notes** for each unit of the Learner's Book and Workbook. Each set of teaching notes contains the following features to help you deliver the unit.

The **Unit plan** summarises the lessons covered in the unit, including the number of learning hours recommended for the lesson, an outline of the learning content and the Cambridge resources that can be used to deliver the lesson.

Lesson	Approximate number of learning hours	Outline of learning content	Learning objective	Resources
1 Celebrating together	1.5–2.5	Ask and answer questions.	3Ld.01 3Ld.02 3Sc.03 3Sc.06 3Rd.01 3Ug.01	Learner's Book Lesson 1.1 Workbook Lesson 1.1 ⬇ Photocopiable 4 **Digital Classroom:** Video and activity sheet – Celebrating the New Year in China; Activity – Activity sounds

The **Background knowledge** feature provides information which helps the teacher to familiarise themselves with the cross-curricular and international content in the unit.

Learners' prior knowledge can be informally assessed through the **Getting started** feature in the Learner's Book.

The **Teaching skills focus** feature covers a teaching skill and suggests how to implement it in the unit.

BACKGROUND KNOWLEDGE

It is useful to have a good understanding of a range different literary genres (historical fiction, traditional folk and fairy tales and myths, science fiction, mystery stories, fantasy fiction, adventure stories, etc.).

TEACHING SKILLS FOCUS

The challenge with active learning is to stop yourself telling learners things that they could discover for themselves.

Reflecting the Learner's Book, each unit consists of multiple lessons.

At the start of each lesson, the **Learning plan** table includes the learning objectives, learning intentions and success criteria that are covered in the lesson.

It can be helpful to share learning intentions and success criteria with your learners at the start of a lesson so that they can begin to take responsibility for their own learning.

LEARNING PLAN

Learning objectives	Learning intentions	Success criteria
3Ld.01, 3Ld.02	• **Listening:** Listen to a description of a festival; listen for specific information; listen for information and instructions.	• Learners can sing a song.

There are often **common misconceptions** associated with particular grammar points. These are listed, along with suggestions for identifying evidence of the misconceptions in your class and suggestions for how to overcome them. At Cambridge University Press, we have unique access to the Cambridge Learner Corpus to help us identify common errors for key language groups.

Misconception	How to identify	How to overcome
Learners add an unnecessary subject pronoun where an imperative form is needed. For example: *You don't forget book. Please you come to my birthday party.*	Write a correct sentence and an incorrect one. Ask learners to compare the sentences. Ask: *What's the difference between the sentences? Which is correct?* Circle the unnecessary pronoun. Say: *Do we need this? Why not? Who am I giving this order to?* Elicit answers.	Learners read the sentence and ask themselves these questions: *Are they giving an order? If they are, who are they talking to? Is it necessary to add the pronoun?*

For each lesson, there is a selection of **starter ideas**, **main teaching ideas** and **plenary ideas**. You can pick out individual ideas and mix and match them depending on the needs of your class. The activities include suggestions for how they can be differentiated or used for assessment. **Homework ideas** are also provided, with home-school link suggestions to enable learners to continue their learning at home.

Starter ideas

Team players (15–20 minutes)

- In order to focus learners' attention back on the topic of team activities, ask the class what team activities they like to do at school and in their English class, for example play games, look for information, do an exercise together.
- Elicit the meaning of 'team'. Ask: *How many children are in a team – one, two, more? And in a basketball team? What sports do we play in teams? How many players are there in each team?*
- This lesson incorporates a review of numbers (1–100) for the first time in Stage 3. You could play a few rounds of Bingo to cover these numbers again. Prepare one blank bingo grid for each learner, and numbers 1–100 on pieces of paper. Put the numbers in a bag or small box. Ask learners to write numbers 1–100 in their grid. Randomly call out the numbers and learners cross out the numbers on their Bingo grids. The winner is the first learner to get a line or full house.

The **Language background** feature contains information to help you present the grammar in the unit.

The **Cross-curricular links** feature provides suggestions for linking to other subject areas.

> **Differentiation ideas:** This feature provides suggestions for how activities can be differentiated to suit the needs of your class.

> **Critical thinking opportunity:** This feature provides suggestions for embedding critical thinking and other 21st-century skills into your teaching and learning.

> **Assessment ideas:** This feature highlights opportunities for formative assessment during your teaching.

> **Digital Classroom:** If you have access to Digital Classroom, these links will suggest when to use the various multimedia enhancements and interactive activities.

Answers: Answers to Learner's Book exercises can be found integrated within the lesson plans and Learner's Book and Workbook answer keys are also available to download.

Note: Some texts used in the Learner's Book and Workbook have been abridged, so please be aware that learners may not be presented with the full version of the text.

Digital resources to download

This Teacher's Resource includes a range of digital materials that you can download from Cambridge GO. (For more information about how to access and use your digital resource, please see inside front cover.) This icon ⬇ indicates material that is available from Cambridge GO.

Helpful documents for planning include:

- **Letter for parents:** a template letter for parents, introducing the Cambridge Global English resources.
- **Lesson plan template:** a Word document that you can use for planning your lessons. Examples of completed lesson plans are also provided.
- **Curriculum framework correlation:** a table showing how the Cambridge Global English resources map to the Cambridge Primary English as a Second Language curriculum framework.
- **Scheme of work:** a suggested scheme of work that you can use to plan teaching throughout the year.

Each unit includes:

- **Differentiated worksheets:** these worksheets cater for different abilities. Worksheet A is designed to support learners who don't feel confident about the topic. Worksheet B is designed for learners who have a general understanding of the topic. Worksheet C is aimed at learners who want a challenge. Answer sheets are provided.
- **Photocopiable resources:** these include communicative language game, templates and any other materials that support the learning objectives of the unit.
- **Sample answers:** these contain teacher comments, which allow learners and teachers to assess what 'good' looks like in order to inform their writing.
- **Project checklists:** checklists for learners to use to evaluate their writing and project work.

Additionally, the Teacher's Resource includes:

- **Progress test 1:** a test to use at the beginning of the year to discover the level that learners are working at. The results of this test can inform your planning. Answers are provided.
- **Progress test 2:** a test to use after learners have studied Units 1-5 in the Learner's Book. You can use this test to check whether there are areas that you need to go over again. Answers are provided.
- **Progress test 3:** a test to use after learners have studied all units in the Learner's Book. You can use this test to check whether there are areas that you need to go over again, and to help inform your planning for the next year. Answers are provided.
- **Progress report:** a document to help you formatively assess your classes' progress against the learning intentions.
- **Audioscripts:** available as downloadable files.
- **Answers to Learner's Book questions**
- **Answers to Workbook questions**
- **Wordlists:** an editable list of key vocabulary for each unit.

In addition, you can find more detailed information about teaching approaches.

 Audio is available for download from Cambridge GO (as part of this Teacher's Resource and as part of the digital resources for the Learner's Book and Workbook).

 Video is available through the Digital Classroom.

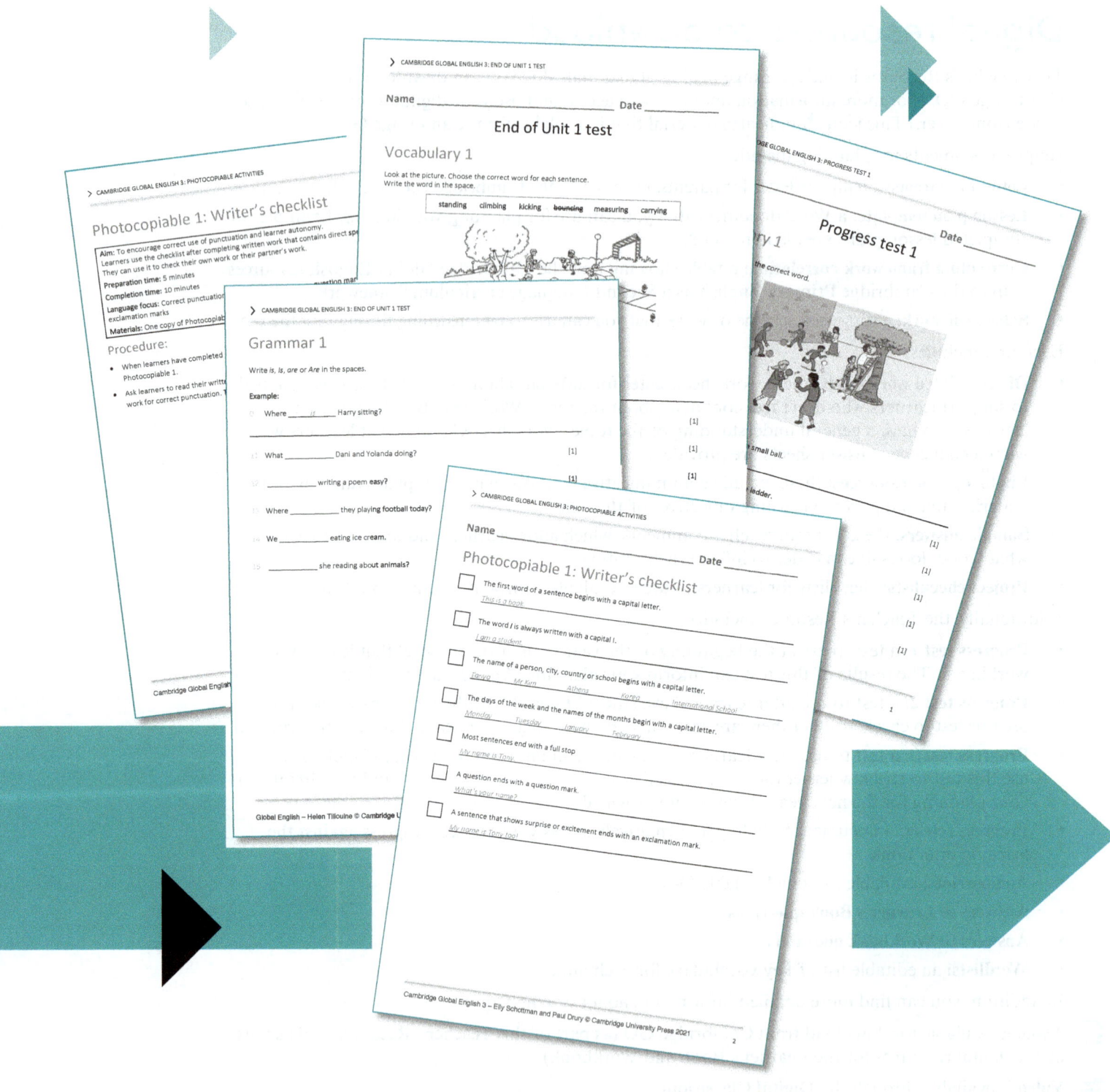

> CAMBRIDGE GLOBAL ENGLISH 3: PHOTOCOPIABLE ACTIVITIES

Photocopiable 1: Writer's checklist

Aim: To encourage correct use of punctuation and learner autonomy.
Learners use the checklist after completing written work that contains direct speech.
They can use it to check their own work or their partner's work.

Preparation time: 5 minutes
Completion time: 10 minutes
Language focus: Correct punctuation,
exclamation marks
Materials: One copy of Photocopiable

Procedure:

- When learners have completed
  Photocopiable 1.
- Ask learners to read their writt
  work for correct punctuation. T

Cambridge Global Engli

> CAMBRIDGE GLOBAL ENGLISH 3: END OF UNIT 1 TEST

Name _____ Date _____

End of Unit 1 test

Vocabulary 1

Look at the picture. Choose the correct word for each sentence.
Write the word in the space.

| standing | climbing | kicking | ~~bouncing~~ | measuring | carrying |

> CAMBRIDGE GLOBAL ENGLISH 3: END OF UNIT 1 TEST

Grammar 1

Write *is*, *Is*, *are* or *Are* in the spaces.

Example:

0   Where _____ _it_ ____ Harry sitting?

_____

1   What _____ Dani and Yolanda doing?   [1]

2   _____ writing a poem **easy?**   [1]

3   Where _____ they playing football today?   [1]

4   We _____ eating ice cream.   [1]

5   _____ she reading about **animals?**   [1]

Global English – Helen Tiliouine © Cambridge U

> CAMBRIDGE GLOBAL ENGLISH 3: PROGRESS TEST 1

Progress test 1 ____ Date ____

ry 1

the correct word.

small ball.

ladder.

[1]
[1]
[1]
[1]
[1]

1

> CAMBRIDGE GLOBAL ENGLISH 3: PHOTOCOPIABLE ACTIVITIES

Name _____
Date _____

Photocopiable 1: Writer's checklist

☐ The first word of a sentence begins with a capital letter.
   This is a book.

☐ The word *I* is always written with a capital I.
   I am a student.

☐ The name of a person, city, country or school begins with a capital letter.
   Tanya   _Mr Kim_   _Athens_   _Korea_   _International School_

☐ The days of the week and the names of the months begin with a capital letter.
   Monday   _Tuesday_   _January_   _February_

☐ Most sentences end with a full stop
   My name is Tony.

☐ A question ends with a question mark.
   What's your name?

☐ A sentence that shows surprise or excitement ends with an exclamation mark.
   My name is Tony too!

Cambridge Global English 3 – Elly Schottman and Paul Drury © Cambridge University Press 2021   2

> About the curriculum framework

This series supports the Cambridge Primary English as a Second Language curriculum framework from 2020. You should always refer to the appropriate curriculum framework document to confirm the details of the framework and for more information. Visit www.cambridgeinternational.orglprimary to find out more.

The Cambridge Primary English as a Second Language curriculum framework is designed to enable young learners from an ESL background (who speak little or no English at home) to communicate effectively and with confidence in English. Cambridge Global English is designed to deliver this curriculum. It does this by developing the skills to access and understand a wide range of information, media and texts. It achieves this by focussing on active learning, developing critical thinking skills and intellectual engagement with a range of topics.

Our scheme is designed to fully support teachers to deliver the framework by providing an integrated approach to planning and teaching to develop effective communication skills in English. The five strands, and their respective learning objectives, work together to support the development of knowledge, skills and understanding in:

- Reading
- Writing
- Use of English
- Listening
- Speaking.

The new curriculum framework includes some important changes. For example, there is a new sub-strand of learning objectives within the Speaking strand, with new learning objectives concerning accuracy of pronunciation.

> About the assessment

Information concerning the assessment of the Cambridge Primary English as a Second Language curriculum frameworks is available on the Cambridge Assessment International Education website: **www.cambridgeinternational.org/primary**.

The resources provide support for the Cambridge Primary English as a Second Language curriculum framework from 2020.

> Approaches to learning and teaching

The following are the teaching approaches underpinning our course content and how we understand and define them.

Active learning

Active learning is a teaching approach that places student learning at its centre. It focuses on how students learn, not just on what they learn. We, as teachers, need to encourage learners to 'think hard', rather than passively receive information. Active learning encourages learners to take responsibility for their learning and supports them in becoming independent and confident learners in school and beyond.

Assessment for Learning

Assessment for Learning (AfL) is a teaching approach that generates feedback which can be used to improve learners' performance. Learners become more involved in the learning process and, from this, gain confidence in what they are expected to learn and to what standard. We, as teachers, gain insights into a learner's level of understanding of a particular concept or topic, which helps to inform how we support their progression.

Differentiation

Differentiation is usually presented as a teaching approach where teachers think of learners as individuals and learning as a personalised process. Whilst precise definitions can vary, typically the core aim of differentiation is viewed as ensuring that all learners, no matter their ability, interest or context, make progress towards their learning intentions. It is about using different approaches and appreciating the differences in learners to help them make progress. Teachers therefore need to be responsive, and willing and able to adapt their teaching to meet the needs of their learners.

Language awareness

For many learners, English is an additional language. It might be their second or perhaps their third language. Depending on the school context, students might be learning all or just some of their subjects through English.

For all learners, regardless of whether they are learning through their first language or an additional language, language is a vehicle for learning. It is through language that students access the learning intentions of the lesson and communicate their ideas. It is our responsibility, as teachers, to ensure that language doesn't present a barrier to learning.

Metacognition

Metacognition describes the processes involved when learners plan, monitor, evaluate and make changes to their own learning behaviours. These processes help learners to think about their own learning more explicitly and ensure that they are able to meet a learning goal that they have identified themselves or that we, as teachers, have set.

Skills for Life

How do we prepare learners to succeed in a fast-changing world? To collaborate with people from around the globe? To create innovation as technology increasingly takes over routine work? To use advanced thinking skills in the face of more complex challenges? To show resilience in the face of constant change? At Cambridge, we are responding to educators who have asked for a way to understand how all these different approaches to life skills and competencies relate to their teaching. We have grouped these skills into six main Areas of Competency that can be incorporated into teaching, and have examined the different stages of the learning journey and how these competencies vary across each stage.

These six key areas are:

*   Creativity – finding new ways of doing things, and solutions to problems
*   Collaboration – the ability to work well with others
*   Communication – speaking and presenting confidently and participating effectively in meetings
*   Critical thinking – evaluating what is heard or read, and linking ideas constructively
*   Learning to learn – developing the skills to learn more effectively
*   Social responsibilities – contributing to social groups, and being able to talk to and work with people from other cultures.

Cambridge learner and teacher attributes

This course helps develop the following Cambridge learner and teacher attributes.

Cambridge learners	Cambridge teachers
Confident in working with information and ideas – their own and those of others.	**Confident** in teaching their subject and engaging each student in learning.
Responsible for themselves, responsive to and respectful of others.	**Responsible** for themselves, responsive to and respectful of others.
Reflective as learners, developing their ability to learn.	**Reflective** as learners themselves, developing their practice.
Innovative and equipped for new and future challenges.	**Innovative** and equipped for new and future challenges.
Engaged intellectually and socially, ready to make a difference.	**Engaged** intellectually, professionally and socially, ready to make a difference.

Reproduced from Developing the Cambridge learner attributes with permission from Cambridge Assessment International Education.

More information about these approaches to learning and teaching is available to download from Cambridge GO (as part of this Teacher's Resource).

> Setting up for success

Our aim is to support better learning in the classroom with resources that allow for increased learner autonomy while supporting teachers to facilitate student learning. Through an active learning approach of enquiry-led tasks, open-ended questions and opportunities to externalise thinking in a variety of ways, learners will develop analysis, evaluation and problem-solving skills.

Some ideas to consider to encourage an active learning environment are as follows:

- Set up seating to make group work easy.
- Create classroom routines to help learners to transition between different types of activity efficiently, e.g. move from pair work to listening to the teacher to independent work.
- Source mini-whiteboards, which allow you to get feedback from all learners rapidly.
- Start a portfolio for each learner, keeping key pieces of work to show progress at parent–teacher days.
- Have a display area with learner work and vocab flashcards.

Planning for active learning

We recommend the following approach to planning. A blank lesson plan template is available to download to help with this approach.

1   **Plan learning intentions and success criteria:** these are the most important feature of the lesson. Teachers and learners need to know where they are going in order to plan a route to get there.

2   **Plan language support:** think about strategies to help learners overcome the language demands of the lesson so that language doesn't present a barrier to learning.

3   **Plan starter activities:** include a 'hook' or starter to engage learners using imaginative strategies. This should be an activity where all learners are active from the start of the lesson.

4   **Plan main activities:** during the lesson, try to: give clear instructions, with modelling and written support; coordinate logical and orderly transitions between activities; make sure that learning is active and all learners are engaged ; create opportunities for discussion around key concepts.

5   **Plan assessment for learning and differentiation:** use a wide range of Assessment for Learning techniques and adapt activities to a wide range of abilities. Address misconceptions at appropriate points and give meaningful oral and written feedback which learners can act on.

6   **Plan reflection and plenary:** at the end of each activity and at the end of each lesson, try to: ask learners to reflect on what they have learned compared to the beginning of the lesson; build on and extend this learning.

7   **Plan homework:** if setting homework, it can be used to consolidate learning from the previous lesson or to prepare for the next lesson.

To help planning using this approach, a blank lesson plan template is available to download from Cambridge GO (as part of this Teacher's Resource).

For more guidance on setting up for success and planning, please explore the Professional Development pages of our website **www.cambridge.org/education/PD**

> 1 Working together

Unit plan

Lesson	Approximate number of learning hours	Outline of learning content	Learning objectives	Resources
1 Celebrating together	1.5–2.5	Ask and answer questions.	3Ld.01 3Ld.02 3Sc.03 3Sc.06 3Rd.01 3Ug.01	Learner's Book Lesson 1.1 Workbook Lesson 1.1 ⬇ Photocopiable 4 **Digital Classroom:** Video and activity sheet – Celebrating the New Year in China; Activity – Activity sounds
2 Let's play together	1.5–2.5	Give and follow directions.	3Sc.04 3Sc.05 3Rd.02 3Rd.03 3Wc.01 3Ug.02	Learner's Book Lesson 1.2 Workbook Lesson 1.2 ⬇ Photocopiable 5 **Digital Classroom:** Activity – What should you say?
3 Team fun	2.0–3.0	Talk about what people are doing.	3Ld.04 3Sc.04 3Sc.05 3Rd.01 3Ug.05 3Uv.01	Learner's Book Lesson 1.3 Workbook Lesson 1.3 **Digital Classroom:** Grammar presentation – Present continuous; Activity – Rhyming words
4 Let's put on a play!	1.45–3.0	Write about things we like and don't like.	3Sc.02 3Rd.01 3Rd.02 3Wca.02 3Wca.03 3Wca.05	Learner's Book Lesson 1.4 Workbook Lesson 1.4 ⬇ Sample answer for Unit 1 ⬇ Photocopiable 1 ⬇ Photocopiable 6 ⬇ Differentiated worksheets 1A, B and C **Digital Classroom:** Video and activity sheet – Let's put on a play; Activity – What do you like doing?
5 *Whose team are you on?*	2.25–3.5	Read and act out a play.	3Ld.04 3Lo.01 3So.01 3Sor.02 3Ro.01 3Wc.03	Learner's Book Lesson 1.5 Workbook Lesson 1.5 ⬇ Photocopiable 1 **Digital Classroom:** Activity – Whose team are you on?

(continued)

Lesson	Approximate number of learning hours	Outline of learning content	Learning objectives	Resources
6 Project challenge	1.0–1.5	Make a 'follow the instructions' or 'find the animal' game	3Sc.05 3Sc.07 3Rd.02 3Wca.02 3Wca.03 3Wc.01	Learner's Book Lesson 1.6 Workbook Lesson 1.6 ⬇ Photocopiable 1 ⬇ Photocopiable 7
7 What do you know now?	0.45–1.0	Self-assessment and reflection.		Learner's Book Lesson 1.7

Cross-unit resources

⬇ Unit 1 Audioscripts

⬇ End of Unit 1 test

⬇ Progress test 1

⬇ Unit 1 Progress report

⬇ Unit 1 Wordlist

BACKGROUND KNOWLEDGE

New Year around the world

In Lesson 1, learners read and talk about New Year celebrations.

Most countries around the world use the Gregorian calendar with 365 days and 12 months. Eleven of the months have 30 or 31 days and one – February – has 28 days. Every four years, February has 29 days. In the countries that use the Gregorian calendar, the year ends on 31st December and begins on 1st January, New Year's Day.

Some cultures celebrate New Year's Day on a different day because they follow lunar, solar or other calendars. These countries are China, Korea, Indonesia, Iran, Sri Lanka, India, Israel and Islamic countries.

Chinese New Year

Chinese New Year is based on the Chinese lunar calendar, and is a very special occasion. Families prepare the celebrations seven days before New Year's Eve. They clean their homes to remove any bad luck from the old year. They also buy decorations, presents and new clothes – all of which are mostly red, as red is seen as a lucky colour in China.

The Dragon Dance

This is a form of traditional dance performed in Chinese culture. It is usually performed during Chinese New Year. Dragons are a symbol of Chinese culture, and they are believed to bring good luck. The longer the dragon is in the dance, the more luck it will bring.

The lunar calendar

The lunar calendar is based on the phases of the Moon. There are 29 days, 12 hours and 44 minutes in a lunar month – which is the time it takes for the Moon to go around the Earth. The Islamic calendar follows the lunar calendar, and is calculated from one crescent moon to the next crescent moon.

TEACHING SKILLS FOCUS

Active learning

Keeping learners actively involved in the learning process is probably one of the biggest challenges that teachers face, and traditional teaching methods seldom help achieve that. Therefore, it is necessary to look for alternative approaches, such as active learning.

Active learning is an instructional approach that aims to actively engage learners with the learning through a variety of activities such as discussions, think-pair-share, problem solving and role play, among others.

The benefits of using this approach include:

- it helps to promote higher-order thinking skills
- it engages learners in deep learning – detecting patterns, applying knowledge and skills to new contexts or in creative ways, and developing critical thinking
- it helps learners to transfer knowledge better
- it increases motivation
- it improves interpersonal communication.

Your challenge

Finding the best way to keep learners actively involved can be quite challenging at times. In each unit of the Learner's Book, opportunities to practise and develop strategies that keep learners involved are highlighted.

Look through Unit 1 and highlight opportunities for introducing some of the ideas below. Then use these to help learners to learn actively.

Implementation ideas:

1 Choose meaningful activities. When planning your class or what you want your learners to do, ask yourself:
  - What is the most important thing my class should learn from the lesson/activity?

- What misconceptions or difficulties do they usually have (or could have) with this content/activity?
- What kind of practice will help learners to prepare for the next step or a more advanced stage?

2 Avoid asking simple recall questions. Instead, choose meaningful questions that will:
  - challenge learners to elaborate and provide explanations, reasons or evidence, e.g. *What makes you say that? Can you give us an example? What do you mean by that?*
  - discover alternative points of view, e.g. *Can anyone give another / an alternative explanation? Can anyone add to this? Is there another way of doing/explaining this?*
  - challenge learners' assumptions, e.g. *Is this always the case? Does this always happen in this way?*
  - explore consequences, e.g. *What would happen if …?*

3 Invite the class to respond by providing alternative solutions or viewpoints.

4 Keep activities short and meaningful. If you allow an activity to lag, learners will lose interest.

5 After learners have worked in pairs or groups, provide a conclusion to the activity.

6 Give clear instructions and share the aims of the lesson/activity with the class.

As you continue with the following units, tick off the relevant points where you can introduce active learning strategies.

Reflection

How successful was the implementation of these ideas? How can you improve them?

1.1 Think about it: Celebrating together

LEARNING PLAN

Learning objectives	Learning intentions	Success criteria
3Ld.01, 3Ld.02	• **Listening:** Listen to a description of a festival; listen for specific information; listen for information and instructions.	• Learners can sing a song.
3Sc.03, 3Sc.06	• **Speaking:** Describe a festival; practise topic vocabulary; talk about festivals; sing a song; give opinions; describe what people are doing.	• Learners can listen and understand the description of a festival.
3Rd.01	• **Reading:** Read about the Dragon Dance; read and follow directions.	• Learners can give opinions.
		• Learners can describe what people are doing.
3Ug.01	• **Language focus:** Questions: *Where …?, What …?, How …?, Who …?*	• Learners can read and understand a text about the Dragon Dance.
	• **Vocabulary:** *up, down, left, right, cymbals, slowly, quickly, twist, turn, dance, easy, hard, ladder, paper, pole, rings, rope, swing, stairs*	• Learners can follow instructions.

21st-century skills

Critical thinking opportunity: Compare and contrast festivals.

Communication: Ask for clarification when they have difficulties in understanding what others have said, take turns appropriately in a conversation, interrupt others politely.

Values: Work as a team.

Materials: Learner's Book pages 11–13; Workbook pages 8–9; map of the world; wall calendar; **Photocopiable 4**

Starter ideas

All together! (5–10 minutes)

- Ask each learner what sports they like. Elicit some answers.
- Discuss with the class if they are team sports or individual sports.
- Ask learners what they prefer to do in class: work on their own or in groups with other learners. Elicit some answers. Ask them about things they can do with other learners.

Getting started (10–15 minutes)

- Focus on the photograph on page 11 of the Learner's Book. Then read questions a–c and elicit answers from the class.

- You could add some extra questions, such as: *What are the children wearing? What do you think they are celebrating? What days do you celebrate at school or at home? How do you work together with your classmates or family to prepare for those celebrations?*

- Supply additional vocabulary if necessary, for example *practise, parade.*

- Ask learners where they think the photograph was taken. Why do they think so? Elicit ideas.

Answers

Learner's own answers.

Sing along! *Working together* (10–15 minutes)

- **Values:** Ask: *What can we achieve when we work together?* Elicit ideas.

- Encourage the class to think about cooperation and collaboration, and how working together helps to develop friendship, loyalty and responsibility.

- Tell the class they are going to listen to a song. Give each learner a copy of **Photocopiable 4**: Sing along! *Working together*.

- Play the song at least twice. Ask the class what it is about. Elicit answers.

- Play the song again and encourage learners to clap along. You could also add gestures to it, for example join hands for *Working together / Helping each other,* mimic laughter for *laughing together,* touch your head for *share ideas,* etc.

- Sing the song and encourage learners to join in.

Audioscript: Track 01

Learner's Book page 11

Working together

Chorus:

Working together, getting better and better

Helping each other as we go along.

Learning together, laughing together,

Planning and building – together we're strong.

Verse:

We can tidy the room, put on a play,

Build a space station, plan a parade.

We can make the world better, share ideas on the way.

Working, building, learning ... let's start today!

Chorus:

Working together, getting better and better

Helping each other as we go along.

Learning together, laughing together,

Planning and building – together we're strong.

⟩ **Digital Classroom:** Use the video 'Celebrating the New Year in China' and the activity sheet to explore the subject of Chinese New Year. The i button will explain how to use the video and activity sheet.

Main teaching ideas

1 Talk about the picture (15–20 minutes)

- Ask learners what festivals they celebrate in their country or region. Ask if they wear special clothes or make special decorations. Encourage the class to describe them.

- Ask the class how they celebrate the New Year. Elicit suggestions from the class.

- Open the Learner's Book at page 12 and focus on the picture. Read the instructions.

- Ask learners to describe what they think the people in the picture are doing and what they are wearing, etc. Supply additional vocabulary as needed, for example *pole, cymbals*.

- Ask learners when they celebrate New Year in their country. Is New Year celebrated on the same day everywhere? Encourage learners to find out when it is celebrated in different parts of the world, for example China, India, Israel, Europe and the Americas. Bring a large wall calendar and ask learners to circle and label the days when New Year is celebrated in different parts of the world.

CROSS-CURRICULAR LINK

Geography

Display the map of the world and ask the class to find China on the map. What do learners know about this country?

If learners are from China, bring a map of the country and ask them to find their city and province on the map.

Answers

Learner's own answers.

2 Listen. Choose a question. Listen for the answer, then share it with your class (10–20 minutes)

- Ask learners to read the questions and choose one. Explain that you are going to play the audio and they have to listen for the answer to that question.

- Play the audio a few times.

- Ask the class who has chosen the first question. Ask learners to share the information with the class.

- Proceed in the same way with the other questions.

- You may wish to ask learners to write the answers on the board. The class copies them in their notebooks.

- Play the audio again. Focus on the last part of the audio. Elicit the meaning of *easy* and *hard*.

- Discuss the meaning of *practise*, i.e. to do something again and again so that you get better at it.

- Ask the class to give examples of things they can practise, for example speaking English, playing the piano, playing football, etc.

- Talk about the English expression '*Practice makes perfect*'. Ask learners what they think it means.

- **Listening strategy:** Play the audio (at least) twice. The first time, learners could listen to understand the gist of the narration. Then have them choose a question. The second time that children listen, they will be listening for specific information (the answer to the question they chose).

> **Critical thinking opportunity:** This activity requires learners to focus on a question and look for specific information. Focusing on one question at a time helps them select the information they really need. This is especially useful when they work with long texts.

> **Differentiation ideas:** When learners have finished doing the task, you may wish to share copies of the transcript with them. Ask them to read it and circle the new words. Can they guess the meaning from the context? Encourage them to explain or mimic the words, e.g. *taps the drum*.

CROSS-CURRICULAR LINK

Social science

Ask learners how they would dance the Dragon Dance. Ask volunteers to mimic it. You may wish to show them videos of people doing the Dragon Dance during the Chinese New Year.

Audioscript: Track 02

Learner's Book page 12

Hello! My name's Steve. We're learning the Dragon Dance. Our city celebrates Chinese New Year and the Dragon Dance is an important part of the celebration. People love watching it.

My friends are holding up the dragon with long poles. Our teacher showed them how to make the dragon move. They are moving the poles up and down, right and left. They are practising moving together. Look – the dragon is dancing in the air!

Our dragon is beautiful. It has big eyes and a big mouth, sharp teeth and a long body. Julia is the leader. She's holding up the dragon's head. My other friends are holding up the dragon's body.

My teacher's playing the drum. I'm learning to play the cymbals. The dancers move to the sound of the drum, too: when my teacher taps the drum quickly, the dancers move quickly. When he taps the drum slowly, the dancers move slowly.

Learning the Dragon Dance is fun, but it's also difficult. We have to practise a lot. My friends want to dance really well. We want our Dragon Dance to be perfect.

Answers
Suggested answers:

- *How do the children make the dragon move?* They hold up the dragon with long poles. They move the poles up and down, and right and left to make the dragon move.

- *What is Steve doing?* Steve is learning to play the cymbals.

- *Is learning the Dragon Dance easy or hard?* It is hard.

3 Vocabulary: Adverbs (10–15 minutes)

- Focus on the word box on page 13 of the Learner's Book. Ask the class to stand up, and pretend that they are holding up the dragon on a pole. They act out the words in the box.

- Say the words in turn and ask individual learners to act them out.

- You may wish to play a round of *Simon Says* to practise the words. Tell the class to listen to your instructions. If you say '*Simon says …*', for example '*Simon says dance slowly*', learners do as they are told. If you don't say '*Simon says …*', they don't move. When a learner makes a mistake, they must sit out until the next round.

Answers
Learners act out each word.

4 Read and listen to the text (10–20 minutes)

- Focus on the picture. Ask learners to describe the dragon.

- Tell learners they are going to listen to and read about the Dragon Dance. If necessary, introduce and explain any new vocabulary.

- Play the audio at least twice.

- Then ask the class to write a question about the text using one of the question words. Circulate, giving help if necessary.

- Prompt each learner to ask their question to the class. Elicit answers.

- Ask learners what they know about dragons. Why are dragons so important in Chinese culture? You may wish to have learners visit suitable webpages such as *Kiddle* or *China Highlights* and find out about dragons.

CROSS-CURRICULAR LINK

Geography

Explain 'lunar New Year': it is celebrated in many Asian countries, as well as other countries where Asian communities continue the traditional celebration.

Ask learners: *Are there lunar New Year celebrations where you live?*

Audioscript: Track 03

See Learner's Book page 13

Answers
Learner's own answers.

5 Read and follow directions (5–10 minutes)

- Tell the class that they are going to learn a new dance. Ask them to stand in a line, one behind the other.

- Give the instructions and ask the class to say the words as they act out your instructions.

- Do it slowly at first and increase the speed progressively.

- Ask: *Is it easy or hard?* Elicit opinions from the class.

Answers
Learners learn and perform the dance.

> **Digital Classroom:** Use the activity 'Activity sounds' to practise activity vocabulary. The i button will explain how to use the activity.

6 Talk: What do you think? Are these things easy or hard? (5–15 minutes)

- Ask learners to work in pairs. They take it in turns to ask and answer if the activities indicated are easy or hard for them.

- Ask them to consider what they need to do if they are hard, i.e. practise doing them.

> **Critical thinking opportunity:** Build on this by encouraging learners to speak about the other activities they do.

> **Assessment ideas:** Circulate, listening to the learners' interactions. Take note of recurrent mistakes for remedial work.

Answers
Learner's own answers.

Plenary ideas

Consolidation (10–15 minutes)

- When learners have finished doing the task in pairs, ask them to share their opinions with the class.

> **Critical thinking opportunity:** Ask the class to think of ways that they could make the difficult activities easier.

- Ask the class: *What did you find interesting in this lesson? What would you like to learn more about? What was the most difficult thing to do?* Elicit ideas.

Homework ideas

> **Workbook**
>
> Learners do Activities 1–4 on pages 8–9.

- Learners could find out about Chinese New Year, for example what food people eat, what special clothes they wear, if there are special decorations, etc. They can look for pictures and write a few sentences about it.

- Alternatively, learners choose a festival from their country or region. They search the internet for information and pictures. They can also ask parents for information. They prepare a poster and a short presentation for the class.

- **Home–school link:** Learners tell their family what they have learned about Chinese New Year.

1.2 Physical education: Let's play together

LEARNING PLAN

Learning objectives	Learning intentions	Success criteria
3Sc.04, 3Sc.05 3Rd.02, 3Rd.03 3Wc.01, 3Ug.02	• **Speaking:** Give and follow directions; give opinions. • **Reading:** Read and understand directions. • **Writing:** Fill in a chart. • **Language focus:** imperatives and *must / mustn't* • **Vocabulary:** *back to back, link, together, elbow, cross, step, hold out, add up, Don't give up!, Let's try again, That's good, We've done it*	• Learners can read and understand directions. • Learners can give and follow directions. • Learners can fill in a bar graph. • Learners can play in teams.

21st-century skills

Critical thinking opportunity: Work with a bar graph, do a survey.

Communication: Communicate how well others are contributing to the group task by giving positive comments.

Values: Work as a team, encourage others.

Materials: Learner's Book pages 14–15; Workbook pages 10–11; pieces of paper for learners to stand on; a set of red, yellow and blue cards for each pair of learners; a set of red, green and yellow cards for each learner; **Photocopiable 5**

Starter ideas

Presentations (5–15 minutes)

- If learners have done the homework activities from the previous lesson, ask them to present their work to the class.

- Display the posters or pictures around the classroom.
- If appropriate, you may wish to video-record learners as they present their work. You can then share the recordings with learners and their families.

Main teaching ideas

1 Read the directions. Then play the games (15–25 minutes)

- Focus on the illustration of the game on page 14 of the Learner's Book and ask learners what the girls are doing. Elicit some descriptions.
- Tell the class that they are going to learn the game in the first illustration (Stand up. Sit down.).
- Ask learners to read the instructions for the game. Then ask them to circle the new words, e.g. *back to back, link,* and guess what they mean.
- Choose some volunteers to try the game and model it for the class.
- Divide the class into groups to try playing the game. When they have finished, ask: *Was the game difficult or easy?* Elicit opinions and encourage learners to justify them.
- **Values:** Emphasise the importance of working together – what happens if one person stands up and the other tries to sit down? Elicit ideas. Learners can even try this in pairs to see how important it is that they work together.
- As the class play the game, you may wish to introduce these expressions at suitable points: *Don't give up!, Let's try again, That's good, We've done it!*
- Now focus on the second game Eleven fingers: a game for three people. Read the directions as a class. Mime as you read to make the meaning clear.
- Ask for three volunteers to model the game. Say the instructions and have them follow them.
- If they cannot add up to 11, say: *Don't give up! Try again!*
- When they have managed to add up to 11, say: *That's good! How many tries does it take?*
- Have the class play in groups of three.

> **Assessment ideas:** Circulate, focusing on how learners work together, and how they interact and communicate.

Answers
Learners play the game.
You *must* not step on the floor!

Language detective – Giving directions (5–10 minutes)

- Focus on the example sentences in the box and ask the class to identify the verbs in each.
- Read the explanation – directions start with a verb that tells you what to do.
- Read the question and encourage learners to think of a direction that starts with a different verb.
- Then direct learners' attention to the new game they have just played. Ask learners to identify the 'verb' that each direction starts with*: sit, link, sit.*

2 Read the directions and play the game. Remember, you must not step on the floor! (15–20 minutes)

- Read the instructions with the class and explain new words, e.g. *need, cross, step on.*
- Bring the pieces of paper and ask two volunteers to try the game as you read out the directions.
- Mime to make the meaning of *must / must not clear.* You could say, for example, *You must wait* and make a signal to stop.
- Ask the class to try playing the game in pairs. When they have finished, ask: *Was the game difficult or easy?* Elicit opinions and encourage learners to justify them.
- As the pairs play the game, remind them of these expressions at suitable points: *Don't give up!, Let's try again, That's good, We've done it!*

Answers
Learners play the game in pairs.

3 Write: Finish the sentences (5–15 minutes)

- As a class, look again at the directions for the game 'Step on the paper'. Then focus on the sentences and ask learners to finish them.
- Check learners' sentences as a class.

> **Differentiation ideas:** If less confident learners find it difficult to think of the words, you could mime or ask some questions, for example signal

'cross' and ask: *Cross or run? Must or mustn't?* More confident learners could write some more sentences using 'must' and 'mustn't', such as classroom rules: *You mustn't run in the classroom. You must pay attention.*

- Give each learner a copy of **Photocopiable 5** and ask learners to make their own chatterbox and write their own directions.

Answers

You **must** cross from one side of the room to the other.
You *must* only step on the paper.
You *must* **not** step on the floor!

4 Values: Good things to say (15–20 minutes)

- Start to introduce the expressions while learners are playing the games in Activities 1 and 2, and explain the meaning as necessary.
- Remind the class of these expressions.
- Highlight the importance of practising and not giving up, and of encouraging those who have more difficulty doing things.
- Encourage learners to use these expression themselves as they play or do activities together.

Answers

Learners use the expressions themselves when playing 'Eleven fingers'.

> **Digital Classroom:** Use the activity 'What should you say?' to reinforce the values in the lesson. The i button will explain how to use the activity.

5 Draw a class bar graph (25–30 minutes)

- Tell learners to look at questions a–c. Discuss the first question as a class.
- Then look at the bar graph and discuss which game most children in that class like best. How do they know?
- Tell the class that they are going to make a bar graph for their class and they are going to find out about the opinions of the class.
- They copy the bar graph on a sheet of paper. Then they circulate, asking and answering questions about the games.

- Set a limit of interviewees, for example five learners, to avoid making the activity too long.
- Ask individual learners what results they got.

> **Critical thinking opportunity:** See Cross-curricular link below.

CROSS-CURRICULAR LINK

Maths

Focus on the chart. Discuss the results shown and how they are reflected on the chart. Ask the class how the results are noted, i.e. using a block per person, what the colours are used for, etc.

Answers

Learner's own answers.

Plenary ideas

Consolidation (10–20 minutes)

> **Critical thinking opportunity:** Make a chart on the board. Ask learners to copy the results of the survey in Activity 5. Ask them which game has been the most popular. How do they know? Elicit answers.

> **Assessment ideas: Stoplight:** Give each learner a set of three cards – one red (difficult), one green (easy) and one yellow (more or less difficult). Explain what the colours mean. Tell learners that they are going to use the cards to show how easy or difficult each of the games were.

Ask: *Was 'Stand up sit down' difficult, more or less difficult, or easy?* Learners display their chosen cards to show their answers. Do the same with all of the games.

> **Critical thinking opportunity:** Ask the class to think of ways that they could make the games easier.

Homework ideas

Workbook

Learners do Activities 1–3 on pages 10–11.

- Ask learners to choose a game they know, write a few simple instructions and draw a picture to illustrate the game.
- **Home–school link:** Learners teach the games to their family.

1.3 Talk about it: Team fun

LEARNING PLAN

Learning objectives	Learning intentions	Success criteria
3Ld.04	• **Listening:** Listen to a poem; listen to and understand questions; listen to and understand a conversation.	• Learners can listen to and understand a conversation.
3Sc.04, 3Sc.05	• **Speaking:** Talk about what people are doing; talk about team activities; recite a poem; find rhyming words.	• Learners can talk about what people are doing. • Learners can talk about team activities.
3Rd.01	• **Reading:** Read instructions; read a poem; find synonyms.	• Learners can recite a poem. • Learners can find synonyms.
3Ug.05	• **Language focus:** action verbs, *What is / are … doing?*	• Learners can find rhyming words.
3Uv.01	• **Vocabulary:** *push, pull, climb, tie, carry, pass, stand, rope, through, count, giggle, bounce,* numbers to 100	• Learners can ask and answer questions using the present continuous.

21st-century skills

Critical thinking opportunity: Compare different types of information; create rules based on observation.

Communication: Take turns appropriately in a conversation; interrupt others politely.

Learning to learn: Join in with learning activities with other children; look at pictures to help them understand a text.

Materials: Learner's Book pages 16–17; Workbook pages 12–13; Blank bingo cards – one per learner; numbers 1–100 on separate pieces of paper; a bag or small box

LANGUAGE BACKGROUND

Present continuous

Remind the class of the use and the form of the present continuous.

Use: We use the present continuous to describe actions that are happening *now*, at the same time as we are speaking.

Form:

- The present continuous is made using the present tense of the verb **be**, and the **-ing** form of a verb, for example: *I **am** play**ing** tennis. You **are** cook**ing** lunch.*

- In questions, we put **am**, **is** or **are** in front of the subject, for example: ***Are** you going to the cinema? **Is** the apple on the left? **Am** I winning the game?*

- We make negative sentences by putting **not / n't** after **am**, **is** or **are**, for example: *She **isn't** doing the homework. We **are not** getting the train today.*

Spelling: We form the present continuous by adding **-ing** to verbs, e.g. *talk**ing**, cook**ing**.*

- If a verb ends in **-e**, drop the **-e** and add **-ing**, for example: *make – mak**ing**, take – tak**ing**.*

- If a verb ends in **-w**, **-x** or **-y**, simply add **-ing**, for example: *draw – draw**ing**, play – play**ing**, buzz – buzz**ing**.*

- With short, one-syllable verbs that end with CVC (consonant + vowel + consonant), double the last consonant and then add **-ing**, for example *put – put**ting**, run – run**ning**, swim – swim**ming**.*

Common misconceptions

Misconception	How to identify	How to overcome
Learners add an unnecessary subject pronoun where an imperative form is needed. For example: *You don't forget book. Please you come to my birthday party.*	Write a correct sentence and an incorrect one. Ask learners to compare the sentences. Ask: *What's the difference between the sentences? Which is correct?* Circle the unnecessary pronoun. Say: *Do we need this? Why not? Who am I giving this order to?* Elicit answers.	Learners read the sentence and ask themselves these questions: *Are they giving an order? If they are, who are they talking to? Is it necessary to add the pronoun?*

Starter ideas

Team players (15–20 minutes)

- In order to focus learners' attention back on the topic of team activities, ask the class what team activities they like to do at school and in their English class, for example play games, look for information, do an exercise together.

- Elicit the meaning of 'team'. Ask: *How many children are in a team – one, two, more? And in a basketball team? What sports do we play in teams? How many players are there in each team?*

- This lesson incorporates a review of numbers (1–100) for the first time in Stage 3. You could play a few rounds of Bingo to cover these numbers again. Prepare one blank bingo grid for each learner, and numbers 1–100 on pieces of paper. Put the numbers in a bag or small box. Ask learners to write numbers 1–100 in their grid. Randomly call out the numbers and learners cross out the numbers on their Bingo grids. The winner is the first learner to get a line or full house.

Main teaching ideas

1 Read and listen (15–20 minutes)

- Ask learners to look at the picture. Can they describe any of the activities the children are doing? Elicit a few answers.

- Focus on the instructions and ask the class to match them to the correct activity. Explain vocabulary as necessary.

- Ask which team is doing what activity.

- Tell the class that they are going to listen to a conversation about the picture. They listen and point to parts of the picture as they are mentioned in the audio.

- Play the recording. Circulate to check that learners are pointing to the correct parts of the picture.

- Divide the class into two groups. Learners are going to listen again and repeat the words: Group 1 repeats what the first speaker says; Group 2 repeats what the second speaker says.

- Swap roles and play the recording again, so that all learners have the chance to repeat the whole dialogue.

Answers

Carry the mats to the table. *Blue*
Climb to the top of the wall. *Red*
Build and measure a tall bridge. *Green*
Pass a glass of water through the hoop. *Yellow*

› **Differentiation ideas:** You could give less confident learners a copy of the transcript, so that they can read it as they listen and say their part. You could ask more confident learners to work in pairs and act out the dialogue, reading it from the transcript.

Audioscript: Track 04

Learner's Book page 16

Speaker 1:   Look at those two boys. What are they doing?

Speaker 2:   They are carrying mats.

Speaker 1:   How many mats are they carrying?

Speaker 2:   One, two, three, four, five. Five mats!

Speaker 1:   Where are they taking the mats?

Speaker 2:   To the table, I think.

Speaker 1:   What are they going to do with the mats?

Speaker 2:   I don't know!

2   Talk with a partner: What are they doing? (10–20 minutes)

*   Point at different children in the picture and ask a few questions, for example: *What's this boy doing? What's girl with number X doing?*

*   Ask learners to work in pairs and read the questions and answers in the activity. They look at the picture and match them.

*   Check answers as a class.

*   Ask learners to look at the picture again and take turns asking at least two more questions about what the children are doing.

> **Assessment ideas:** Circulate, listening to the learners' interactions. Check that learners are using word order correctly in this type of question, i.e. split verb with subject in the middle. Make a mental note of mistakes for remedial work.

> **Differentiation ideas:** You could model a few questions to encourage less confident learners: *What is the boy with number 10 doing? What are the girls with 11 and 16 doing?* Accept answers like 'climbing'. Echo the correct answer, for example 'They are climbing the wall', and ask learners to repeat after you.

Answers

1b   2c   3a

Learner's own answers.

Language detective (10–20 minutes)

*   Focus on the examples in the box. Remind the class of the use and form of the present continuous.

*   Look at each example sentence in turn, and point to the present tense *be*, and then the *-ing* form of the verb.

> **Critical thinking opportunity:** Ask learners to read the sentences. Write the infinitive form of the verbs on the board. What do they notice about the spelling of the verbs? Elicit ideas from the class.

> **Assessment ideas:** Encourage learners to write the spelling rules and provide examples of verbs for each one.

> **Digital Classroom:** Use the grammar presentation 'Present continuous' to revise the present continuous. The i button will explain how to use the grammar presentation.

3   Think and talk (10–15 minutes)

*   Ask learners to look at the picture again and then focus on the first question. Elicit the answer.

*   Then focus on the second question: *What else can you climb?* Ask the class to give as many answers as possible. Supply additional vocabulary if necessary.

*   Proceed in the same way with the other questions.

*   You could ask learners to help you make a list of things for each verb on the board.

> **Differentiation ideas:** Ask more confident learners to add more verbs of their choice and continue asking and answering questions. You may give less confident learners a choice of two or three verbs and a copy of the audioscript, and use it as a model for asking and answering more questions.

Answers

*   A wall. Learner's own answers.
*   Mats. Learner's own answers.
*   A bridge. Learner's own answers.

05

4 Read and listen to the poem (20–30 minutes)

> **Critical thinking opportunity:** Focus on the title of the poem and the picture. Ask learners what they think the poem is about and what the relation with the picture is. By doing this, learners will establish the relationship between the picture and the text, and draw conclusions about the content of the text. Emphasise the fact that pictures can be a useful tool to help them understand the meaning of a text.

CROSS-CURRICULAR LINKS

Literature

Ask the class to explain what a poem is. Elicit ideas. Ask: *What is the difference between a poem and a story?* Remind learners of what a verse, rhyme and rhyming words are.

- Tell the class that they are going to read and listen to the poem. Play the audio at least twice.
- Focus on the first set of words and ask the class to read them aloud. Play the audio again. Learners find words that rhyme.
- The word 'again' rhymes with 'ten' here, though it can also be pronounced with a long *a* sound.
- Ask the class to read the poem again and find words that mean the same as the ones listed. Explain the meaning of 'synonym'.
- Check answers as a class.
- Have a Readers' Theatre lesson: divide the class into five groups. Each group will practise reading two lines of *Rope Rhyme*. Then do a class reading of the poem together. Encourage the class to mime or act out their lines as they say them.

Audioscript: Track 05
See Learner's Book page 17

Answers

a in – spin, ground – sound, to – do, ten – again, about – out
b laugh – giggle, turn around – spin, begin – start
c Learners perform a class reading of the poem.

> **Digital Classroom:** Use the activity 'Rhyming words' to revise rhyming words that appear in the poem. The i button will explain how to use the activity.

5 Stand up and move! (10–20 minutes)

- Review the numbers the class has learned so far.
- Focus on the activity and explain the rules of the game.
- Play the game as a class. If conditions permit, take the class to the schoolyard and play the game there.

Answers
Learners play the game. They count up to 100 and kick their legs every time they say a number that ends in nought or five.

6 Picture dictionary: Action verbs (15–20 minutes)

- Ask learners to turn to the Action Verb page in the Picture dictionary (Learner's Book page 171).

> **Critical thinking opportunity:** Ask the class to look at the title of the section: *Action verbs*. Ask: *Why are these words called 'action verbs'?* Elicit ideas, i.e. action verbs show some kind of action; they express something that a person, animal or object can do, for example run, walk, shout, jump. Ask the class to find more of these words on pages 12 and 13 of the Learner's Book.

- Ask learners to work in pairs to play a guessing game. One learner acts out an action, and their partner asks questions to guess which verb they are miming.
- You may wish to tell the class to begin a list of 'Action verbs' in their notebooks. Tell them to start a section in their notebooks and record any new action verbs they learn. They can add to the list as they progress through this unit and beyond.

Answers
Learner's own answers.

Plenary ideas

Consolidation (10–20 minutes)

- As an extension, play the 'Action verbs' guessing game as a class. Divide the class into two teams. Teams take turns acting out sentences with action verbs. They ask the other team: *What am I doing? Guess!*

> **Assessment ideas:** Ask learners what they have found the most interesting or exciting in the lesson. Ask if there was something they found difficult to do. Can the class give ideas about how to help each other overcome these difficulties?

Homework ideas

Workbook

Learners do Activities 1–4 on pages 12–13.

- Learners look for rhyming pairs in the Learner's Book. Tell them to use the Picture dictionary for help. More confident learners may write a simple poem with some of the pairs. Less confident learners could write one or two sentences. In both cases, ask learners to illustrate their work.

- **Home–school link:** Learners teach the poem to their family.

1.4 Write about it: Let's put on a play!

LEARNING PLAN

Learning objectives	Learning intentions	Success criteria
3Sc.02	• **Speaking:** Speak about what you like or don't like doing; speak about animals; describe animals.	• Learners can read and understand a text about birds and mammals.
3Rd.01, 3Rd.02	• **Reading:** Read and understand a text about birds and mammals.	• Learners can speak about animals.
3Wca.02, 3Wca.03, 3Wca.05	• **Writing:** Write about things we like and don't like; use correct spelling and punctuation; use simple structures correctly.	• Learners can speak about what they like or don't like doing.
	• **Language focus:** *like* + gerund	• Learners can write about things they like and don't like doing.
	• **Vocabulary:** *owl, bat, kangaroo, bear, hen, fox, parrot, mammal*	

21st-century skills

Collaboration: Take part in tasks by interacting with others and staying on task; communicate own knowledge of a topic; ask others questions about a topic.

Communication: Contribute in lessons by asking questions, attempting responses and explaining understanding.

Learning to learn: Complete tasks in class as required; join in with learning activities with other children.

Materials: Learner's Book pages 18–19; Workbook pages 14–15; A3 or larger sheets of paper; drawing materials; scissors; glue; circular stickers in various colours; Sample answer for Unit 1; **Photocopiable 1, 6; Differentiated worksheets 1A, B and C**

Starter ideas

Class poster (10–20 minutes)

- If learners have done the homework activities from the previous lesson, ask them to share their poems and sentences with the class.

- They can glue their poems together to create a class poster. Display the poster in the class for a few days.

- If the school has a website, you could also upload their work to it. Alternatively, you may wish to start a class blog where learners can publish their work and then share it with the family and other classes.

Main teaching ideas

1 Read, write and talk (15–30 minutes)

- Ask the class if they like acting. Have they ever taken part in a school play? What was it like? Did they dress up? Do they like dressing up?

- Focus on the picture on page 18 of the Learner's Book. Encourage learners to describe it. What do they think the children are doing? Elicit some ideas.

- Tell learners that these children are going to act in a play and they are making signs for the animal characters in the play.

- As a class, read the paragraph about mammals and ask learners to write the names of three mammals on the chart.

- Discuss the meaning of any new words. Encourage learners to discover the meaning by themselves.

- Do the same with the paragraph about birds.

- Ask learners to read the last paragraph. Then focus on the question. Discuss what sort of animal a bat is. Encourage learners to justify their answers.

- Ask learners to add more examples of mammals and birds to the chart. Supply names in English, and help with additional vocabulary as necessary.

CROSS-CURRICULAR LINK

Science

You could direct learners to suitable websites such as Kidzone and read more about the different types of animals. Alternatively, they may look up information in books. Ask them to find out different classes of animals, for example mammals, birds, fish, reptiles, etc. Then divide the class into groups and assign an animal class to each group. Ask them to write some sentences about their class of animals, add pictures and make a poster. Display the posters around the class.

Answers

A bat is a mammal. It has fur, not feathers; it does not lay eggs. It is the only mammal that can fly. To find out, the children could look in a book or on the internet.

---

2 Play an animal spelling game (10–15 minutes)

- Ask learners to work in groups. They take it in turns to spell the name of one of the animals on the Learner Book's page aloud.

- The rest of the group writes the word of the animal. Then they have to make a sound like that animal or act like the animal.

> **Assessment ideas:** When all groups have finished, ask them how happy they are with what they did. Is there something they could have done better or differently? Elicit ideas.

Answers

Learner's own answers.

> **Workbook**
>
> Learners do Activities 1, 2 and 3 on pages 14 and 15.

> **Digital Classroom:** Use the video 'Let's put on a play' and the activity sheet to explore the subject of putting on a play. The i button will explain how to use the video and activity sheet.

3 Write. Imagine your class is putting on a play (60–90 minutes)

- Tell the class to imagine that they are going to act in a play. They have to decide if they want to be a mammal or a bird. Which mammal or bird would they like to play? Encourage them to explain their choice. Hand out copies of **Photocopiable 6** for the learners to use as they write.

- **Step 1:** Tell the class that there are many things they can do in a play besides acting. Focus on the table and read the options.

- Divide the class into pairs. Ask learners to think about things they like doing and things they don't like doing. Give examples about yourself, for example *I like singing but I don't like acting.*

- Ask learners to turn back to the table and answer the questions about themselves by ticking the boxes. Then they ask their friend and record the answers in the table.

- **Step 2:** Tell learners that they are now going to write sentences about themselves and their partner using the answers in the table.

- Focus on the highlighted words in the model. Explain the rules of using 'and' and 'or', and give some more examples. Ask learners to give some more examples as well, for example *I like playing with my friends and reading. I don't like eating soup or getting up early.*

- Learners work independently and write their sentences using the information in their table.

- **Step 3:** When they have finished, ask what they need to look for in order to make sure everything is correct. Focus on the questions. Ask learners to think of the answers while they are reading their text aloud.

- **Step 4:** Focus on the checklist and read it with the class. Ask learners to check their text with the checklist. Then give each learner a copy of **Photocopiable 1:** Writer's checklist. Read it as a class and ask them to use it to check other aspects of their writing.

- When they have finished revision, direct learners to write the final draft of their sentences.

- See the **Sample answer for Unit 1** for an example answer to this writing task.

Answers

Learners plan, write and check their sentences.

> **Digital Classroom:** Use the activity 'What do you like doing?' to revise *like/don't like* + verb *-ing*. The i button will explain how to use the activity.

> **Workbook**
>
> Learners do Activities 4 and 5 on page 15.

Plenary ideas

Consolidation (10–20 minutes)

> **Assessment ideas:** Ask pairs to write their sentences on a sheet of paper (A3) and add a picture to it. Display them around the class or leave them on their desks.

- Give each learner an allocation of circular stickers, i.e. one-third the number of dots as there are learners in the class.

- Learners walk around the class and place their dots on work that they think is good, and write a comment next to the dot saying what they think is good about it.

- Tell them they can't give more than two dots to a single piece of work. In this way, you ensure that everyone gets one positive comment.

Homework ideas

- Ask learners to search the internet and find out about mammals and birds that live in their region or country. They draw or print a picture and write two sentences about the animals.

- Hand out copies of **Differentiated worksheets 1A, B and C** depending on each learner's ability, and ask them to complete the activities at home.

- **Home–school link:** Learners tell their family about mammals, birds and other animals. They could also play an animal spelling game with their parents or siblings.

1.5 Read and respond: *Whose team are you on?*

LEARNING PLAN

Learning objectives	Learning intentions	Success criteria
3Ld.04, 3Lo.01	• **Listening:** Listen to a story, listen and understand the plot.	• Learners can listen to a story.
3So.01, 3Sor.02	• **Speaking:** Discuss rules for fair play; discuss a story; discuss the characters in a story; act out a play.	• Learners can discuss rules for fair play.
3Ro.01	• **Reading:** Read a play; understand the meaning of unfamiliar words using the context; understand the feelings of characters; understand stage directions.	• Learners can act out a play. • Learners can understand the meaning of unfamiliar words using the context.
3Wca.03	• **Writing:** Write a letter; use correct layout; use correct spelling and punctuation. • **Language focus:** rules • **Vocabulary:** *match, winning, losing, score (n), score a goal, draw (n), grumpy, switch, fair, rules, loser, winner*	• Learners can write a letter.

21st-century skills

Critical thinking opportunity: Explain why things happened (for example, identifying cause and effect in a story).

Learning to learn: Learn from mistakes and feedback, listen attentively and resist distraction.

Values: Be a good sport; discuss rules for fair play.

Materials: Learner's Book pages 20–23; Workbook pages 16–17; large sheet of poster paper; drawing supplies; index cards or small sheets of paper; A4 sheets of paper or card; **Photocopiable 1**

Starter ideas

Animals I know (15–25 minutes)

- If learners have done the homework activity, ask them to read out their research to the class.

- Then collect the mini-posters and create a class poster.

- Play a matching game in pairs or small groups. Ask learners to make animal word cards and

picture cards. Then put them face down on the table. They take it in turns to turn over two cards. If they have a match of picture and words, they say the name of the animal or bird. Then they can add, for example: *It's a mammal. / It's a bird.*

Main teaching ideas

1 Talk about it (10–15 minutes)

- Ask learners to look at the text and pictures, and guess what this story might be about.

- Tell learners to look at the pictures and read the questions. Allow them a few moments to think about their answers.

> **Critical thinking opportunity:** The questions will help learners develop useful reading strategies, such as previewing text for general information, and using text features and illustration to predict the content.

- Ask learners to look at the pictures and read the title. What do they think is the relationship between the title and the picture? Who are these animals? What is the story about?

CROSS-CURRICULAR LINKS

Literature

- Tell the class to look at the title of the story and the characters again. Discuss what kind of story it could be.

- Talk about fables. What makes a fable different from other stories? Ask the class to think about this as they read it. Elicit that fables are stories with animals as the main characters and they have a moral, i.e. they teach values.

- Ask learners if they have ever read a fable. Encourage them to retell the fable.

- You may wish to bring in extracts from popular fables, such as Aesop's fables, to share with the class.

Answers

The characters in the play are Fox, Kangaroo, Bear, Goose, Owl, Parrot and Bat.
The two teams in this play are the Mammals and the Birds.

---

 2 Read and listen (5–10 minutes)

- Tell the class they are going to listen to the play 'Whose team are you on?'

- While they listen, they read the text in the Learner's Book.

- Play the audio at least twice. Ask the class if their predictions were correct.

- Play the audio again. Learners follow in their books.

Audioscript: Track 06

See Learner's Book pages 20–22

> **Digital Classroom:** Use the activity 'Whose team are you on?' to reinforce comprehension of the play. The i button will explain how to use the activity.

3 Talk about the story (10–20 minutes)

- You may wish to do this activity as Think-Pair-Share. Tell learners to read the questions and give them some time to think about their answers. Ask them to make notes of their ideas.

- Then they discuss the answers with a partner.

- After a few minutes, have an open class discussion. Encourage learners to justify their opinions.

> **Assessment ideas:** Circulate and check how well learners are performing, paying special attention to vocabulary use and how they communicate, for example respect of turns to speak, solving communication breakdowns, etc.

- You may wish to play the recording again before learners answer the questions. More confident learners could think of their own questions to ask their partner.

Answers

a Because he thinks the Mammals team will win.
b Bat feels happy when his team is winning.
c Bat feels frustrated when his team is losing.
d Because the Mammals team is losing, and he doesn't want to be on the losing team.
e The other animals feel annoyed when Bat switches teams because it is not fair.
f They say Bat is not a good team player, and that they do not want to play with him if he won't follow the rules.
g Learner's own answers.

---

4 Values: Playing fair and being a good sport (10–15 minutes)

- Focus on the list of rules. Ask learners to discuss the question with their partner.

- Allow some time and then ask pairs to share their decision with the rest of the class. Encourage them to give reasons for their choice.

> **Differentiation ideas:** Play this last part of the audio again, if necessary, or share the audioscript with less confident learners.

Answers
Learner's own answers.

Workbook
Learners do Activities 1 and 2 on page 16.

---

5 Word study: Sports words and Reading tip (15–20 minutes)

- Focus on the word in blue in the speech bubble: *match*. Ask learners what they think the word means. Elicit simple explanations from the class.

- Ask them to find the words in blue in the text (*match, winning, draw, losing, rules*) and to work out the meaning of each word.

- Encourage learners to use the context and other clues like the pictures to help them understand these new words.

- Allow time for this, while you circulate and offer help where necessary, before offering class feedback.

> **Differentiation ideas:** When learners have to explain the meaning of words, you could accept equivalents in the learners' first language from less confident learners. You can then echo the explanation in simple English for them to repeat.

> **Critical thinking opportunity:** Focus on the Reading tip and explain that we don't have to look up all the new words in a dictionary when we read a text – this would be boring and distracting. Remind learners of what they do when they read a story in their own language: they use the context, i.e. the text that surrounds the word and illustrations, to work out the meaning. Afterwards, they can check in the dictionary if they wish.

Answers
Suggested answers:
match: a sports game between two teams or two people
winning: having more points than the other team/person
draw: an equal score: two teams/players have the same number of points
losing: having fewer points than the other team/person
rules: the instructions that everyone must follow

---

6 Act out the play! (30–45 minutes)

- Tell learners that they are going to act out the play 'Whose team are you on?' as a class. Ask them to choose a character.

- You may wish to double cast all characters except Bat. In this way, you would be involving all students in the production – so there can be two (or more) Bears, two Parrots, etc., with learners reading and acting out the lines in chorus. There can be several narrators as well, taking turns.

> **Differentiation ideas:** You could also have one set of learners miming the roles of the seven characters, while other learners read the script off-stage. This could help differentiate with learners who are less confident reading aloud or memorising; they could do the acting while the more confident read the script.

- As a class, discuss what costumes learners could wear. They could make character placards to hang around their necks, or wear coloured t-shirts or hats to show which team they are on.

- Divide the class into groups according to the character that learners have chosen.

- They act out the play.

> **Critical thinking opportunity:** Draw attention to the stage directions. What do learners think they are for? Point out that they don't read these words aloud, but they give information about how to perform the lines. Remind learners about the *-ly* ending on words, which tell you *how* to do something (e.g. *loudly, quietly*).

- You may wish to record the performance and share the video with learners' families.

Answers
Learners act out the play as a class.

7 Write a letter (20–40 minutes)

- Tell the class that they are going to pretend that they are Bat. They are going to write a letter to the Mammals and the Birds, saying they are sorry that they switched teams.

- Read the instructions with the class. Also remind them of how to begin and end a letter.

- Support learners with appropriate language, for example how to say sorry (*'I'm really sorry that …'*); how to make a promise (*'I promise that I will …'*).

- As a class, brainstorm things that learners need to remember when writing, for example correct spelling, use of capital letters at the beginning of sentences and for names, full stops at the end of sentences.

- Tell the class to use the instructions to organise their letter. Ask them to write up to three sentences.

> **Differentiation ideas:** You could give less confident learners some sentence openings to help them build the letter, for example *I'm writing to tell you …, I wasn't …, Will you …?* More confident learners may add more details to the letter, for example Bat could explain how he was feeling when his team was losing.

> **Assessment ideas:** When learners have written the first draft, ask them to exchange it with a partner. They read each other's letter, make comments on what has been done well and suggest how to improve it. Ask learners to get their copy of **Photocopiable 1:** Writer's checklist. Ask them to use it to check each other's work. When learners get their letter back, ask them to make corrections and then write the final draft. When learners have finished, ask them to write their name and the date on their work. Then file the sheets in the learners' portfolios.

Answers
Learners write their own letters.

> **Workbook**
>
> Learners do Activities 3, 4 and 5 on pages 16 and 17.

Plenary ideas

Consolidation (15–20 minutes)

- When learners have written their final draft, they read their letter to the class.

- They could then upload them to the class blog.

> **Assessment ideas:** As a class, encourage learners to discuss how easy or difficult the lesson has been for them. What were the most difficult things to do? As a class, have them discuss how to overcome the difficulties next time. What did they enjoy most? Elicit ideas.

Homework ideas

- Learners search the internet or visit the school library and find a fable to tell the class.

- **Home–school link:** Learners read the play to their family. They show them the letter they have written.

1.6 Project challenge

LEARNING PLAN

Learning objectives	Learning intentions	Success criteria
3Sc.05, 3Sc.07	• **Speaking:** Discuss a project; organise work; play an instructions game.	• Learners can read and understand instructions.
3Rd.02	• **Reading:** Read and understand instructions.	• Learners can give instructions.
3Wca.02, 3Wca.03, 3Wc.01	• **Writing:** Write instructions; spell words correctly; use correct punctuation; write a description.	• Learners can plan a project. • Learners can write a description of an animal.
	• **Language focus:** Unit 1 review	• Learners can play an instructions game.
	• **Vocabulary:** Unit 1 review	

21st-century skills

Creative thinking: Design new items based on a model.

Collaboration: Respect the importance of doing a fair share of group work; keep to the instructions to complete the task; invite others to give their opinions during the task.

Learning to learn: Listen and respond positively to feedback; understand why a correction was given and learn from mistakes and feedback.

Materials: Learner's Book pages 24–25; Workbook pages 18–19; Project A: writing/drawing supplies, file cards; Project B: file cards, writing and drawing supplies, A4 sheets of paper; **Photocopiable 1, 7**; End of Unit 1 test

Starter ideas

Fables galore! (15–20 minutes)

- If learners have looked for a fable at home, ask them to retell it to the class.

- Learners can then vote for the most interesting/funniest fable.

- You may also wish to discuss the values illustrated in each fable.

Main teaching ideas

Learners choose an end-of-unit project to work on. Look at the examples in the pictures and help learners to choose. Provide materials.

Project A: Make a 'Follow the instructions' game (30–45 minutes)

- Read the directions in the Learner's Book. Give out drawing and writing supplies.

- Learners work with a group to make a set of 20 cards, following the example in the Learner's Book. Suggest they brainstorm instructions and make a draft before making the actual cards.

- Ask learners to get their copy of **Photocopiable 1:** Writer's checklist. Ask them to use it to check their work.

- Circulate, checking for correct grammar and spelling.

- Groups then make the cards.

- They explain the game to the class and play it together.

Project B: Make a 'Find the animal' game (30–45 minutes)

- Read and explain the instructions. Learners draw the pictures.

- When they have finished, they write the descriptions.

- Tell them to use the questions as a guide.

- Encourage learners to find out words for things they don't already know by looking them up in the Picture dictionary (pages 161–173 of the Learner's Book). Circulate and give extra help as needed.

- Ask learners to get their copy of **Photocopiable 1:** Writer's checklist. Ask them to use it to check their work.

- When they have finished, they display the animal pictures on the wall. They read the descriptions.

- The class guesses which animal is described.

〉 **Assessment ideas:** When learners have finished their work on Projects A and B, give them a copy of **Photocopiable 7** and read the instructions as a class. Ask them to work independently and think about their work on their project. They reflect and answer the questions. Ask them to tick off the aims they have achieved. Insist on the importance of giving honest answers.

Workbook

Learners do the Check your progress quiz on pages 18–19.

Plenary ideas

Reflect on your learning (5–10 minutes)

- Draw learners' attention to the 'Reflect on your learning' questions in the Learner's Book.

- Learners answer the questions to reflect on their project work.

Consolidation (10–15 minutes)

- Ask learners to reflect on and discuss what they liked most about this unit, and encourage them to explain why. This may also be a good opportunity for them to think about what aspects of the unit they have found most difficult and why.

- You may wish to keep a record of their comments to see how they progress over time.

〉 **Assessment ideas: Portfolio opportunity:** If you have been filing learners' work for Unit 1, you may find it useful to put all the work of this unit together. You could ask learners to make a cover for their Unit 1 work, decorating it with an image that represents what they have learned.

Homework ideas

- Learners draw a picture of what they have liked most about this unit.

- **Home–school link:** Learners show their family their projects.

1.7 What do you know now?

What can we achieve when we work together? (30–40 minutes)

- Learners work in pairs. They work together through all the tasks set in this section.

- They write the answers in their notebooks. You may ask them to have a special section in their notebooks where they record the answers.

- Whenever their opinion is requested, encourage them to be honest in their answers.

Answers
1–6 Learner's own answers.

Look what I can do! (15 minutes)

- Review the five '*I can ...*' statements on page 26 of the Learner's Book. Learners demonstrate what they can do.

- Learners colour in the faces to show which things they can do.

- Encourage them to be honest in their answers.

Workbook

Learners answer the Reflection questions on page 19.

> 2 Families

Unit plan

Lesson	Approximate number of learning hours	Outline of learning content	Learning objectives	Resources
1 A family wedding	1.5–2.25	Talk about families and family events.	3Ld.01 3Sc.05 3Sc.07 3Rd.01 3Rd.02 3Wca.02 3Uv.04 3Uv.07	Learner's Book Lesson 2.1 Workbook Lesson 2.1 ⤓ Photocopiable 8 ⤓ Photocopiable 9 **Digital Classroom:** Video – Family time; Activity – Who's at the wedding?
2 Birthday customs	1.5–2.5	Ask and answer questions about events in the past.	3Ld.02 3Sc.01 3Sc.02 3Sc.03 3Rd.01 3Ug.01	Learner's Book Lesson 2.2 Workbook Lesson 2.2 **Digital Classroom:** Grammar presentation – Past simple questions
3 It's nice to meet you!	1.0–1.75	Practise polite greetings and conversations.	3Ld.04 3Lm.01 3Sc.06 3Rd.01 3Rm.01	Learner's Book Lesson 2.3 Workbook Lesson 2.3 **Digital Classroom:** Activity – Introductions; Activity – Wedding quiz
4 What's your favourite month?	1.5–2.25	Write about our favourite months.	3Ld.04 3Sc.07 3Wca.03 3Wca.04 3Wor.02 3Us.04	Learner's Book Lesson 2.4 Workbook Lesson 2.4 ⤓ Sample answer for Unit 2 ⤓ Photocopiable 1 ⤓ Photocopiable 10 ⤓ Differentiated worksheets 2A, B and C **Digital Classroom:** Activity – Find the dates
5 Special memories	1.5–2.5	Read and talk about family memories.	3Ld.04 3Sc.01 3Sor.02 3Rd.03 3Ro.01 3Wca.02 3Wca.03	Learner's Book Lesson 2.5 Workbook Lesson 2.5 ⤓ Photocopiable 11 **Digital Classroom:** Activity – Past or present?; Activity – School memories: matching

(continued)

Lesson	Approximate number of learning hours	Outline of learning content	Learning objectives	Resources
6 Project challenge	1.5–2.25	Make a 'memories' scrapbook or a pop-up birthday card.	3Sc.07 3Rd.02 3Wca.03 3Wca.04 3Wc.01	Learner's Book Lesson 2.6 Workbook Lesson 2.6 ⬇ Photocopiable 12 ⬇ Photocopiable 13
7 What do you know now?	0.75–1.0	Self-assessment and reflection.		Learner's Book Lesson 2.7 ⬇ Photocopiable 14

Cross-unit resources
⬇ Unit 2 Audioscripts
⬇ End of Unit 2 test
⬇ Unit 2 Progress report
⬇ Unit 2 Wordlist

BACKGROUND KNOWLEDGE

Birthday celebrations around the world

Birthday foods

In China, people eat *chang shou mian* on their birthday, which is a type of egg noodles. These noodles symbolise having a long and happy life (longevity).

In South Korea, people eat *miyeok-guk* for breakfast on their birthday, which is a seaweed soup. It contains lots of nutrients.

In the Netherlands, people eat *Taarties* on their birthday, which are tarts filled with fruit and topped with whipped cream.

Birthday traditions

In Mexico, there is a fun tradition for children's birthdays: the birthday piñata, which is filled with sweets.

In India, Hindus perform a head-shaving ritual called the *mundun* on or before a child's first or third birthday. This is because they believe that shaving the hair removes any negativity that the child has from a past life, and protects them from evil.

In Vietnam, people celebrate their birthdays collectively on New Year's Day, also known as *Tet*. All babies turn one year old on the day of Tet, regardless of when they were born that year. Children are given bright red envelopes as presents; they are filled with 'lucky money'.

In Japan, people enjoy a birthday festival called Shichi-Go-San, which means 'seven-five-three'. It gets its name because three-year-old children, five-year-old boys and seven-year-old girls are taken to the temple and given special sweets by the priest.

Name days

In some countries in Europe and America, as well as in Roman Catholic and Eastern Orthodox countries, many people celebrate name days as well as birthdays. There is a day of the year that is associated with their name, and they celebrate their name and life on this day. People named after a saint would also celebrate their saint's feast day.

TEACHING SKILLS FOCUS

Formative assessment: the plenary

At some point during a lesson, teachers need to know (and be able to show) what learners have learned. They therefore need to carry out some form of assessment – this is usually most appropriate at the end of the lesson in the form of a performance task plenary that is specifically related to the learning objectives. However, despite their usefulness, plenaries are often not given enough time and thought, and therefore are ineffective.

In order to be really effective, a plenary needs to have the following features:

- It needs to occur at the most appropriate time – this is quite often at the end of the lesson; however, mini-plenaries can be introduced at transition points during a lesson.
- It should allow teachers to assess the class as a whole, as well as individual learners.
- It needs to be differentiated, and include assessment on what learners know as well as what they still do not know.
- It should highlight misconceptions, which can then be addressed immediately or in the next lesson.
- It should give learners the chance to reflect on what they have learned and how they have learned it. Learners should also be able to use the plenary to assess how successful they have been in achieving the aims of the lesson, and what – if anything – they need to improve.

Your challenge

Planning good plenaries can be challenging at times. In each unit of the Learner's Book, opportunities to introduce plenary activities at the end of a lesson are highlighted.

Look through Unit 2 and use the activities below to introduce more opportunities for plenary assessment.

1 **Exit tickets**

These are linked to the objective of a lesson or activity, and can pose one or more questions. Questions can be *Wh-* questions, for example *What did you learn today? What are you still unsure of? What do you still need to review?*, or multiple-choice questions, for example *The most interesting thing I learned today was* + a choice of items to tick off. Learners can be asked to write *X* number of facts they know now that the lesson is over. They can use the traffic lights technique or tweet an exit ticket, i.e. write what they have learned and what they still feel unsure of in 280 characters or fewer. Exit tickets can be written on sticky notes, file cards, smartphones, tablets or laptops.

2 **Give me five**

This is a well-known technique in which learners draw a hand on a sheet of paper and assign a label to each finger, for example thumb: *In this lesson I have learned …*; index finger: *I have used* + a skill; middle finger: *Today, I found … hard*; ring finger: *Today I have improved on …*; pinkie: *For next time, I need to remember …*

3 **K-W-L chart**

Learners use a three-column grid where 'K' is what learners *know* already, 'W' is what they *want* to learn in the lesson and 'L' is what they have *learned*. This K-W-L chart is provided as **Photocopiable 3**. Learners fill in the K and W columns at the beginning of the class, and the L column during the plenary at the end.

Reflection

How successful was the implementation of these ideas? How can you improve them?

2.1 Think about it: A family wedding

Learning objectives	Learning intentions	Success criteria
3Ld.01	• **Listening:** Listen to a description of a celebration; listen for specific information.	• Learners can listen and understand a description of a celebration.
3Sc.05, 3Sc.07	• **Speaking:** Describe a wedding; practise topic vocabulary; talk about family celebrations; sing a song; talk about families and family events; describe people; describe what they are wearing.	• Learners can describe a wedding. • Learners can talk about family celebrations.
3Rd.01, 3Rd.02	• **Reading:** Read and follow instructions; read and understand an information text.	• Learners can sing a song. • Learners can talk about families and family events.
3Wca.02	• **Writing:** Describe people; describe what they are wearing; use correct spelling and punctuation.	• Learners can follow instructions.
	• **Language focus:** *after, first, next, then*	
3Uv.04, 3Uv.07	• **Vocabulary:** *happy, peaceful, contented, excited, proud, bride, groom, photographer, sister, grandson, grandmother, grandfather, granddaughter, aunt, uncle, cousin*	• Learners can write a description.

21st-century skills

Critical thinking opportunity: Compare and contrast different families and celebrations.

Collaboration: Take part in tasks by interacting with others and stay on task; keep to the instructions to complete the task.

Values: Understand and respect different types of family and different celebrations.

Materials: Learner's Book pages 27–29; Workbook pages 20–21; map of the world, slips of paper, strips of paper, scissors, sticky tape; **Photocopiable 8, 9**

Starter ideas

Let's celebrate! (5–10 minutes)

- If appropriate, show photographs of you and your family celebrating special occasions. Explain briefly what you were celebrating.

- Ask learners what special dates their families celebrate. Elicit some answers.

- Ask the class how they celebrate special occasions. Encourage them to talk about the food they eat, clothes they wear, music played, etc.

Getting started (10–15 minutes)

- Focus on the Big Question: *What are some of your favourite family memories?*

- You may wish to tell the class about yours and then invite them to contribute.

- Focus on the photograph. Read questions a–c and elicit answers from the class.

- Encourage the class to identify the probable family members (grandfather, grandson), talk about what the family is doing (action verbs), and how the child in the photo is (probably) feeling.

- Supply additional vocabulary if necessary. You may wish to introduce useful vocabulary to encourage children to use in discussion, e.g. feeling words: *happy, peaceful, contented, excited, proud.*

Answers

Learner's own answers. Suggested answer:
This is a grandfather and his grandson. They are fishing. The boy looks relaxed and happy. He is enjoying himself. He's focused, concentrated. His grandfather is teaching him to fish.

> **Digital Classroom:** Use the video 'Family time' to introduce the theme and vocabulary in the lesson. The i button will explain how to use the video.

 Sing along! *Families all over the world* (10–15 minutes)

- Talk to the class about your family, how many siblings, cousins, uncles, aunts you have, how old they are, etc. Then ask learners to talk about their families.
- Tell the class you are going to listen to a song. Give each learner a copy of **Photocopiable 8**: *Sing along! Families all over the world.*
- Play the song *Families all over the world* at least twice. Ask the class what it is about and elicit answers.
- Sing the song and encourage learners to join in.
- **Values:** You may wish to show the YouTube video of this song. In the video, learners can see families from different parts of the world, from different ethnic groups, etc. You could take advantage of this video to have learners discuss, for example: *Are all families the same? Do they have the same numbers of members? Do all family members look alike?* Elicit answers.

Audioscript: Track 07

Learner's Book page 27

Families All Over the World

Chorus: There are families all over the world,
          All over our beautiful world
          Families like yours and families like mine
          Are living all over the world.

Verse: Around and across to the other side
          Through the ebb and flow of the ocean tide
          A different place and there you'll find
          Families like yours and families like mine.

Chorus: There are families all over the world,
          All over our beautiful world
          Families like yours and families like mine
          Are living all over the world.

Verse: It's the same bright moon, we all can see
          Glowing with the stars in harmony
          We're different yet the same, what a grand design, for families like yours and families like mine.

Chorus: There are families all over the world,
          All over our beautiful world
          Families like yours and families like mine
          Are living all over the world.

Verse: All over our big wide world today
          Living our lives in our own way
          Children playing in the warm sunshine,
          with families like yours and families like mine.

Chorus: There are families all over the world,
          All over our beautiful world
          Families like yours and families like mine
          Are living all over the world.

Main teaching ideas

1   **Talk about the wedding picture (10–15 minutes)**

- Ask learners if they have ever been to a wedding.
- Ask them where a wedding takes place. Supply vocabulary as necessary, for example *church, mosque, temple.*

- Encourage the class to speak about things they remember about a wedding they have attended. Introduce vocabulary, such as *bride, groom, wedding dress, wedding cake,* etc.

- Ask them to describe something they liked about the wedding.

- Ask learners to focus on the picture and describe what they see, what they think the people in the picture are doing, what they are wearing, etc. Supply additional vocabulary as needed.

- Ask the class to compare how the wedding in the image is similar to or different from weddings they have been to in their country. Ask questions such as: *Was there a cake? What did people wear? What did the bride wear? Was there a photographer?*

- Explain the preposition of time *after* to state when things happen. Ask: *What do people do **after** the wedding ceremony? Is there a special meal? A party?* (The word *after* occurs again in Lessons 2.2 and 2.6.)

- **Values:** This activity requires learners to compare different customs, paying attention to detail. Focus on similarities and differences between both cultures. Highlight the importance of respecting cultural differences.

CROSS-CURRICULAR LINK

Geography

The picture shows a wedding in Greece. Display the map of the world and ask the class to find Greece on the map. If learners are from Greece, bring a map of the country. Ask them to find their city on the map. What province/region is it in?

Answers

Learner's own answers.

2 Listen. Choose a question. Listen for the answer (5–10 minutes)

- Ask learners to read the questions. Explain that you are going to play the audio and they have to listen for the answers to the questions.

- Play the audio a few times. Elicit the answers from the class.

Audioscript: Track 08

Learner's Book page 28

Hello, my name is Christina. This is my sister's wedding. My sister's name is Alexia and she just got married. The photographer is taking lots and lots of photos, and so am I. I am taking photos with my mum's phone. Do you see me?

Let me introduce my family! My sister Alexia is the bride. Isn't she pretty? She is standing next to her husband, Georgios. He is the groom. He's really nice. The bride and groom are both wearing flower crowns on their heads.

My mum and dad are standing next to the groom. My mum is carrying a purple bag. My uncle and aunt are standing next to the bride. My uncle is wearing glasses and my aunt is wearing a big orange hat. They have two children, a son and a daughter. Those are my cousins. My cousin Elias is a little boy, just four years old. He's very excited and can't stand still. He's running around and waving. Do you see him? His sister is my cousin Luisa. Luisa is seven years old, one year younger than me. She is standing in front of my aunt and next to our grandmother.

Grandma is sitting in a chair. Do you see her? Grandma is very clever. She made my sister's wedding dress. Isn't it beautiful? She also made the flower crowns.

After the photos we are going to have a big meal. There will be lots of delicious food and a big wedding cake.

Answers

Christina is taking photos with her mum's phone. Grandma made the bride's dress. After the photo, the family is going to have a big meal.

3 Vocabulary. Family members (5–10 minutes)

- Focus on the box in the Learner's Book. Play the audio again and ask the class to put up their hands every time they hear the people described (you may want to explain that words like 'mum' and 'mother' mean the same thing, as does 'grandma' and 'grandmother').

- Stop the audio and ask the class to repeat the words.

- Play the audio again and ask the class to check who is who in the picture.

- Ask learners to work with a partner. They use words in the box to describe each person in the picture.

⟩ **Differentiation ideas:** You may wish to extend the activity by asking more confident learners to use the words to talk about their families. Less confident learners may draw a picture of their family and label members with name and family words, for example *Ali, brother.*

Answers
Learners use the words to describe the people in the picture.

⟩ **Digital Classroom:** Use the activity 'Who's at the wedding?' to revise family vocabulary. The i button will explain how to use the activity.

4 Picture dictionary: Clothes (5–10 minutes)

- Ask learners to turn to the Clothes page in the Picture dictionary (Learner's Book page 164) and talk about the words.

- Ask them to imagine they are going to a wedding. They tell each other what they are wearing.

- Encourage them to be as creative and funny as they wishs.

Answers
Learner's own answer.

5 Write a description of what one person is wearing in the picture (10–15 minutes)

- Ask learners to look at the picture on page 28 carefully and choose one person. They will write a short description of what this person is wearing.

- As a class, brainstorm things that learners need to remember when writing the description, for example capitalisation, final punctuation, spelling.

- Read the instructions and the example sentence. You could elicit a few additional examples from the class.

- Focus on the examples in the Language focus box. Explain the relation with personal pronouns *he/she.* You may wish to draw a two-column table on the board. Write *he/she* in the column

on the left and the corresponding *him/her* in the column on the right. Give some examples and elicit a few from the class. Ask learners to write the examples in their notebooks.

- Then ask the class to work on their own to write their own descriptions.

- Tell the class that when they finish their writing, they should proofread their work, checking for and correcting their mistakes.

- Then they pair up with a partner or partners in a small group and read each other's description(s). Can they guess which person is described?

⟩ **Assessment ideas:** Circulate, asking learners questions about their work. Take notes of mistakes for remedial work. You could ask the class to write the descriptions on a separate sheet of paper. Ask learners to write their name and the date on them and file the work in their portfolios.

Answers
Learner's own answers.

Workbook

Learners do Activities 1, 2 and 3 on page 20.

---

6 Make linked paper hearts! (20–25 minutes)

- Tell the class that they are going make linked paper hearts (also known as Mobius strip hearts). Explain that they are sometimes used as ornaments.

- Hand out copies of **Photocopiable 9** and focus on the instructions. Give each learner strips of paper, scissors and tape.

- Model each step of the process yourself, making the sequencing words clear by using mime, for example: *First, …* – show one finger; *Next, …* – make a circular movement forward, etc. (When taping the heart strips together, it is helpful to put tape on both sides.)

- When you have finished modelling, say the instructions aloud again as the class makes their own paper hearts.

- When learners have finished, collect all the hearts and ask learners to help you decorate the classroom with them.

> **Assessment ideas:** To give learners further practice in the use of sequencing words, ask them to work in pairs and prepare an explanation of a simple processes, for example making a sandwich, making a collage, laying the table for dinner, etc. They make their notes and give the instructions to the class.

Answers

Learners make their own paper hearts.

> **Workbook**
>
> Learners do Activities 4, 5 and 6 on page 21.

Plenary ideas

Consolidation (10–15 minutes)

- Ask learners to draw the outline of a hand or a foot. They label each finger or toe with something they've gained from the lesson.

> **Critical thinking opportunity:** Ask these questions:

1 Thumb: *What have you learned this lesson?*

2 Index finger: *What skills have you used?*

3 Middle finger: *What did you find difficult?*

4 Ring finger: *What have you improved on today?*

5 Pinkie: *What do you need to remember for next time?*

Homework ideas

- Give learners a list of suitable websites or books they can find in the school library, so they can look for information about Greece. They can also look for pictures. They prepare a poster and a short presentation for the class.

- **Home–school link:** Learners take home copies of **Photocopiable 9** and teach their family how to make the linked hearts.

2.2 Global awareness: Birthday customs

LEARNING PLAN		
Learning objectives	**Learning intentions**	**Success criteria**
3Ld.02	• **Listening:** Listen to a description of a birthday celebration.	• Learners can read and understand a description of a birthday party.
3Sc.01, 3Sc.02, 3Sc.03	• **Speaking:** Talk about families and family events; ask and answer questions about past events.	• Learners can listen and understand a description of a birthday celebration.
3Rd.01	• **Reading:** Read a description of a birthday party; read and listen for information.	• Learners can talk about families and family events.
3Ug.01	• **Language focus:** questions in the past simple	• Learners can ask and answer questions about past events.
	• **Vocabulary:** *coin, string, rice cake, clever*	

21st-century skills

Collaboration: Listen attentively while other learners are contributing; respectfully wait for their turn to speak.

Communication: Use simple techniques to start, maintain and close conversations of various lengths.

Learning to learn: Participate sensibly and positively in learning activities in class.

Materials: Learner's Book pages 30–31; Workbook pages 22–23; map of the world

Starter ideas

My birthday party (5–10 minutes)

Ask the class how they celebrate their birthday. Do they organise something special, such as games? Do they decorate their home in a special way? What food do they eat? Elicit answers.

Main teaching ideas

1 Read about a birthday party (10–15 minutes)

- Focus on the picture. Encourage learners to describe it. Ask: *What are the children doing?* Elicit some ideas.

- Explain what a 'piñata' is: a container made of cloth, clay or papier mâché, decorated with bright colours and filled up with small toys and sweets. It is commonly used in celebrations in Latin America, mainly in Mexico. Similar objects are used in India, Japan or the Philippines.

- Tell learners to read and listen about Maria's birthday. Play the audio at least twice while learners follow in their books.

- Ask learners to read the text again and discuss the meaning of the new words. Encourage them to discover the meaning by themselves.

> **Critical thinking opportunity:** Ask learners how they think they can get the sweets and toys from the piñata.

Audioscript: Track 09

See Learner's Book page 30

Key words (5–10 minutes)

- Focus on the question words in the Key words box, and the pictures.

- Ask learners to explain the relation between the words and the pictures next to them, i.e. we use *who* to ask about people, *what* to ask about things, etc.

- Ask learners to look at Lessons 2.1 and 2.2 for examples of these question words. Ask: *What do they ask about?* Elicit the answers.

2 Write. Answer each question with a full sentence (10–20 minutes)

- Ask learners to read the questions. Explain that the words for the answers are in the wrong order. Learners write the words in the correct order to form each answer.

- Check answers as a class.

> **Assessment ideas:** Ask learners to work in pairs. They write some questions on a sheet of paper. They then write the answers on slips of paper, cut them up and shuffle the pieces. They give the questions and the pieces to another pair. They have to read the questions and order the words to form the answers. Each authoring team checks that the answers are correct.

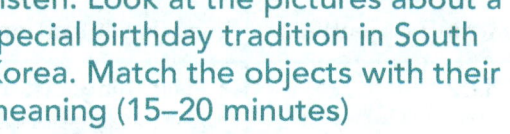

Answers

When was Maria's birthday? *It was yesterday.*
Who was at the birthday party? *Maria's grandparents and friends were at the party.*
How many candles were there on the birthday cake? *There were nine candles.*
Where was the piñata? *It was in the garden.*
What was inside the piñata? *There were sweets inside the piñata.*

3 Listen. Look at the pictures about a special birthday tradition in South Korea. Match the objects with their meaning (15–20 minutes)

- Tell learners that they are going to hear about a special tradition in South Korea.

- Focus on the words and the pictures. What celebration do they think they are used for? (*birthdays*) Elicit ideas.

- Play the recording at least twice.

> **Differentiation ideas:** You may ask more confident learners to explain what the celebration is and what it involves. With less confident learners, you may ask questions to help them explain the celebration.

- Ask learners to compare this celebration with celebrations in their own country. How similar or different are they?

Audioscript: Track 10

Learner's Book page 31

We have a special custom in Korea. When a child is one year old, we have a birthday party with lots of food. The child wears special, very colourful clothes. We put some things on the table in front of the child: a coin, a long piece of string, a rice cake and a book. We wait to see which thing the child chooses. If the child chooses the coin, they will be rich. If they choose the string, they will have a long life. If they choose the rice cake, they will always have lots of food. If they choose the book, they will be very clever.

Answers

Coin – You will be rich.
String – You will have a long life.
Rice cake – You will always have lots of food.
Book – You will be very clever.

4 Listen to Jongmin's grandmother (15–20 minutes)

- Tell learners that they are going to hear about Jongmin's family, who live in South Korea. Jongmin's grandmother is talking about his first birthday.

- They have to listen and find out what object Jongmin chose.

- Ask the class to predict what he will choose.

- Play the audio at least twice. Were they right?

Audioscript: Track 11

Learner's Book page 31

When Jongmin was one year old, we had a big birthday party. The whole family was there. We had lots of lovely food. Jongmin was not very happy that day; he was very cross. He didn't smile and he didn't eat the lovely food.

We put the coin, the string, the rice cake and the book in front of Jongmin. At first, he didn't choose anything. Then he grabbed all four things at the same time: the coin, the string, the rice cake and the book! We thought, this child will have a very long, special, happy life!

Answers

Jongmin grabbed all four things at the same time.

5 Read and talk (5–10 minutes)

- Focus on the questions and the answers. Divide the class into pairs and ask learners to match each question with its answer.

- Check answers as a class.

Answers

Was my grandfather at my party? – Yes, he was.
Were my cousins at my party? – Yes, they were.
Was there any ice cream at my party? – No, there wasn't any ice cream.
Was I happy? – No, you were very cross!
Did I cry? – No, you didn't.

Language detective – *yes/no* questions in the simple past tense (5–10 minutes)

- Remind learners of the past simple tense. Elicit examples.

- Focus on the question openings in the box.

- Elicit more examples from the class of using the past simple to ask *yes/no* questions.

⟩ **Digital Classroom:** Use the grammar presentation 'Past simple questions' to revise past simple *yes/no* and *Wh-* questions. The i button will explain how to use the grammar presentation.

6   Talk with your partner (10–15 minutes)

- Ask learners to make up questions for a partner about his or her last birthday using *was / were*.

- They can ask the questions in the activity and add more questions.

> **Assessment ideas:** Circulate, listening to learners' exchanges. Take notes of mistakes for remedial work. You may wish to ask questions to help if you notice that a pair is stuck.

> **Differentiation ideas:** You could give less confident learners sentence starters. Alternatively, they could write down their answers in preparation for the pair activity. They could also write down the extra questions. More confident learners could extend the answers offering more details, for example: What was your favourite present? *It was a white and purple dress. My grandmother made it for me.*

- After learners have finished the activity, ask them to share with the class what they have learned about their partner's birthday.

Answers
Learner's own answers.

Workbook
Learners do Activities 1–5 on pages 22–23.

Plenary ideas

Consolidation (10–15 minutes)

> **Assessment ideas: Exit tickets:** You can use this simple technique to assess what learners have learned at the end of a lesson. Before the class is over, give them a 'ticket', i.e. a slip of paper or card where they answer one or two questions about the lesson.

Homework ideas

- Learners write about birthday celebrations in their family or in their region.

- **Home–school link:** Learners tell their family about South Korean birthday customs. They can ask them about birthday customs or other special family celebrations in their country.

2.3 Talk about it: It's nice to meet you!

Learning objectives	Learning intentions	Success criteria
3Ld.04, 3Lm.01	• **Listening:** Listen and understand an information text about wedding customs.	• Learners can listen and read about wedding customs.
3Sc.06	• **Speaking:** Practise polite conversations; perform a role play; discuss ways of addressing adults and family members; discuss wedding customs.	• Learners can practise polite conversations. • Learners can perform a role play.
3Rd.01, 3Rm.01	• **Reading:** Read and understand an information text about wedding customs.	• Learners can discuss wedding customs.
	• **Language focus:** *from* + country *to* indicate origin	
	• **Vocabulary:** titles: *Mr, Mrs, Miss, Ms; kimono, henna, patterns, lei, necklace, name, surname, married, unmarried*	• Learners can discuss ways of addressing adults and family members.

21st-century skills

Critical thinking opportunity: Compare and contrast wedding traditions and forms of address.

Creative thinking: Take part in a role play.

Collaboration: Take part in tasks by interacting with others and stay on task.

Values: Address adults politely.

Materials: Learner's Book pages 32–33; Workbook pages 24–25; map of the world

How to address people in English

How to address people in English properly may be confusing for learners. Many languages have a formal and an informal pronoun for addressing an interlocutor. However, in English, 'you' is both formal and informal, therefore you can say 'Thank you' to both your sister and your head teacher, even if the degree or formality is different. However, there are a few ways in which we can show the level of formality.

• If the interlocutor is in a position of authority (because of age, profession, etc.), their surname will be used, and will be preceded by: *Mr, Mrs, Miss* or *Ms.*, e.g. *Mr Jackson, Mrs Murray, Miss Huang, Ms Zhao.* In some English-speaking countries, women may change their surname and adopt their husband's surname when they get married.

• When you greet someone you can say: *Good morning, Madam/Sir.* If you want to get someone's attention, you can say: *Excuse me, Sir/Madam.*

• Sometimes, if there is a closer relationship with a teacher, a more informal greeting may be used, e.g. *Good morning Miss Alicia*, especially by young children.

CONTINUED

Use of *was* and *were*

Was / were are the past forms of the verb *to be*.

	Present	Past
I	*am*	*was*
He She It	*is*	*was*
We You (singular and plural) They	*are*	*were*

For example: *Peter **was** tired after the match yesterday. I **wasn't** tired but I **was** hungry.*

*They **were** late for the class again so they **weren't** allowed to go in.*

When asking questions with *was / were*, we change the order of words; for example:

***Was** the shop closed at 7 p.m.? Where **were** you at midday yesterday?*

*What **was** that noise?*

Common misconceptions

Misconception	How to identify	How to overcome
Learners sometimes make agreement mistakes with *was*. For example: *The clothes **was** very cheap.* *I **were** very happy to see them.* *There **was** 13 people in my birthday party.* *I had a birthday party yesterday and there **was** a lot of presents.*	Write a correct sentence and an incorrect one. Ask learners to compare the sentences. Ask: *What's the difference between the sentences? Which is correct? Are we talking about one thing or many? If this is a plural/singular noun, what should we use?* Circle the mistake and elicit answers.	Ask learners to make a poster and write the correct forms in colour, for example *I was / You were*, etc. Keep the poster on display so learners can look and check when they are completing sentences. Ask learners to circle the nouns and decide whether they are singular or plural. What pronoun should they use to replace the noun? They decide and write the correct form.
Learners sometimes make word order mistakes when using adverbs of definite time. For example: *I left my wallet last night at your place.* *I left my purse last night in your house.*	Write a correct sentence and an incorrect one. Ask learners to compare the sentences. Ask: *What's the difference between the sentences? Which is correct? Why? What comes first in a sentence time or place?*	Revise the correct order of sentences. Write on the board: *Subject + verb + object (what or who?) + manner (How?) + place (Where?) + time (When?)* Ask learners to identify these elements with different colours. When they write the sentences, they ask themselves the questions, for example: *He wrote what? A letter, where? In his notebook, when? In the English class.* They write the corresponding parts in colour.

Starter ideas

Wedding time! (5–10 minutes)

- To generate interest in the idea of wedding customs, remind the class of the Greek wedding they read about in Lesson 2.1. Ask learners what they remember about it.

- Ask learners about weddings in their country or region. Encourage them to talk about the clothes people wear, the food they eat, decorations, presents given, etc.

Main teaching ideas

1 Talk (5–10 minutes)

- Ask learners what their name is. Ask them which is their first name and which is their surname.

- Focus on the explanations in the activity. Ask learners to say your name in English. What title do they use?

- Ask learners to think of three other teachers in your school. What title do learners use to say their names in English? Do they use the same form of address for teachers in their own language?

- Compare and contrast how names and surnames are used in the learners' language.

- Point out that in English the titles are not used on their own, but are always followed by a surname.

Answers
Learner's own answers.

Language focus – Mr, Mrs, Miss, Ms (5–10 minutes)

- Focus on the titles and model the pronunciation.

- Point out that the same title is used for a man, no matter whether he is married or not. However, with women, a different title is used if she is married.

2 Listen and talk (5–15 minutes)

- Tell the class that they are going to listen to some children practising introductions and polite conversations.

- Play the audio recording once. They listen and point to the picture as they hear the children.

- Then play the audio again and ask learners to repeat the words.

- Ask learners to get together in groups of three. They role play the mini dialogues.

Audioscript: Track 12

Learner's Book page 32

Girl 1: This is my grandmother, Mrs Abed.

Girl 2: It's very nice to meet you, Mrs Abed.

Girl 3: Well, thank you. It's nice to meet you, too.

Boy 1: I'd like you to meet my uncle, Mr Dabiri.

Boy 2: How do you do. My name is Farhad.

Boy 3: How do you do, Farhad. I'm pleased to meet you.

Answers
Learners point to the pictures and repeat the words.

3 Perform a role play: *I'd like you to meet my aunt* (10–15 minutes)

- Ask learners to imagine that they are going to introduce a 'family adult' to their friend.

- Divide the class into groups of three – one learner plays him or herself, one plays their friend and one plays the family adult. Tell them to use some of the phrases in their Learner's Book.

> **Differentiation ideas:** Less confident learners may write the dialogues before acting them out. More confident learners may add more lines to the conversation.

- Swap roles so that every learner gets a chance to play each role.

Answers
Learners role play introducing a family member to their friend.

> **Digital Classroom:** Use the activity 'Introductions' to revise introductions and polite conversations. The i button will explain how to use the activity.

4 Compare customs (5–10 minutes)

- Focus on the explanation in the activity, and explain that in different countries there are different customs.

- Ask learners what the custom is in their country and in their family when they talk to an adult. Elicit answers.

- Ask learners to compare and see if there are differences in how families address members.

Answers
Learner's own answers.

Language detective (5–10 minutes)

- Focus on the explanation in the box about when we use the word *from*. Explain that we use *from* when we name the country where we live or the countries we are from.

- Say what country you are from / countries where you live. Then ask learners to say where they are from, and to name someone who is from a different country (this could be a family member, a friend or a famous person).

5 Read and talk (10–20 minutes)

- Focus on the pictures and explain that these people are all from different countries. Ask the class to describe what they see.

- Focus on the introductory lines. Ask: *Who are the 'bride' and the 'groom'?* Elicit answers.

- Tell the class that they are going to read about wedding customs from around the world.

- Ask the class if these customs are similar to customs in their country, or different. Elicit ideas from the class.

- Ask the class to vote for the wedding tradition they like most, and the clothes they like most.

CROSS-CURRICULAR LINK

Geography

Bring a map of the world to class and ask learners to locate the countries mentioned in the text. What do they know about them? How far are they from their country? If there are learners from those countries in your class, invite them to talk about their countries.

Answers
Learner's own answers.

Workbook

Learners do Activities 1–4 on pages 24–25.

› **Digital Classroom:** Use the activity 'Wedding quiz' to revise wedding customs around the world and reinforce comprehension of the text. The i button will explain how to use the activity.

Plenary ideas

Consolidation (10–15 minutes)

› **Assessment ideas:** Play noughts and crosses – draw the grid on the board. Divide the class into two groups. Ask each group questions about the lesson, for example to give a definition of a key word, a synonym, a sentence, etc. The team that gives a correct answer can put an X or O on the grid.

Homework ideas

- Learners write a few sentences about wedding customs in their own region or country.

- **Home–school link:** Learners tell their family about the customs they have read about. They ask their parents, carers or family friends about their wedding.

2.4 Write about it: What's your favourite month?

LEARNING PLAN

Learning objectives	Learning intentions	Success criteria
3Ld.04	• **Listening:** Listen to a chant; listen for information.	• Learners can listen and do a chant.
3Sc.07	• **Speaking:** Do a chant; ask and answer questions about dates.	• Learners can ask and answer questions about dates.
3Wca.03, 3Wca.04, 3Wor.02	• **Writing:** Write about favourite months; use correct spelling and punctuation.	• Learners can write about favourite months.
3Us.04	• **Language focus:** *because*	• Learners can join sentences using *because*.
	• **Vocabulary:** *cold, cool, warm, hot, sunny, windy, rainy,* ordinal numbers	

21st-century skills

Creative thinking: Respond to songs, rhymes and poems in a variety of ways.

Communication: Take turns appropriately in a conversation; interrupt others politely.

Learning to learn: Complete tasks in class as required; join in with learning activities with other children.

Materials: Learner's Book pages 34–35; Workbook pages 26–27; wall calendar showing each month of the year; sticky notes; Sample answer for Unit 2; **Photocopiable 1**, **10**; **Differentiated worksheets 2A, B and C**

Starter ideas

Vocabulary game (15–20 minutes)

*   Divide the class into two teams. On the board, draw a table with two columns – one for each team, to record their points.

*   Write words you would like the class to review on slips of paper. A learner from Team A comes up to the front, chooses a slip of paper and draws a picture to represent the word. Tell learners they cannot use words, symbols or hand gestures. Set a time limit, for example 30 seconds maximum. Each correct word gets the team a point, and the first team to get 10 points is the winner.

Main teaching ideas

1 Say the months of the year (5–10 minutes)

*   Focus on the months of the year. Tell the class that they are going to listen to a chant.

*   Play the audio twice. Then ask the class to say the chant as a class.

*   Point out the use of capital letters in names of months. Also explain the multiple meaning of *March* (noun) and *march* (verb).

*   Ask the class to stand up and join in with the chant. When they get to the month of March, they begin to march along.

Audioscript: Track 13

Learner's Book page 34

Man:	January!
Children:	January!
Man:	February!

Children:	February!
Man:	March!
Children:	March!
Man:	April!
Children:	April!
Man:	May!
Children:	May!
Man:	June!
Children:	June!
Man:	July!
Children:	July!
Man:	August!
Children:	August!
Man:	September!
Children:	September!
Man:	October!
Children:	October!
Man:	November!
Children:	November!
Man:	December!
Children:	December!

Answers
Learners say a chant and march along.

2 Talk. Discuss these questions (10–20 minutes)

- Display a wall calendar. Ask learners to work in small groups to answer the bulleted questions on page 34 of the Learner's Book. They can use the words from the box to help them answer the questions.

- Then discuss the answers as a class.

- Ask learners when their birthday is. Ask them to write their name on a sticky note and position it on their birthday date on the wall calendar.

Answers
Learner's own answers.

Language focus (5 minutes)

- Look at the Language focus and explain how to read dates.

- Explain that *1st, 2nd, 3rd, 21st, 22nd, 23rd* and *31st* do not follow the rule of adding 'th'.

> **Digital Classroom:** Use the activity 'Find the dates' to revise dates. The i button will explain how to use the activity.

3 Read, listen and say (10–15 minutes)

- Focus on the calendar in the Learner's Book. Explain that it shows when some children have their birthdays. Tell the class that they are going to listen to an audio. They point to each birthday and date as they hear it.

- Play the audio twice. Ask the class, e.g. *When's Magda's birthday?* Elicit the answer.

- Draw attention to the use of apostrophe *'s* to show ownership/possession, e.g. *Magda's birthday, Kevin's birthday*, etc.

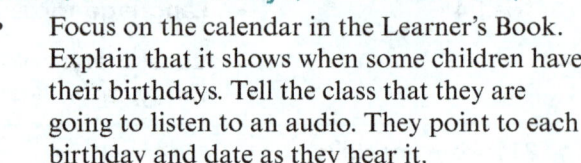

Audioscript: Track 14

Learner's Book page 34

Magda's birthday is on the first of October. Happy birthday, Magda!

Kevin's birthday is on the second of October. Have a lovely day, Kevin!

Danika's birthday is on the third of October. Enjoy your special day, Danika!

Zander's birthday is on the fifth of October. Many happy returns, Zander!

Answers
Magda's birthday is on 1st October.

4 Talk and write (5–10 minutes)

- Divide the class into pairs. Learners ask their partner when his or her birthday is.

- They write down their partner's name and birthday.

- Choose learners in turn to then read out their partner's name and birthday. Encourage them to say it in a sentence as in the example, e.g. *Michael's birthday is on the 5th of December*.

Answers
Learner's own answers.

> **Workbook**
>
> Learners do Activity 1 on page 26.

5 Write about your favourite month (20–30 minutes)

- Tell learners that they are now going to write sentences about their favourite month.

- Hand out copies of **Photocopiable 10** and follow the steps with the class.

- **Step 1:** Learners circulate, asking each other what their favourite month is. Then they form a group with other learners who have the same favourite month as them. Ask each group to brainstorm ideas about why this is their favourite month, and write the ideas in a mind map. They can use the questions to help them discuss.

- **Step 2:** Tell learners that they are now going to write a sentences about their favourite month by answering the questions in the Learner's Book, and using their ideas from their mind map. They can use the sample mind map and sentences as a model. Explain the use of *because*, and tell learners to use it in their answer. Learners work independently and write their sentences using the information in their mind maps.

- **Step 3:** When they have finished, ask groups to read their sentences aloud and decide if they want to add or take away any words. Learners check that they have answered the questions, and that they have used 'because'.

- **Step 4:** Focus on the checklist and read it with the class. Learners then use it to check their work – that they have used capital letters and full stops correctly. You may also ask learners

to check the spelling, and spelling of months in particular. Remind learners of their Writer's checklist (**Photocopiable 1**). Ask them to get their copy and use it to check their work.

- See **Sample answer for Unit 2** for an example answer to this writing task.

Answers
Learners plan, write and check their sentences.

> **Workbook**
>
> Learners do Activities 2, 3 and 4 on pages 26–27.

Plenary ideas

Consolidation (10–20 minutes)

- When learners have finished, ask groups to read out their text to the class.

- Then they can upload them to the class blog.

> **Assessment ideas:** You may wish to collect the texts and file them in the learners' portfolios.

- As a class, do a survey. Ask learners to check the wall calendar and find out which month has the most birthdays. Draw a table on the board and record the results.

Homework ideas

- Learners choose a family member and write about their favourite month using the model in Activity 5.

- Hand out copies of **Differentiated worksheets 2A, B and C** depending on each learner's ability, and ask them to complete the activities at home.

- **Home–school link:** Learners do the Challenge activity (Activity 5) on Workbook page 27. They can also ask the family about their favourite month. They can make a mini-poster for each family member with the name, the birthday and the favourite month. They can add a picture if it is appropriate.

2.5 Read and respond: Special memories

LEARNING PLAN

Learning objectives	Learning intentions	Success criteria
3Ld.04	• **Listening:** Listen and read about children's memories of family events.	• Learners can read about children's memories of family events.
3Sc.01, 3Sor.02	• **Speaking:** Discuss children's memories of family events; discuss own memories of family events; discuss personal examples of trying hard and not giving up.	• Learners can discuss children's memories of family events.
3Rd.03, 3Ro.01	• **Reading:** Read about children's memories of family events, scan texts; use text features to understand the meaning of new words.	• Learners can discuss own memories of family events.
3Wca.02, 3Wca.03	• **Writing:** Write about memories of family events; use correct spelling and punctuation.	• Learners can discuss personal examples of trying hard and not giving up.
	• **Language focus:** *could/couldn't*; *and* to join sentences	
	• **Vocabulary:** *teddy bear, beach, proud, get married, bridesmaids, petals, banquet, hide and seek, necklace*	• Learners can write about memories of family events.

21st-century skills

Critical thinking opportunity: Compare different types of information (for example, looking for similarities and differences); make predictions and estimations from given information.

Communication: Share ideas with a peer before writing and speaking tasks in order to improve the quality of their work, where necessary; can tell a story or describe something in a simple way, using simple connectors such as 'and', 'but' or 'because' to link groups of words.

Learning to learn: Show awareness of own progress in learning English (for example, by reflecting on what went well in a class).

Values: Trying hard and not giving up.

Materials: Learner's Book pages 36–39; Workbook pages 28–29; **Photocopiable 11**

Starter ideas

Memories (5–10 minutes)

• Remind learners of their discussions about memories of birthdays and special celebrations from previous lessons.

• What other memories do they have, for example of early childhood, holidays, etc. Are they happy or sad memories?

• Some learners may be reluctant to answer about difficult times. Be sensitive about this and do not press for an answer.

Main teaching ideas

1 Talk about it (5–10 minutes)

- Tell the class that they are going to read a collection of three stories.

- Ask them to read the titles and look at the pictures, and predict what memories they are going to read about. What do they think is the relationship between the titles and the pictures? Why do they think a photo is clipped to each story? What else does each story include? Elicit answers from the class.

  > **Critical thinking opportunity:** This activity offers the opportunity to practise pre-reading strategies: previewing selections by scanning text and using text features for general information/gist.

Answers

The titles are: A sad memory, A proud memory, A happy memory.
The photo clipped to each story shows the child who wrote the story.
Each story includes an illustration with a caption.

2 Read and listen (10–15 minutes)

> **Critical thinking opportunity:** How realistic do learners think the texts will be? Encourage them to give reasons for their answers.

- Tell the class that they are going to read and listen to the texts.

- Play the audio at least twice. Stop after each section and ask learners if their predictions were correct.

Audioscript: Track 15
See Learner's Book pages 36–38.

Language focus (5 minutes)

Focus on the word **memory**. Highlight the fact that it has the same root as the word **remember**.

3 Word study: Nouns (10–20 minutes)

- Point out the words in blue in the text. Ask learners to find them all and work out the meaning.

- Explain to the class that these words are all nouns. Read the explanations in the activity: that

learners can use the context (sentences and words around the noun) and other clues like the pictures to help them understand these new words.

- Then ask learners to draw a picture to help them remember the meaning of each word.

- Allow time for this, while you circulate and offer help where necessary, before offering class feedback.

Answers

Words and suggested definitions:
- *Teddy bear*: a soft toy bear.
- *Beach*: the land next to the sea (covered with sand or small stones).
- *Peak*: the highest part of a mountain.
- *Picnic*: a meal that you prepare at home and eat outside, away from home.
- *Parents*: your mother and father.
- *Necklace*: a piece of jewellery that you wear around your neck.

Learners draw pictures to represent each blue noun in the text.

4 Read and talk (15–25 minutes)

- Ask learners to work with a partner and read and discuss the questions.

- Encourage them to make notes of their answers.

  > **Assessment ideas:** Circulate, listening to the learners' conversations. Take notes of performance and mistakes for remedial work. If necessary, help with additional vocabulary.

- When pairs have finished, ask them to get together with other pairs and compare their answers.

- Finally, discuss answers as a class.

Answers

A sad memory: **a** The boy lost his teddy bear called Bruno. **b** Learner's own answers.
A proud memory: **c** Ling's mother. **d** Ling and her grandfather. A happy memory: **e** (Various possible answers: those supplied are followed by textual clues). She liked the long dresses ('beautiful long dresses'), she liked decorating the car with balloons ('It was fun!') and she liked the necklace ('I still have my necklace.').
f To say 'thank you' to them and to help them to remember the day. (Other answers possible.)
Language detective: cannot

5 Values: Keep trying! Don't give up! (10–15 minutes)

- Ask learners to work individually. Ask them to think of a time they tried to do something that was difficult, for example play a sport, do a piece of homework, play a musical instrument, etc.

- Direct them to use the questions in the Learner's Book to help them.

- When they have finished, ask them to pair up and discuss their experiences with a partner.

> **Critical thinking opportunity:** When they have finished, ask pairs to tell the class about their experiences. Have they had similar experiences to other learners? How did they overcome the difficulties?

Answers
Learner's own answers.

Language detective (5–10 minutes)

- Remind learners of the use of *can*. Ask them to supply examples of things they can and can't do.

- Focus on the explanation in the box – using *could* as the past form of *can* – and the question. Encourage learners to answer the question.

> **Digital Classroom:** Use the activity 'Past or present?' to reinforce the use of irregular past verbs. The i button will explain how to use the activity.

Answers
Couldn't is the past form of *can't*.

6 Write: *Could* or *couldn't* (10–15 minutes)

- Ask learners to look for sentences with *could* or *couldn't* in the reading texts. Ask them to read these sentences aloud and then write them out themselves.

- Then ask learners to write sentences about themselves in their notebooks using *could* and *couldn't*.

- Offer some examples and elicit a few from the class.

Answers
A sad memory: We **could** play in the sand and swim in the sea all day. I **couldn't** sleep that night without my teddy bear. We went back to look for him the next day, but we **couldn't** find him.
A proud memory: She thought I **couldn't** climb that far. I knew I **could** do it. He said to me, 'I knew you **could**

do it, Ling! I am really proud that you climbed this mountain with me.'
A happy memory: We ate and ate until we **couldn't** eat any more. After dinner our parents said we **could** play. Learner's own answers.

7 Draw and write (10–15 minutes)

- Point to each of the emotion images in turn and explain what each one is. Then ask learners to think of a memory that is one of these emotions.

- Ask learners to draw a picture of their chosen memory and write a title for it. They then write a few sentences about their memory.

- Ask learners to share their sentences with the class. Can they find things in common with other learners?

- When they have finished, display the pictures and sentences around the class. You could also then file them in the learners' portfolios.

Answers
Learner's own answers.

Workbook

Learners do Activities 1–7 on pages 28–29.

> **Digital Classroom:** Use the activity 'School memories: matching' to reinforce special memories vocabulary and listening comprehension. The i button will explain how to use the activity.

Plenary ideas

Consolidation (10–20 minutes)

> **Assessment ideas:** Ask learners what they have found the most interesting/difficult in this unit. What could they do easily? What couldn't they do? Ask them to reflect what they would do differently the next time.

- Hand out copies of **Photocopiable 11** and ask learners to complete the activity in pairs.

Homework ideas

- Learners write about a memory using the texts as a model.

- Learners bring a photo of a memory to the following class.

- **Home–school link:** Learners read the texts to their family. They ask them about sad, proud and happy memories they have.

2.6 Project challenge

LEARNING PLAN

Learning objectives	Learning intentions	Success criteria
3Sc.07 3Rd.02 3Wca.03, 3Wca.04, 3Wc.01	• **Speaking:** Discuss a project; discuss steps of a project; organise work; present their project to the class. • **Reading:** Read and understand instructions. • **Writing:** Write instructions; spell words correctly; use correct punctuation; write greetings; write about memories. • **Language focus:** Unit 2 review • **Vocabulary:** Unit 2 review	• Learners can read and understand instructions. • Learners can give instructions. • Learners can plan a project. • Learners can make a scrapbook. • Learners can make a birthday card. • Learners can write greetings.

21st-century skills

Creative thinking: Design new items based on a model.

Collaboration: Respect the importance of doing a fair share of group work; keep to the instructions to complete the task; invite others to give their opinions during the task.

Learning to learn: Listen and respond positively to feedback and understand why a correction was given; learn from mistakes and feedback.

Materials: Learner's Book pages 40–41; Workbook pages 30–31; Project A: (prior to the lesson, you could ask learners to bring in a photo of a memory – optional), writing/drawing supplies, sheets of paper or file cards; Project B: coloured cards, sheets of paper or file cards, writing/drawing supplies, photos, glue, scissors, wall calendar, **Photocopiable 12**, **13** and **14**; End of Unit 2 test

Starter ideas

Looking back (15–20 minutes)

* Ask the class to choose a lesson from Unit 2 that they liked a lot. Ask them to explain why they liked it.

* Use the wall calendar to revisit saying dates, before moving on to the project of making the birthday card (Project B). Ask learners about their birthdays as well as their families' birthdays.

> **Assessment ideas:** Divide the class into two teams and play a few rounds of charades to revise new vocabulary and useful phrases. This game will give you the opportunity to assess how much learners remember from previous lessons.

Main teaching ideas

Learners choose an end-of-unit project to work on. Look at the examples in the pictures and help learners to choose. Provide materials.

Project A: Make a 'Memories' scrapbook or slideshow (60–90 minutes)

* Read Steps 1–6 in the Learner's Book. Give out drawing and writing supplies.

* Divide learners into groups depending on the memory subject they choose. Ask learners to bring in a photo of a memory, or to draw a picture.

- Each member of the group writes a few sentences for their picture.

- They read their sentences aloud to a partner and check each other's work, for example spelling, punctuation, choice of words, etc.

- Learners could make a group slideshow – they scan the pictures and type the sentences. They then make a title screen, and write the title and all the authors' names.

- Alternatively, learners could make a scrapbook – they staple the pages together to make a group scrapbook. They then create a cover and write their names on it.

- When they have finished, groups share their work with the class.

> **Assessment ideas:** You may wish to video-record groups as they work so that they can then use copies of the recordings to assess what they have done and how they have worked. The copies can then be shared with the family and filed in their portfolios. You may also display the slideshows or the scrapbooks during an open day for families to see.

Project B: Make a pop-up birthday card (60–90 minutes)

- Tell learners that they are going to make a pop-up birthday card for a friend or family member. Give them the necessary supplies.

- Ask them to help each other read and follow Steps 1–8.

- First, ask learners to make a list of the people they would like to make a card for and write down the birthday dates. They choose who they are going to make the card for.

- Then they follow the instructions and make their card.

- When they have finished, they write on the outside of the card who the card is to, and who it is from.

- They choose and write one of the three messages on the inside of the card.

> **Assessment ideas:** More confident learners may wish to add more to the message or write a different one.

- When they have finished, they show their pop-up card to the class and read the messages aloud.

> **Assessment ideas:** You may wish to video-record groups as they work so that they can then use copies of the recordings to assess what they have done and how they have worked. The copies can then be shared with the family and filed in their portfolios. Learners may give the card to the person they have made it for on a special occasion.

> **Differentiation ideas:** When learners have finished their work on Projects A and B, give them a copy of **Photocopiable 13** and read the instructions as a class. Ask them to work independently and think about their work on the projects. They reflect and answer the questions. Ask them to tick off the aims they have achieved. Insist on the importance of giving honest answers.

Workbook

Learners do the Check your progress quiz on pages 30–31.

Plenary ideas

Reflect on your learning (5–10 minutes)

- Draw learners' attention to the 'Reflect on your learning' questions in the Learner's Book.

- Learners answer the questions to reflect on their project work.

Consolidation (10–15 minutes)

If you have been filing learners' work during this unit, you may find it useful to put all the work of this unit together. You could ask learners to make a cover for their Unit 2 work, decorating it with an image that represents what they have learned.

Homework ideas

- Learners draw a picture of what they have enjoyed most about this unit. For learners who completed Project B, you could hand out copies of **Photocopiable 12** if they would like to make additional pop-up cards at home.

- **Home–school link:** Learners show their family their projects.

2.7 What do you know now?

Materials: Photocopiable 14

What are some of your favourite family memories? (35–45 minutes)

* Learners work in pairs. They work together through all the tasks set in this section. Hand out copies of **Photocopiable 14** for learners to use for question 4.

* They write the answers in their notebooks. You may ask them to have a special section in their notebooks where they record the answers.

* Whenever their opinion is requested, encourage them to be honest in their answers.

Answers

1–6 Learner's own answers.

Look what I can do! (15 minutes)

* Review the *I can* … statements on page 42 of the Learner's Book. Learners demonstrate what they can do.

* Learners colour in the faces to show which things they can do.

* Encourage them to be honest in their answers.

Workbook

Learners answer the Reflection questions on page 31.

> 3 The desert

Unit plan

Lesson	Approximate number of learning hours	Outline of learning content	Learning objectives	Resources
1 Deserts around the world	1.5–2.5	Read and talk about deserts around the world.	3Ld.03 3Lo.01 3Sc.02 3So.01 3Rd.01 3Wca.03	Learner's Book Lesson 3.1 Workbook Lesson 3.1 ⤓ Photocopiable 3 ⤓ Photocopiable 15 **Digital Classroom:** Video – Deserts; Activity – The living desert
2 At the oasis	2.25–3.25	Discuss friendship and events in the past.	3Ld.02 3Sc.01 3So.01 3Sc.07 3Rd.03 3Ug.01 3Ug.04	Learner's Book Lesson 3.2 Workbook Lesson 3.2 **Digital Classroom:** Slideshow – What is an oasis?; Activity – Present or past simple; Activity – Opposites: matching; Slideshow – Opposites
3 Desert reptiles	1.25–2.5	Talk about and compare desert reptiles.	3Ld.04 3Sc.03 3So.01 3Sor.01 3Rd.01 3Wca.05 3Ug.09	Learner's Book Lesson 3.3 Workbook Lesson 3.3 **Digital Classroom:** Activity – Which reptile?; Grammar presentation – Comparative and superlative adjectives
4 Desert adaptations	1.75–2.75	Write a report about a desert animal.	3So.01 4Rd.01 3Wca.03 3Wca.05 3Wor.02 3Ug.03 3Us.03	Learner's Book Lesson 3.4 Workbook Lesson 3.4 ⤓ Sample answer for Unit 3 ⤓ Differentiated worksheets 3A, B and C ⤓ Photocopiable 1 **Digital Classroom:** Activity – Which animal?

(continued)

Lesson	Approximate number of learning hours	Outline of learning content	Learning objectives	Resources
5 *Rattlesnake, Mouse and Clever Coyote*	2.0–3.5	Read, discuss and act out a story about a trick.	3Ld.04 3Sc.05 3Rm.02 3Rd.01 3Rd.03 3Wc.02 3Wc.03	Learner's Book Lesson 3.5 Workbook Lesson 3.5 ⬇ Photocopiable 16 **Digital Classroom:** Activity – Rattlesnake, Mouse and Clever Coyote
6 Project challenge	1.5–2.25	Make a desert mural or a weather chart.	3Sc.06 3Sc.07 3Rd.02 3Wca.02 3Wca.04 3Wc.01	Learner's Book Lesson 3.6 Workbook Lesson 3.6 ⬇ Photocopiable 17 ⬇ Photocopiable 18
7 What do you know now?	0.75–1.0	Self-assessment and reflection.		Learner's Book Lesson 3.7 ⬇ Photocopiable 19

Cross-unit resources
⬇ Unit 3 Audioscripts
⬇ End of Unit 3 test
⬇ Unit 3 Progress report
⬇ Unit 3 Wordlist

BACKGROUND KNOWLEDGE

Measuring temperature: Celsius and Fahrenheit

In Lesson 3.1, learners are taught how to measure temperature in degrees Celsius. However, this is not the only scale we can use. Gabriel Fahrenheit created the Fahrenheit scale in the 18th century, which has the freezing point of water as 32 degrees and the boiling point as 212 degrees. Not long after, Anders Celsius invented the Celsius scale, which has the freezing point of water as 0 degree and the boiling point of water as 100 degrees.

The Celsius scale is known as a Universal System Unit, and it is used in science and in most countries. However, the Fahrenheit is still the most used in countries such as the USA, the Bahamas, Palau, Belize, the Cayman Islands, the Federated States of Micronesia, the Marshall Islands, Puerto Rico, the US Virgin Islands and Guam.

Camels

In Lesson 3.4, learners read about camels. Camels are large mammals that live in desert regions of Africa and Asia. They are famous for having humps and for being able to survive for long periods without drinking. The Arabian (dromedary) camel has one hump, while the Bactrian camel has two. Camels have long been used as pack or saddle animals. People also use them for their milk, meat, wool and hide.

About one million domesticated Bactrian camels live in the Middle East, China and Mongolia. Wild Bactrian camels are very rare – most (around 650 adult animals) live in the Gobi Desert.

TEACHING SKILLS FOCUS

Reading strategies: Reading fluency

Reading fluency is much more than simply reading quickly. It involves the ability to read words accurately, at the appropriate speed and with suitable expression and intonation. Reading fluency is also closely linked to comprehension – if a reader is stuck reading individual words, their comprehension of the text can help them to decode the words by creating an overall picture in their mind of what the text is about. Reading fluency also includes reading words with the correct expression; otherwise a reader will be unable to construct meaning, which is the ultimate aim of reading.

Reading fluency can be particularly challenging for learners of English, so we need to help them develop strategies to improve reading fluency. Here are some ideas:

1 Listen to fluent readers, which will provide learners with models for their own reading; for example, audio books, listening to fluent readers reading aloud.

2 Reread familiar texts. After learners have read a text a few times, they may have decoded some or all of the unfamiliar vocabulary so they can focus on improving their fluency.

3 Start with short texts, such as fluency strips – these are simple sentences written on slips of paper. Write one sentence on each slip and have learners choose one to read aloud. As their fluency improves, you may write fluency slips consisting of two or three sentences.

Your challenge

In each unit of the Learner's Book, opportunities to introduce, practise and develop reading fluency are highlighted.

Look through Unit 3 and use the activities below to introduce more opportunities for developing reading fluency.

1 Provide opportunities for reading aloud. Model reading first and then have learners read aloud. They can do so in un-threatening and fun ways, for example silent reading, choral reading, partner reading, games or reader's theatre.

2 Crazy reading: This is a fun game that requires learners to read a text in different ways – as if they were sad, bored, excited or crying, or reading very slowly or very quickly, etc. and adding dramatic gestures. Ask the whole class to read in a particular way, or give each learner (or groups of learners) slips of paper with different feelings.

3 Reader's theatre: Learners are given a script and a role to act out (they do not need to memorise their part). They have to reread it several times – providing opportunities for repeated readings helps to develop word recognition and fluency skills, and also helps to boost reading confidence. Follow these steps:

   - Choose a text from the Learners' Book, other texts of your choice or a text chosen by the class.

   - Choose a prepared script or adapt a text. The best scripts include plenty of dialogue.

   - Assign roles or, if you do this activity in groups, ask group members to choose the roles they would like to play.

   - Group members highlight the lines they have to read.

   - Learners rehearse their lines in their groups.

   - Groups perform.

Reflection

How successful was the implementation of these ideas? How can you improve them? How could you encourage shy or reluctant learners to take part or feel more comfortable? Is more scaffolding necessary?

3.1 Think about it: Deserts around the world

LEARNING PLAN

Learning objectives	Learning intentions	Success criteria
3Ld.03, 3Lo.01	• **Listening:** Listen for general and specific information; listen for detail.	• Learners can read and understand a text about deserts.
3Sc.02, 3So.01	• **Speaking:** Sing a song; share background knowledge about deserts; state and support opinions.	• Learners can listen for specific information.
3Rd.01	• **Reading:** Make predictions based on text features.	• Learners can sing a song.
3Wca.03	• **Writing:** Write notes; write temperatures.	• Learners can talk about deserts and regions in the world.
	• **Language focus:** measuring temperature; comparatives/superlatives.	• Learners can identify deserts and continents on a world map.
	• **Vocabulary:** desert animals and plants, weather and temperature, geographic regions, continents; *at night, during the day, desert, dry, sandy, flat, cactus, waxy, sharp, spine, minus, degrees, Celsius*	• Learners can understand desert weather.
		• Learners can understand temperature.

21st-century skills

Critical thinking: Compare and contrast information; make predictions about a text; understand cause and effect; research information.

Collaboration: Take part in tasks by interacting with others and stay on task; communicate own knowledge of a topic; ask others questions about a topic.

Learning to learn: Take basic notes about key information while reading and listening; engage with practice activities in class.

Materials: Learner's Book pages 43–45; Workbook pages 32–33; map of the world; large sheet of poster paper; index cards or sticky notes; sticky-tack; a wall thermometer or an app where learners can see the temperature (optional); **Photocopiable 3, 15**

Starter ideas

Deserts (5 minutes)

• Write the word *desert* on the board. Ask learners if they know what a desert is. Elicit a few ideas.

• Learners often confuse *desert* with *dessert*. Point out the differences in spelling, pronunciation and meaning.

• You may wish to ask learners to repeat *desert* a few times, making sure they put the stress on the first syllable. Model the pronunciation of *dessert*, with stress on the second syllable, so that they perceive the difference clearly.

Getting started (10–15 minutes)

• Focus on the pictures on Learner's Book page 43 and discuss questions a–c.

• Ask the class if there are any deserts in their country. If there are, help the class locate them on a map.

> **Critical thinking opportunity:** Ask learners to work in small groups. Give them a copy of the K-W-L ('know', 'would like to know', 'learned') chart on **Photocopiable 3**. Brainstorm with the class what they know about deserts. Ask them to write down what they know in the K column. When they have finished, ask them what they would like to learn about deserts in this unit; have them write this in question form in the W column. Explain that you will come back to the table at the end of each lesson to see what questions they have found answers to, and write these in the L column.

Answers
Learner's own answers.

> **Digital Classroom:** Use the video 'Deserts' to introduce the subject of deserts. The i button will explain how to use the video.

Sing along! *Song of the shifting sand* (10–15 minutes)

- Ask the class what sounds they would expect to hear in a desert. Would they hear birds? Animals? Elicit ideas. Supply additional vocabulary as necessary.

- You could play some sound clips from YouTube, for example 'The Desert at Night' Soundscape, and ask learners to identify what they hear. Is it animals? Insects? Birds? Elicit ideas.

- Tell the class you are going to listen to a song about the desert. Give each learner a copy of **Photocopiable 15**: Sing along! *Song of the shifting sand*.

- Play the song at least twice and ask the class what it is about. Elicit answers.

- Sing the song and encourage learners to join in.

> **Critical thinking opportunity:** Ask questions about the lyrics. Ask learners why they think the song is called 'Song of the shifting sand' (The sand in the desert is never still – it moves and shifts.) Ask: *Why is 'the sun beating down'? What's a 'date palm tree'?*

> **Differentiation ideas:** You could give less confident learners copies of the lyrics. You could challenge more confident learners to try to sing without the support of the recording.

- You may wish to show learners some videos of deserts online, for example *Visual Soundscapes – Desert*; search for *Planet Earth II, BBC America* to find this online.

Audioscript: Track 16
Learner's Book page 43

Song of the shifting sand
Walking 'cross the desert with the sun beating down
The sky so blue, the land so brown.
It's peaceful and still, yet there's life all around
Listen, listen to the desert sounds.
I hear
The song of the shifting sand.

Walking 'cross the desert with the sun beating down
The sky so blue, the land so brown.
It's peaceful and still, yet there's life around
Listen, listen to the desert sounds.
I hear
The call of a bird, flying free,
The song of the shifting sand.

Walking 'cross the desert with the sun beating down
The sky so blue, the land so brown.
It's peaceful and still, yet there's life around
Listen, listen to the desert sounds.
I hear
The wind in the leaves of a date palm tree,
The call of a bird, flying free,
The song of the shifting sand.

Walking 'cross the desert with the sun beating down
The sky so blue, the land so brown.
It's peaceful and still, yet there's life around
Listen, listen to the desert sounds.
I hear
The music of my friends where I soon will be,
The wind in the leaves of a date palm tree,
The call of a bird, flying free,
The song of the shifting sand.

Main teaching ideas

1 Talk about the four questions that are headings in the article (5–10 minutes)

- Focus on the article on Learner's Book page 44 and draw learners' attention to the four headings in the article – they are all questions.

- Ask learners to work in pairs to discuss these questions and write down their ideas.

- Then share ideas with the class.

Answers
Learner's own answers.

2 Listen and read the article (5–15 minutes)

- Explain that you are going to play the audio of the article while learners listen and read.

- Play the audio while learners read.

- Then as a class, talk about the new facts they have learned. Which do they think is the most interesting fact?

> **Critical thinking opportunity:** See the Cross-curricular link below.

CROSS-CURRICULAR LINK

Natural sciences

You may ask learners additional questions, for example: *What's the weather like in a desert? What's the land like? What kinds of plants can survive in a desert? What's a cactus? And a saxaul? Why does land turn into a desert? What are the consequences of cutting down too many trees?*

Audioscript: Track 17

See Learner's Book page 44

Answers
Learners read the article and discuss the facts.

> **Digital Classroom:** Use the activity 'The living desert' to reinforce comprehension of the text. The i button will explain how to use the activity.

3 Vocabulary: Geography (10–15 minutes)

- Ask learners what the difference is between a *continent* and a *country*. Elicit ideas.

- Focus on the map of the world you displayed in Activity 3 and ask learners to label the seven continents.

- Focus on the questions and the map in the Learner's Book. As a class, go through the questions one at a time. Elicit answers.

- Ask individual learners to locate the places on the map of the world while the class works on the map in their books. Ask learners to identify a continent where there are no deserts, for example Europe.

Answers
1 South America, 2 Africa, 3 Antarctica, 4 North America, 5 Asia

4 Listen to learn more about deserts (10–15 minutes)

- Ask learners to read questions a–e. Discuss the meaning of the words in bold and give some examples to help the class understand them. Explain the meanings if necessary.

- Ask the class to predict the answers and write their ideas on the board.

- Then tell learners to choose one question. Explain that you are going to play the audio and they have to listen for the answer to their chosen question.

- Ask learners to copy their chosen question in their notebook and take note of the information they need.

- Play the audio a few times. It may be necessary to stop after each desert is described. Allow enough time for the class to write the answers.

- Once everyone has finished taking notes, ask who has chosen the first question; ask those learners to share the information with the class.

- Proceed in the same way with the other questions.

> **Critical thinking opportunity:** Ask learners what helped them find the answers. This activity requires learners to focus on a question and look for specific information. Focusing on one question at a time helps them select the information they really need. This is especially useful when they work with long texts that include new vocabulary or a new topic.

> **Differentiation ideas:** After you have finished the activity, ask more confident learners to write down some more detailed questions about the other deserts. With less confident groups, you may share the transcript with the class. Give each learner a copy of 'their' desert. Learners work in groups of five and take turns to ask and answer questions about the other deserts.

Audioscript: Track 18

Learner's Book page 45

The Atacama Desert is in South America. It is the driest place on Earth. It gets almost no rain – about 1 centimetre each year. It is hot during the day and cold at night. Not many plants grow in the Atacama Desert.

The Sahara Desert is the largest hot desert on Earth. It is a very hot desert. The Sahara Desert is in northern Africa. It covers 12 different countries. Some parts of the Sahara are sandy, but most parts are rocky. The name 'Sahara' means 'great desert' in the Arabic language.

The Sonoran Desert is in North America. Like all other deserts it is a dry place, but there are a few heavy rainfalls in the summer and in the winter. Grown in the Sonoran Desert, the saguaro cactus plant, the tallest cactus on Earth, grows as tall as a six-storey building.

Some deserts are called 'cold deserts.' The Antarctic Desert is the largest cold desert on Earth. The Antarctic Desert is covered with ice!

The Gobi Desert in Asia is also called a 'cold desert'. In the winter, the Gobi Desert is very cold and very windy. But in the summer, the Gobi Desert can get very hot.

Answers

a Sahara is the largest hot desert.
b Antarctica is the largest cold desert.
c Sonoran Desert has the tallest cactus.
d Atacama Desert is drier than the Sonoran Desert.
e Gobi Desert is colder in winter than the Sahara Desert.

5 Read the thermometer. What's the temperature? (10–20 minutes)

- Focus on the picture. Ask the class what it is and what we use it for.

- Explain that temperatures are measured in degrees.

- Write temperatures on the board and ask the class to read them. Explain that we can say both *minus 5 degrees* and also *5 degrees below zero.*

- Explain that we sometimes write a capital C to show that degrees are expressed in Celsius, a scale that measures temperatures.

- Ask learners: *What's the weather like today? Is it cold, cool, warm or hot?* Elicit answers.

- Then ask: *What do you think the temperature is?* Elicit ideas.

- If possible, bring a wall thermometer to the class and show what the temperature is in the classroom. You could take the class to the schoolyard and measure the temperature outside. What difference is there?

- You could also use an app or visit a website such as Weather Channel and show the class what the temperature is in their city or region, as well as in other parts of the world.

CROSS-CURRICULAR LINK

Science

You may wish to explain that, as well as Celsius, there are other ways of measuring temperature, i.e. Fahrenheit. You could explain the difference between Celsius and Fahrenheit, and how temperatures can be converted from one into the other.

Answers

Learner's own answers.

6 Listen and write the temperatures you hear (5–10 minutes)

- Tell the class that they are going to listen to four short dialogues and they have to write the temperatures they hear.

- Play the audio a few times. Stop after each mini-dialogue and ask the class: *What's the temperature? Is it hot, warm, cool or cold?*

- Elicit the answers from the class. Tell the class that what is considered hot, warm, cool or cold is subjective and will depend on the climate where they live.

Audioscript: Track 19

Learner's Book page 45

1   What's the temperature?
    I think it's 30 degrees. Phew!

2   What's the temperature?
    It's 9 degrees. I need my jacket.

3   What's the temperature?
    It's minus 8 degrees. Brrrrr!

4   What's the temperature?
    It's about 17 degrees. That's nice!

Answers

1   The weather is hot.
2   The weather is cool.
3   The weather is cold.
4   The weather is warm.

Workbook

Learners do Activities 1–4 on pages 32–33.

Plenary ideas

Consolidation (10–20 minutes)

- Learners make a temperature poster. They use a thermometer and record the temperature every day for a number of days, e.g. until they finish this unit.

> **Assessment ideas:** Ask learners to get their KWL charts and read the questions they asked. Have they found the answers to any of them? Is there any new information they now know that they didn't know before? Learners write the new information they have learned in the L column.

Homework ideas

- Learners choose one of the deserts they learned about. Give them a list of suitable websites or books from the school library. Learners look for information and pictures about the desert they have chosen and prepare a poster and a short presentation for the class.

- **Home–school link:** Learners could tell their family what they have learned about deserts and temperatures. They can also look for information about the highest and lowest temperatures in their country and in their region, and write a few sentences.

3.2 Language arts: At the oasis

LEARNING PLAN

Learning objectives	Learning intentions	Success criteria
3Ld.02	• **Listening:** Listen to a story; listen to and understand questions; listen and understand opinions.	• Learners can read and understand a story about friendship.
3Sc.01, 3So.01, 3Sc.07	• **Speaking:** Ask and answer questions; discuss a story; discuss friendship; discuss the qualities of a good friend.	• Learners can discuss the qualities of a good friend.
3Rd.03	• **Reading:** Read a story; use context to understand the meaning of new words.	• Learners can ask and answer questions about a story.
3Ug.01	• **Language focus:** past simple of regular and irregular verbs, *Wh-* questions	• Learners can use the past tense of regular and irregular verbs.
3Ug.04	• **Vocabulary:** opposites; *oasis, argue, yell, waterhole, cool off, shore, carve, blow away, kindness, wise, hurt, glad*	• Learners can use opposites. • Learners can give opinions.

21st-century skills

Critical thinking opportunity: Use features of a text to understand its meaning.

Collaboration: Listen attentively while other students are contributing; respectfully wait for their turn to speak.

Values: Identify the value of friendship, the qualities of a good friend.

Materials: Learner's Book pages 46–47; Workbook pages 34–35; large sheet of poster paper, slips of paper or index cards

Starter ideas

Temperatures and deserts (5–10 minutes)

- If learners have done the homework activity, ask them to present their findings to the class.
- When they have finished, make a class display of their work. Alternatively, you may ask them to upload their work to the class blog.
- Ask learners to look at the temperature today and record it in the temperature poster they created in the previous lesson.

Main teaching ideas

> **Digital Classroom:** Use the slideshow 'What is an oasis?' to introduce the subject of desert oases. The i button will explain how to use the slideshow.

1 Read and listen to a traditional tale (10–15 minutes)

- Ask the class who their best friend is. Ask them what they have in common with this friend.
- Have they ever quarrelled with their friend? Were they angry? Was their friend angry? What did they do afterwards? Elicit ideas.

> **Critical thinking opportunity:** Focus on the pictures. Encourage learners to describe them. Ask the class to predict what the story is about. Elicit some ideas.

- Point at the picture of the oasis. Ask the class what they call a place like that. Elicit ideas. Focus on the key word *oasis* and the explanation. Remind the class that pictures and titles can help them establish not only what a story is about but also what new words mean.

- Tell learners to listen and read about the two friends in the picture. As they read, they should think about the lesson it teaches about friendship.

- Play the audio at least twice while learners follow the story in their books.

> **Differentiation ideas:** Ask learners to read the text again and discuss the meaning of the new words. Encourage them to discover the meaning independently and write a definition. Less confident learners may copy the words in their notebooks and draw a picture to remind them of the meaning. You could ask more confident learners to look for synonyms in dictionaries.

Audioscript: Track 20
See Learner's Book page 46.

Language detective: Regular and irregular verbs (10–20 minutes)

- Ask the class to look at the past forms of the verbs and say what they notice about these words.

- Focus on the explanation of how regular verbs are formed. Give some more examples and ask learners to add some more. Have them make some sentences.

- Focus on irregular verbs. Give some more examples and ask learners to add some more. Help them to discover the difference between regular and irregular verbs. Then have them make some sentences.

- You may wish to remind learners of the spelling rules for making the past tense of verbs.

> **Digital Classroom:** Use the activity 'Present or past simple' to reinforce the use of past simple verbs. The i button will explain how to use the activity.

2 Use of English. Find the past simple of these verbs in the story (10–20 minutes)

- Ask learners to read the verbs in the word box. Tell them to find the past simple of these verbs in the story.

- Then ask learners to copy the list into their notebooks and write the past forms of the verbs.

- As an extension, you could ask learners to create an irregular part tense poster. Draw a table with three columns on a large sheet of poster paper – the first for the infinitive forms and the second for the irregular past forms. Tell the class you are leaving the third column blank for now, and fill it in with participle forms when the class learns the present perfect. Ask learners to fill in the irregular verbs they have come across in the story. They can also look back at Units 1 and 2 and try to find verbs that have irregular forms in the past.

Answers
yell – yelled, stop – stopped, jump – jumped, rest – rested, shout – shouted, carve – carved, save – saved, smile – smiled

3 Write. Find the past simple of these verbs in the story (10–15 minutes)

- Ask learners to read the verbs in the list. Tell them to find the past simple of these verbs in the story.

- Then ask learners to copy the list into their notebooks and write the past form of each verb.

Answers
feel – felt, write – wrote, read – read, come – came, see – saw, think – thought, swim – swam, say – said

4 Talk. Discuss the questions (25–30 minutes)

- Focus on the questions. Ask learners to work individually and write the answers.

- When they have finished, ask learners to compare their answers with a partner and discuss any differences. Then hold an open class discussion.

- Tell learners to write four more questions using *What? Why? How?* and *Where?*

- Check correct formation of questions and answers, for example *What did Ibrahim say? He said ... .*

- When learners have finished, they take turns to ask and answer the questions.

> **Differentiation ideas:** Less confident learners may also write the answers to their own questions to help them check their partner's answers. More confident learners may add subsequent questions to the ones they initially asked, and develop a conversation.

Answers
a   Hassan yelled at Ibrahim because he was angry with him.
b   Ibrahim felt hurt and upset.
c   Ibrahim wrote 'Today my friend yelled at me.'
d   Learner's own answers.

5   Write four more questions about the story. Use the question words (15–20 minutes)

- Learners ask their partner four more questions about the story using these question words: *What did...? Why did...? How did...? Where did...?*

- Circulate, checking correct formation of questions.

Answers
Learner's own answers.

6   Word study: Opposites (25–30 minutes)

- Focus on the words. Explain what opposites are and give a few examples.

- Ask learners to think of some opposites in their own language.

- As a class, read the story again and find the opposites of the words in the box.

- Turn to the Picture dictionary: Opposites (Learner's Book pages 168–169). Learners choose three new opposite pairs and make sentences with them.

- Ask learners to write their opposite pairs on slips of paper or index cards, one word per slip or card.

- Divide the class into groups of four. Each group member puts their six slips of paper face down on the table. They shuffle them and take

it in turns to pick two cards or slips of paper and put them face up. If they have a matching opposite pair, they keep both cards. If they don't match, they return the cards face down and reshuffle.

> **Digital Classroom:** Use the activity 'Opposites: matching' to reinforce the concept of opposites. The i button will explain how to use the activity.

> **Digital Classroom:** Use the slideshow 'Opposites' to reinforce opposites. The i button will explain how to use the activity.

Answers
cold – hot, slowly – quickly, whispered – shouted, stupid – wise
Learner's own answers.

7   Values: Friendship (10–15 minutes)

- Read the questions with the class.

- Ask learners to work in pairs and discuss the questions. Tell them to use the words in the box. Encourage them to be very honest in their answers.

> **Assessment ideas:** Circulate, listening to learners' interactions and take notes of mistakes for remedial work. Also pay attention to their interactions, for example respect for turn-taking, use of repair strategies when communication breaks down, encouraging their partner to speak, etc.

Answers
- If you are unkind to your friend, what should you say? Possible answers: *Sorry. I'm sorry. That was unkind.*
- If your friend does something kind to you, what should you say? Possible answers: *Thank you very much. Thank you for being kind. Thank you for helping me.*
- What do you think is the most important thing for a friend to be? Learner's own answers.

> **Workbook**
> Learners do Activities 1–3 on pages 34–35.

Plenary ideas

Consolidation (10–20 minutes)

- Ask learners to pretend that they are Hassan and Ibrahim, and role play a conversation. Hassan should apologise for getting angry and yelling at his friend; Ibrahim should accept Hassan's apology and thank Hassan for saving his life.

- Invite volunteers to perform their role plays for the class.

Homework ideas

- Learners search the internet and look for stories that are similar to the one they have read, or they can ask their family if they know one. They make notes of the story and retell it to the class on the next day.

- **Home–school link:** Learners tell the story to their family.

3.3 Talk about it: Desert reptiles

LEARNING PLAN

Learning objectives	Learning intentions	Success criteria
3Ld.04 3Sc.03, 3So.01, 3Sor.01 3Rd.01 3Wca.05 3Ug.09	• **Listening:** Listen for information; listen for detail; listen to how living things adapt to their habitat. • **Speaking:** Talk about desert animals; talk about how living things adapt to their habitat; compare desert animals; give and justify opinions. • **Reading:** Read about desert animals; read about how living things adapt to their habitat. • **Writing:** Write about animals using superlatives. • **Language focus:** comparative and superlative adjectives • **Vocabulary:** *thick, waxy, skin, sharp, spine, hawk, canyon, lizard, coyote, rocky, trail, thorn, steep, cliff, scurry, keen-nosed, trot, bush, sharp-eyed, dive, cliff top, splash, amidst*	• Learners can talk about how living things adapt to their habitat. • Learners can read and understand a text about desert animals. • Learners can listen to and understand a text about how living things adapt to their habitat. • Learners can give and justify opinions about desert animals. • Learners can compare and contrast desert animals.

21st-century skills

Critical thinking opportunity: Understand cause and effect, state and support opinions, compare and contrast.

Collaboration: Be aware of when and how to take turns and when and how to interrupt; communicate own knowledge of a topic; ask others questions about a topic.

Learning to learn: Take basic notes about key information while reading and listening.

Materials: Learner's Book pages 48–49; Workbook pages 36–37; photos of animals that live in different natural regions, for example monkeys, tigers, lions, buffalo, etc., as well as lizards, Komodo dragons, crocodiles and large snakes, e.g. anaconda; map of the world; sticky notes or index cards and sticky tack

LANGUAGE BACKGROUND

Spelling rules for the past simple of verbs

The '-ed' spelling rules for the formation of the past simple of regular verbs are as follows:

- Add **-ed** to a verb to change it to the past tense, e.g. *walk + ed = walked*.
- When the verb ends in **-e**, add only **d**, e.g. *arrive + d = arrived*.
- When a verb ends in a vowel + **y**, add **-ed**, e.g. *play + ed = played*.

- However, if the verb ends in a consonant + *y*, change the *y* to *i* and add **-ed**, e.g. *carry + ed = carried*.
- If a one-syllable verb ends in a vowel + consonant, double the consonant, e.g. *stop + p + ed = stopped*.
- When the stress is on the final syllable of a verb that ends in vowel + consonant, double the consonant, e.g. *refer + r + ed = referred*.
- However, if the stress is not on the final syllable of a verb that ends in vowel + consonant, add -**ed** only, e.g. *offer + ed = offered*.

Common misconceptions 👁

Misconception	How to identify	How to overcome
Learners make frequent spelling mistakes when writing the past forms of irregular verbs, and they sometimes also make irregular verbs regular, for example: *catched* *swimmed*	Write a correct form and an incorrect one. Ask learners to compare them. Ask: *What's the difference between the two forms? Which is correct? Is this a regular or an irregular verb?* Circle the mistake and elicit answers.	Ask learners to make a two-column poster and have them write the infinite form of irregular verbs on the left-hand column and the irregular past form on the right-hand column. Keep the poster on display so learners can look and check when they are completing sentences. Have learners fill in the table with new irregular verbs as they learn them.
Quite frequently, learners use present simple throughout to refer to past events, for example: *It was very beautiful, so I like it very much. We visit our grandparents first, then we go to the beach.*	Write the incorrect sentences on the board. Ask the class, for example: *This happens when? Today? Every day? Yesterday?* Elicit the answers, such as *Yesterday / Last year.* Ask: *How do you know?* Elicit the answer and ask learners to circle the time reference in the sentence. Ask: *What tense do we use when we speak about the past? Yesterday? Last year?* Elicit the answers and have learners write the correct form.	Tell learners to look for and circle the time references in sentences before deciding what tense they have to use.

Starter ideas

Story time! (5–10 minutes)

If learners have looked for stories about friendship as homework, invite them to share them with the class.

Desert animals (10–20 minutes)

- Remind the class of the natural regions (or biomes) they learned about in Lesson 3.1.

> **Critical thinking opportunity:** Show photos of different animals, for example monkeys, tigers, lions, buffalo, etc. Ask learners where they think these live. Ask: *Would it*

be possible for these animals to live in the desert? Why? Elicit answers.

- Show photos of reptiles from different parts of the world, for example lizards, Komodo dragons, crocodiles, large snakes such as anaconda, etc. Ask learners where they think these animals live. Can they live in a desert? Why? Elicit answers.

- Ask the class what sort of animals these are. Are they insects? Mammals? Elicit the word 'reptile'. Ask learners what a reptile is. Ask them to give examples of reptiles.

- Ask learners if when know which animals are hot-blooded (mammals and birds). Encourage them to give examples of each.

- You may also wish to share appropriate websites with the class to learn more about hot- and cold-blooded animals; examples of suitable sites include Cool Cosmos and Kid's Corner.

> **CROSS-CURRICULAR LINK**
>
> Science
>
> Focus on the introductory text: *What is a reptile?* and read it with the class. Can they think what animals are cold-blooded other than reptiles? (insects, fish, amphibians)

Main teaching ideas

 1 Read, listen and compare (20–30 minutes)

- Focus on the fact cards and photos. Ask the class if they have ever seen these animals.

- Tell them to read the fact cards and learn about them.

- Then ask learners to listen to learn more information about them. As they listen, they make notes.

- Play the audio recording at least twice. Then ask learners to pair up with a partner and answer the questions using the notes they have taken.

- Check answers as a class.

> **Differentiation ideas:** With less confident groups, you may need to play each description two or three times in turn before proceeding to the following one. You could ask more confident learners to write a sentence about what they think of each animal, for example: *Do you like it? What do you find interesting about it?*

> **Critical thinking opportunity:** You could ask learners to create a table on the board to compare the animals (see Cross-curricular link below).

- Bring in a map of the world. Give learners sticky notes or index cards and sticky tack. Ask them to write the name of a reptile and put it in the correct place on the map.

> **Critical thinking opportunity:** Remind the class of the deserts around the world. Remind them that Antarctica is also a desert. Would any of these animals be able to live there, even if they are desert animals? Why? Elicit answers.

> **CROSS-CURRICULAR LINK**
>
> Science
>
> You could ask learners to create a table on the board to compare the animals (see the example below). If any information is not provided in the text, ask learners to search for it on the internet or in books and add it to the table.
>
> | Name | Thorny devil | Gila monster | Frog-eyed gecko |
> | --- | --- | --- | --- |
> | Home | | | |
> | Size | | | |
> | Poisonous? | | | |
> | Diet | | | |
> | Physical features | | | |
> | Special features | | | |

Audioscript: Track 21

Learner's Book page 48

Hello. My name is Professor Patel. I'm a herpetologist. That means I study reptiles. There are snakes and lizards of many different shapes and sizes living in deserts all over the world. Some are venomous and some are not. Today I'm going to tell you about six desert reptiles that I think are the most interesting.

The thorny devil lives in the deserts of Australia. It has some interesting ways to protect itself from large birds and other animals that want to eat it. First, it is covered with sharp prickly spikes. Ouch! Second, it can puff itself up like a balloon so that it looks bigger. Third, it can change colours to help it hide.

The Gila monster is an unusual lizard. It is big and colourful. It eats mice and rabbits and little lizards, swallowing them whole. It stores the food as fat in its thick short tail. Also, the Gila monster has venom in its teeth! When it's threatened, first it hisses, then it bites and chews the animal or person who is attacking it.

I think the frog-eyed gecko is very cute. Do you? They live in the deserts of many Asian and Middle Eastern countries. Like other geckos, the frog-eyed gecko doesn't have eyelids so it keeps its big eyes moist and clean by licking them with its long tongue.

The shovel-snouted lizard is quite tiny. It lives in the Sahara Desert, in Africa. It does a special dance to keep its feet from burning on the hot sand. First it holds up two feet, then it switches and holds up the other two feet. The shovel-snouted lizard has a special organ in its body where it can store water. That's very important in the hot dry desert!

The sidewinding adder is a venomous snake that also lives in the Sahara. It digs itself into the sand and hides with just its eyes peeking out, waiting to catch lizards to eat. It especially likes to eat shovel-snouted lizards because of the unusual organ in that lizard that stores water. It's like a built-in water bottle! Yum!

The Indian sand boa is a big snake. It can be 100 centimetres long. It is sometimes called a 'two-headed snake' because its tail looks very much like its head. When it is threatened, the Indian sand boa hides its head and waves its tail in the air. That way, the predator will hopefully bite the snake's tail, rather than its head!

Answers
- The frog-eyed gecko and the shovel-snouted lizard are smaller than the thorny devil.
- The Indian sand boa is bigger than the sidewinding adder.
- The Gila monster is more dangerous than the Indian sand boa.

> **Digital Classroom:** Use the activity 'Which reptile?' to reinforce comprehension of the reading/listening texts about desert animals. The i button will explain how to use the activity.

2   Listen and talk: What's your opinion? (10–20 minutes)
- Focus on the explanation in the Learner's Book and read it with the class.
- Tell learners that they are going to listen to some children share their opinions and explain their reasons.
- Play the recording twice.

> **Differentiation ideas:** You could ask more confident learners to listen and identify expressions the children on the audio use to give their opinions.

- Ask learners to work in small groups. They look at the reptiles on the fact cards and discuss their opinions. Ask them to use the expression words from the Learner's Book.
- When they have finished, ask groups to share their opinions with the class.

> **Assessment ideas:** You could ask groups to audio or video-record themselves as they work. When they have finished, they can then reflect on how well they have done. Ask them to think if they have used the language they were required to use and respected turn-taking, how they have reacted to different opinions, and whether they justified their opinions, etc.

Audioscript: Track 22

Learner's Book page 49

Teacher:	Let's compare these six desert reptiles. Which reptile do you think is the strangest? Annie, what's your opinion?
Child 1:	Hmm. I think the frog-eyed gecko is the strangest.
Child 2:	So do I! It's really strange!
Child 3:	I don't agree. Why do you think that the frog-eyed gecko is the strangest?
Child 1:	Because it licks its eyes with its tongue. Weird!
Child 2:	And it has scales like a fish.

Child 1:	Which animal do you think is the strangest?
Child 3:	I think the Gila monster is the strangest.
Child 4:	So do I!
Child 2:	Why?
Child 3:	Because it is so big. It looks like a little dinosaur.
Child 4:	And it is poisonous!

Answers

Learners listen to track 22 and give their own opinions.

Language detective – Comparing things (10–20 minutes)

- Focus on the examples in the Language Detective box, using *-er* and *-est* words. Remind the class of the use of superlatives.

- As preparation for the next activity, focus on the explanations and examples, and remind the class of how the superlative is used, i.e. when we compare three or more things.

- Ask the class to look at the examples carefully and say why the superlative forms are different.

- Encourage learners to discover the rule by themselves. Then they complete it. They write the rule in their notebooks and supply some more examples.

- Ask the class to work in pairs. Learners read through the previous lessons or units and look for adjectives. You could set a limit of words.

- They make two lists – one for adjectives that make superlatives with *-est* and another for adjectives that make superlatives with the ***most***, and write them in their notebooks.

> **Digital Classroom:** Use the grammar presentation 'Comparative and superlative adjectives' to revise comparative and superlative adjectives. The i button will explain how to use the grammar presentation.

3 Talk about your opinions (15–30 minutes)

- Divide the class into pairs. Ask learners to think of the reptiles again. They read the questions and answer by giving their opinion.

Ask them to explain their reasons, and remind them of the correct forms of the superlatives.

- Have learners ask one more question using the words in the boxes.

- When they have finished, have learners draw a table on the board and record the opinions in the form of votes.

- When they have finished, they record the opinions in the table. Which is the most popular reptile?

> **Differentiation ideas:** Less confident learners may write their questions before attempting to ask them. More confident learners may decide to use other adjectives too, such as *strange*, *dangerous*, *ugly*, etc.

Workbook

Learners do Activities 1, 2 and 3 on pages 36–37.

Plenary ideas

Consolidation (10–20 minutes)

> **Assessment ideas:** Bring the K-W-L poster to the board. Have learners found the answers to their questions in W. Elicit answers and have learners note the answers in the L column.

Ask learners if they have learned new things they hadn't thought about. Ask them to add a new column: VN (Very New information) to the K-W-L poster, and add the new information there.

Homework ideas

- Give learners a list of suitable websites or books they can find in the school library and ask them to look for information about animals.

- They make a mini-poster, write a few sentences and bring it to the next class.

- **Home–school link:** Learners tell their family about the animals they have learned about. They ask their family which they think is the cutest, most dangerous, etc.

3.4 Write about it: Desert adaptations

LEARNING PLAN

Learning objectives	Learning intentions	Success criteria
3So.01	• **Speaking:** Talk about desert animals; interpret and discuss a diagram.	• Learners can read and understand a text about camels.
4Rd.01	• **Reading:** Read for detail, read for information, read information texts.	• Learners can talk about desert animals.
3Wca.03, 3Wca.05, 3Wor.02	• **Writing:** Write a report about a desert animal; turn notes into full sentences; use correct spelling and punctuation; use correct layout for a report.	• Learners can interpret and discuss a diagram. • Learners can turn notes into full sentences.
3Ug.03, 3Us.03	• **Language focus:** present simple, pronouns	• Learners can write a report about a desert animal.
	• **Vocabulary:** *store, fat, eyelashes, hump, wide, round, hop, thick, fur*	

21st-century skills

Critical thinking opportunity: Read information and draw conclusions, understand cause and effect.

Collaboration: Take part in tasks by interacting with others and stays on task.

Communication: Take turns appropriately in a conversation; interrupt others politely.

Materials: Learner's Book pages 50–51; Workbook pages 38–39; photos of camels (both dromedary and Bactrian); Sample answer for Unit 3; **Differentiated worksheets 3A, B and C; Photocopiable 1**

Starter ideas

Animal records (10–15 minutes)

If learners have done the homework activity from the previous lesson, ask them to present their animal records to the class. Then collect their mini-posters and display them around the class. You could also ask them to upload their work to the class blog.

Main teaching ideas

1 Read about camels (10–20 minutes)

- Ask the class what they know about camels. Show photographs of the two species of camels (the Arabian camel or dromedary, and the Bactrian camel).

- Ask the class what parts of the animal they can name. Introduce the word *hump*.

- Ask the class how they think camels survive in the desert. Elicit ideas. Then tell the class to read and listen to learn more about them.

- Play the recording as learners read.

- When they have finished, ask the class what new information they have learned about camels.

> **Critical thinking opportunity:** Draw attention to the use of pronouns *it* and *they*. Encourage the class to think why they are used instead of just repeating *camels / a camel*. Elicit some ideas.

- Point out that we use *its* for an animal, instead of *his/her*, when we don't know if it is male or female.

CROSS-CURRICULAR LINK

Science

Focus on the photos of the two species of camels again, and ask the class to find the differences between the two. You may point out that the two species of camels are the Arabian camel or dromedary, which has one hump, and the Bactrian camel, which has two humps and lives in Central Asia.

Audioscript: Track 23

See Learner's Book page 50

Answers

Learner's own answers.

Language focus – Present simple (5 minutes)

- Focus on the explanation in the Learner's Book. Explain that reports are usually written in the present tense.
- Remind the class of the form of the present tense for affirmative, interrogative and negative sentences.

2 Study the diagram (10–15 minutes)

- Before doing the activity, ask learners to work in pairs. Ask: *How do you think each part of the camel's body helps it adapt to living on the dry, hot, windy desert?*
- After a few minutes, have an open class discussion in response to this question.
- Then ask learners to look at the explanations in the activity. They read the diagram and the explanations, and match the parts of the body to the correct statement.

Answers

It helps the camel reach leaves on tall trees: *3 a long neck*

They help a camel walk on top of the sand: *5 wide round feet*

They keep sand out of the camel's eyes: *1 long eyelashes*

It stores fat for when there is no food or water: *6 a hump*

They keep the camel's body away from the hot sand: *4 long legs*

They help the camel eat spiny desert plants: *2 lips with thick skin*

Workbook

Learners do Activities 1 and 2 on pages 38–39.

---

3 Write a report about a desert animal using a fact card (60–90 minutes)

- Tell learners that they are going to write a report about a desert animal using information from a fact card.

> **Critical thinking opportunity:** Remind the class of the fact cards about reptiles they read in Lesson 3.3. Then ask them to read the fact cards about the jerboa and the fennec fox. Draw their attention to the note-style of the texts, and ask them why we use it and what kinds of words are missed out. Elicit answers.

- **Step 1:** Ask the class to work in pairs. Learners read the fact cards to gather information, and then look at the sample report about the jerboa. Ask them to read and answer the questions. As a class, discuss the questions in the Learner's Book and write a bullet point list of the features of the report, for example: organised in paragraphs; each paragraph has a heading; written in full sentences; no personal opinion is given. Keep this list on the board and ask learners to copy it in their notebooks. They can use it later to check their work.
- **Step 2:** Ask learners to write a report of the fennec fox in the present simple, using information from the fact card. Tell them to use the sample report about the jerboa as a model – they can use similar headings or think of some themselves.
- **Step 3:** When they have finished, learners read their report aloud. Tell them it is important to listen to their sentences to find out if they are missing any words.

> **Assessment ideas:** At this point, learners can get together with another pair. They read their report to each other and give feedback, e.g. Are any words missing? Have they included all the information?

- **Step 4:** Learners re-read their reports then check and correct them using the checklist they created at the beginning of the activity and the checklist in Step 4 in the Learner's Book. Remind learners of their Writer's checklist (**Photocopiable 1**); ask them to get their copy and use it to check their work.

- When they are happy with their report, they can read it to the class.

- See the **Sample answer for Unit 3** for an example answer to this writing task.

- You might want to use this as extension material as discussion about writer's intention is beyond the requirements of the Cambridge Primary English as a Second Language curriculum framework.

Answers

Learners plan, write and check their animal report.

Workbook

Learners do Activity 3 on page 39.

> **Digital Classroom:** Use the activity 'Which animal?' to reinforce comprehension of the reading/listening texts about desert animals. The i button will explain how to use the activity.

Plenary ideas

Consolidation (15–20 minutes)

> **Assessment ideas:** Bring the K-W-L poster to the board. Ask learners whether they have found the answers to their questions in W. Elicit answers and have learners note the answers in the L column. Ask learners if they have learned new things they hadn't thought about. They add the new information in the VN column.

- Ask the class how easy or difficult the writing activity was. How can they overcome the difficulties? Elicit ideas from the class.

Homework ideas

- Give learners a list of suitable websites or books from the school library.

- Learners look for information about camels. They write a fact card and then use it to write a report.

- **Home–school link:** Learners tell their family about the desert animals they have read about.

- Hand out copies of **Differentiated worksheets 3A, B and C** depending on each learner's ability, and ask them to complete the activities at home.

3.5 Read and respond: *Rattlesnake, Mouse and Clever Coyote*

LEARNING PLAN

Learning objectives	Learning intentions	Success criteria
3Ld.04 3Sc.05 3Rm.02, 3Rd.01, 3Rd.03 3Wc.02, 3Wc.03	• **Listening:** Listen to a traditional tale. • **Speaking:** Discuss a trickster tale; act out a trickster tale; discuss the characters in the tale; give and justify opinions, discuss values. • **Reading:** Read and understand a trickster tale, understand the meaning of words in context; understand the use of speech marks; make predictions using text features. • **Writing:** Write about a favourite story character; use correct grammar, spelling and punctuation. • **Language focus:** direct speech, speech marks, questions in the past simple • **Vocabulary:** *rattlesnake, push, let out, roll over, fair, trot, slither, pretend, evening, trapped, confused, explain*	• Learners can listen and read a trickster tale. • Learners can discuss a trickster tale. • Learners can discuss the characters in a tale. • Learners can discuss what is fair. • Learners can write about a favourite character.

21st-century skills

Critical thinking opportunity: Predict what a story is going to be about; understand the difference between fiction and non-fiction; state and support opinions.

Collaboration: Understand that others can be shy, less confident speaking English or unhappy about something and reassure them.

Values: Discuss what is fair and unfair.

Materials: Learner's Book pages 52–55: Workbook pages: 40–41; K-W-L poster from previous lesson; pictures of a rattlesnake and a coyote; materials to make simple costumes or masks (optional); big box or floor cushion (optional); puppets for the story re-enactment (optional); **Photocopiable 16**

Starter ideas

Looking back (10–20 minutes)

• If learners have done the homework activity from the previous lesson, have them share their reports with the class. Collect the reports and upload them to the class blog. Alternatively, make a class poster.

❯ **Assessment ideas:** Bring the K-W-L-VN poster from the previous lesson to the board. Have learners discuss what information they found the most interesting or surprising. What would they like to learn more about? Are there any questions they still have not found answers to? Where could they find the answers? Elicit ideas.

• Remind learners of the animals and plants that live in the desert. Ask them which they liked or found the most interesting, and which they did not.

Fiction or non-fiction? (10–15 minutes)

- You might want to use this as extension material as this is beyond the requirements of the Cambridge Primary English as a Second Language curriculum framework.

> **Critical thinking opportunity:** Ask learners to look at the title and the pictures of the characters. Discuss what kind of text it could be – fiction or non-fiction, and how realistic they think it will be. What helped them decide? Elicit ideas, for example: fiction; animals are doing things that real animals would not do (e.g. a mouse pushing the rock), the animals are speaking.

- Help learners understand the meaning of 'fiction' and 'non-fiction'. Establish what makes a fictional text. Elicit examples from the class.

Main teaching ideas

Reading tip (5 minutes)

- Tell the class that this story is a folktale from the Sonoran Desert, in Mexico.

- Bring a map of the world and ask learners to find Mexico and the Sonoran desert. Remind them of the kinds of animals that might live there.

CROSS-CURRICULAR LINK

Literature

Ask learners what they think a folktale is. Elicit answers, for example a folktale is an old story that has been told again and again, often for generations. They are tales that people tell each other, rather than write. They usually involve animals, magic, and ordinary people living ordinary lives.

---

1   Talk about it: Making predictions (5–20 minutes)

- Read the rubric with the class – it introduces the character of Coyote. Ask learners who they think Coyote will trick in this story. Elicit ideas and encourage learners to justify them.

- In one of the pictures, Mouse is pushing a rock. Ask: *Why is he doing this?* Invite the class to predict what happens.

CROSS-CURRICULAR LINKS

Science

Show pictures of a rattlesnake and a coyote and explain what they are, e.g. a coyote is a member of the canine family, similar to but smaller than a wolf. A rattlesnake is a poisonous snake that has 'rattles' on its tail. Rattlesnakes rattle to tell other animals they are coming.

You may wish to show learners some age-appropriate websites where they can find information about the Sonoran Desert, rattlesnakes and coyotes, e.g. Arizona Sonora Desert Museum, Live Science, National Geographic Kids.

Answers

Learners talk about their predictions for the story.

---

2   Read and listen (5 minutes)

- Tell the class to read and listen to the story.

- Begin the recording of the story, but get ready to stop the audio – please see Activity 3 below for details.

Audioscript: Track 24

See Learner's Book pages 52–54.

Stop, think, predict! (5–10 minutes)

- Play the recording up to: *'OK,' said Mouse. Mouse pushed and pushed until the big rock rolled over. Out came Rattlesnake!*

- Focus on the questions and discuss them as a class. Invite learners to predict what will happen next.

- Then play the rest of the recording.

Answers

Rattlesnake said 'Help, help! I'm trapped under this rock.'
Rattlesnake promised Mouse that she would not eat him.
Mouse did help Rattlesnake.
Learner's own answers.

> **Digital Classroom:** Use the activity 'Rattlesnake, Mouse and Clever Coyote' to reinforce comprehension of the story. The i button will explain how to use the activity.

3 Talk about the story (10–20 minutes)

- Focus on questions a–f.

- Ask learners to think about the answers individually. Have them make notes of the answers.

- When learners have finished, they pair up with a partner and compare their answers, before checking answers as a class.

Answers

a Rattlesnake was stuck under a rock.
b Rattlesnake was stuck under a rock.
c Mouse helped Rattlesnake by lifting the rock off and setting her free.
d Rattlesnake wanted to eat Mouse.
e Mouse had been kind when he saved Rattlesnake from under the rock, so it was unfair that Rattlesnake wanted to then eat him.
f Coyote pretended to not understand so Rattlesnake would get back into the hole to show him. Coyote could then put the rock over to trap her underneath again.

4 Talk: Ask and answer questions (10–20 minutes)

> **Assessment ideas:** Remind learners of the use of the past simple and *was/were*. Ask them to explain in their own words how to use the past simple and how to answer questions.

- Focus on the questions and answers and ask learners to choose the correct option.

- Check answers as a class.

- When they have finished, ask learners to make up some more questions about the story. They take it in turns to ask and answer the questions with a partner.

> **Differentiation ideas:** You may wish to pair up learners of different abilities so that the more confident help their less confident partners to write the questions. Once they have written the questions, they can pair up with another pair of learners and take it in turns to ask and answer the questions.

Answers

Was Rattlesnake kind? *No, she wasn't.*
Was Mouse helpful? *Yes, he was.*
Did Rattlesnake eat Mouse? *No, she didn't.*
Did Coyote save Mouse's life? *Yes, he did.*
Learner's own answers.

5 Values: Fair or unfair? (15 minutes)

- Do this activity as Think-Pair-Share. Ask the class to read the questions and reflect on the answers individually. They can make notes of the answers.

- Then learners pair up with a partner and discuss their ideas.

- When they have finished, ask them to get together with another pair and compare what they think.

- Finally, have an open class discussion. Encourage learners to be honest and to justify their opinions.

> **Critical thinking opportunity:** The first question is likely to cause some debate. You may also ask if what Rattlesnake did was fair or unfair. Ask learners to compare both behaviours. Can Coyote and Rattlesnake be justified in any way? For example, one is hungry and the other wanted to teach the snake and the mouse a lesson.

- When you have finished discussing the questions, ask the class what happened after the snake was trapped again. Did the other animals disappear or just wait until she had learned her lesson? Elicit opinions and ask learners to justify their ideas.

> **Differentiation ideas:** This discussion can be quite challenging for less confident groups in terms of the vocabulary they may need. Allow some use of L1. Echo in simple English and write any key vocabulary on the board for reference.

Answers

a–d Learner's own answers.

6 Word study (5–15 minutes)

- Ask the class to find the blue words in the story.

- They read the sentences in context to check the meaning.

- Then they read the sentences in both columns and match them.

- Check answers as a class.

> **Differentiation ideas:** Ask learners to re-read the story and find other words they may not understand. Can they guess the meaning from the context? If not, share some dictionaries and have them look up the words. They can write the words and their meanings in their notebooks.

Answers
1c, 2a, 3e, 4b, 5d

7   Readers' theatre: Act it out! (30–60 minutes)

- You might want to use this as extension material as this is beyond the requirements of the Cambridge Primary English as a Second Language curriculum framework.

- Tell the class that they are going to act out the story. Ask learners to choose a character.

- Learners then look through the story and find all the places where their character speaks. They may underline or highlight their parts.

- Tell them that you will read all the words that are said by their characters i.e. the words that are said by the narrator.

CROSS-CURRICULAR LINKS

Drama

Ask learners to get together with the learners who have chosen the same character and rehearse their parts. Remind them to be dramatic, to 'live' their character, and to use body language as well as their voice for effect. Model if necessary.

When learners feel that they are ready, have the class act out the play.

Actors can use the cut-out puppets on **Photocopiable 16** as they act out their parts. Alternatively, they can make simple costumes or masks, or just wear a placard with the name of their character. A big box or floor cushion can be used as a rock prop. You can also use puppets to act out the story.

> **Differentiation ideas:** With mixed ability classes, you could ask more confident learners to read the story while others mime the action. More confident groups may act out the story, improvising the lines. You can also divide the class into groups of four and assign each group member a role. The narrator can also act as the prompter to help actors if they forget what's next.

> **Assessment ideas:** If appropriate, you could video-record learners as they act out the story.

Answers
Learners perform the story as a play.

8   Write your opinion (5–15 minutes)

- Ask learners to read the questions and write the answers. Ask them to explain their answers.

- When they have finished, ask them to draw a picture of their favourite animal in the story.

- Ask volunteers to read their answers to the class.

- Ask: *Which is the most popular character? Why?* Discuss answers as a class.

Answers
Learner's own answers.

Workbook

Learners do Activities 1–4 on pages 40–41.

Plenary ideas

Consolidation (10–15 minutes)

- Share the recording of the play with the class.

- Ask learners to watch and discuss what they did well and what could be improved for the next time.

Homework ideas

- Learners look for a folktale in their country's tradition. They write a summary in English and bring it to the next class.

- **Home–school link:** Learners read the stories to their family and discuss the questions with them.

3.6 Project challenge

LEARNING PLAN

Learning objectives	Learning intentions	Success criteria
3Sc.06, 3Sc.07	• **Speaking:** Discuss a project; discuss steps of a project; organise work; present their project to the class.	• Learners can read and understand instructions.
3Rd.02	• **Reading:** Read and understand instructions.	• Learners can give instructions.
3Wca.02, 3Wca.04, 3Wc.01	• **Writing:** Write sentences; write temperatures and a report on an experiment.	• Learners can plan a project.
	• **Language focus:** Unit 3 review	• Learners can make a desert mural.
	• **Vocabulary:** Unit 3 review	• Learners can chart the weather.

21st-century skills

Creative thinking opportunity: Design new items based on a model.

Collaboration: Respect the importance of doing a fair share of group work; keep to the instructions to complete the task; invite others to give their opinions during the task.

Learning to learn: Listen and respond positively to feedback and understand why a correction was given; learn from mistakes and feedback.

Materials: Learner's Book pages 56–57; Workbook pages 42–43; Project A: writing/drawing supplies, large sheets of paper; Project B: writing supplies, outdoor thermometer; **Photocopiable 17**, **18** and **19**; End of Unit 3 test

Starter ideas

1 Looking back (15–20 minutes)

- Ask the class to choose a lesson from Unit 3 that they liked a lot. Ask them to explain why they liked it.

- As a class, sing *Song of the shifting sand.*

> **Assessment ideas:** Divide the class into two teams and play a few rounds of *Catch a fish!* to revise new vocabulary and useful phrases. To play this game, divide the class into two teams. One team chooses a word that the other team will guess. Draw a fishing rod and a bucket on the board. Ask one learner to

come to the board and draw a line for each letter in the word they have chosen. The other team then guess one letter at a time to fill in the word. As letters in the word are guessed, the learner writes them above the corresponding line. If a letter is not in the chosen word, the learner draws part of a fish on the rod – one part per wrong guess. A basic drawing would allow for six guesses, e.g. the head, the body, the tail, two fins and the eyes. Once the word has been guessed or the fish is fully drawn, switch teams. This game will give you the opportunity to assess how much learners remember from previous lessons.

Main teaching ideas

Learners choose an end-of-unit project to work on. Look at the examples in the pictures and help learners to choose. Provide materials.

Project A: Make a desert mural (60–90 minutes)

- In groups, learners choose a desert and find out where it is. Hand out some relevant source texts for learners to find information about the desert they have chosen. They use the questions in the Learner's Book as a guide to plan their work.

- Each group member chooses a different plant or animal to draw and write about. They do more research to find information about their chosen animal or plant.

- They write two sentences about it.

> **Differentiation ideas:** Less confident learners may write a fact card using the ones in this unit as models. Then they can use the information to write their sentences. Tell them to use the report they wrote in Lesson 3.4 as a model.

- Give out drawing supplies and sheets of paper. Learners draw a desert background on a large sheet of poster paper.

- Then they draw the picture of their chosen animal or plant and paste it on the desert background. They write the name of their plant or animal next to the picture.

- As a group, learners share their desert mural with the class. They read the facts about their plant or animal aloud.

> **Assessment ideas:** You could video-record groups as they work, so that learners can self-assess what they have done and how they have worked. The copies can then be shared with learners' families and filed in their portfolios. You may also display the slideshows or the scrapbooks during an open day for families to see.

Project B: Make a weather chart (5 days of out-of-class work, 60–90 minutes of class work)

- Learners work in groups and make two charts: a chart to record the weather where they live, and a second to record the weather in another place far away. They agree what place they will find out about.

- Learners should use **Photocopiable 17** as a support to complete the charts.

- Learners record the weather for five days. For each day, they draw a picture that shows the weather, write the temperature and then record whether it is hot, warm, cool or cold.

- To record the weather where they live, learners can check a weather app, read the information online or in newspapers, or look out the window and use an outdoor thermometer.

- To record the weather in another place, they look up information on a weather website, such as The Weather Channel.

- After five days, learners compare the weather on the two charts and answer the questions.

> **Differentiation ideas:** More confident groups may include answers to additional questions, for example: *Which place was windier? Which place had the most extreme weather? Were there any storms or extreme weather conditions?*

- Learners show the finished charts to the class. They display the chart that shows the weather in a place far away with the weather charts that other groups have made.

- They then answer the questions in the Learner's Book together.

> **Assessment ideas:** You may wish to video-record groups as they work, so that they can then use copies of the recordings to assess what they have done and how they have worked. The copies can then be shared with the family and filed in their portfolios. Learners may give the cards to the person they have made it for on a special occasion.

> **Assessment ideas: Think about your work on this project:** When learners have finished, give them a copy of **Photocopiable 18** and read the instructions as a class. Ask them to work independently and think about their work on their project. They reflect and answer the questions. They tick off the aims they have achieved. Insist on the importance of giving honest answers.

Workbook

Learners do the Check your progress quiz on pages 42–43.

Plenary ideas

Reflect on your learning (5–10 minutes)

* Draw learners' attention to the 'Reflect on your learning' questions in the Learner's Book.

* Learners answer the questions to reflect on their project work.

Consolidation (10–15 minutes)

* Encourage learners to think about and comment on aspects of the unit they feel they are good at and what they have found most difficult and why. You may wish to keep a record of their comments to see how they progress over time.

* If you have been filing learners' work during this unit, you may find it useful to put all the work of this unit together. You could ask learners to make a cover for their Unit 3 work, decorating it with an image that represents what they have learned.

Homework ideas

* Learners draw a picture of what they have liked most about this unit.

* **Home–school link:** Learners show their family their projects.

3.7 What do you know now?

What makes a desert special? (35–45 minutes)

* Learners work in pairs. They work together through all the tasks set in this section.

* They write the answers in their notebooks. You may ask them to have a special section in their notebooks where they record the answers.

Answers
1–6 Learner's own answers.

Look what I can do! (15 minutes)

* Review the six *I can …* statements on page 58 of the Learner's Book. Learners demonstrate what they can do.

* Learners colour in the faces to show which things they can do.

* Encourage them to be honest in their answers.

Workbook

Learners answer the Reflection questions on page 43.

Check your progress 1

Starter ideas

Revision of vocabulary

- **Materials:** a set of word cards of the vocabulary you want learners to review, and picture cards to match – one per group
- Play a game to revise the verbs and language of instructions of Units 1–3.
- **Pelmanism:** Divide the class into groups of three. Give each group a set of word cards and picture cards of the vocabulary you want learners to review.
- Players take turns to play. They put the cards face down on the table – put all of the word cards on one side and all of the picture cards on the other side. They take turns to turn one card of their choice from each group face up. If the cards match, the player takes these two cards, stores them and takes another turn. If they do not match, the player turns them face down, without changing their position in the layout, and it is the next player's turn.

Main teaching ideas

What did you do last week?

- **Use of English:** past simple, regular and irregular verbs
- **Materials (per pair):** five small objects to use as game markers (e.g. buttons, paper clips, coins, etc.) for each player; a piece of paper (for learners to cut out nine squares of paper); markers; game board in Learner's Book (page 59); **Photocopiable 19**.
- **Preparation:** Have learners play in pairs. Give each player a set of five small objects to use as game markers. Each pair cuts out nine squares of paper and writes 'A' on three of the squares, 'B' on three of the squares and 'C' on the three remaining squares. They then place the letter cards face down.
- **How to play:** With the class, read through the rules of the game. Model and explain if necessary. Remind learners that some of the verbs are irregular in the past simple. They can use the Verb pages in the Picture dictionary for help (Learner's Book pages 172–173).
  The first player to place three game markers in a row – across, down or diagonal – is the winner.

1 Give and follow directions: Simon says

- **Use of English:** action verbs
- **How to play:** As a class, brainstorm directions using the words *up, down, left, right, slowly, quickly*. Remind learners that directions start with a verb that tells them what to do, e.g. 'turn left' or 'stand up', etc.
  After a few minutes of brainstorming ideas, use the directions to play a game of Simon says. Remind the class of the rules: they have to carry out the instructions only if they are preceded by 'Simon says'.

2 Play a partner action verb game

- **Use of English:** action verbs
- **How to play:** Learners work in pairs. They act out an action verb as partners, and the rest of the class try to guess the word. Whoever guesses first correctly then acts out another action verb with their partner.

3 Make a class bar graph

- **Use of English:** *like + -ing forms*
- **How to play:** As a class, choose a verb to complete the question: *Do you like …ing?* Learners enter their answer on the graph by colouring in one space to show their answer – 'Yes, I do' or 'No, I don't'. When all learners have finished, they count the squares and talk about the results of their graph.

4 Comparisons: Two group games

- **Use of English:** comparatives, superlatives
- **Materials:** a set of animal picture cards for each learner (pictures can be from the internet or you can draw them yourself)
- **Game 1:** Learners play in groups. They place the picture cards face down. Learners take it in turns to turn two cards over. They compare the two animals by answering the questions in their Learner's Book (page 60). Everyone in the group should give their opinion. They discuss their answers.
- **Game 2:** The rules are the same as for Game 1, except that learners turn three cards over instead of two. They compare the animals by answering the questions in their Learner's Book (page 60). Everyone in the group should give their opinion. They discuss their answers.

>4 Look again!

Unit plan

Lesson	Approximate number of learning hours	Outline of learning content	Learning objectives	Resources
1 Optical illusions	1. 25–2.0	Learn and talk about optical illusions.	3Ld.01 3Sc.06 3Sc.07 3So.01 3Rd.02	Learner's Book Lesson 4.1 Workbook Lesson 4.1 ⬇ Photocopiable 20 ⬇ Photocopiable 21 **Digital Classroom:** Slideshow – Photo tricks; Video – Optical illusions; Activity – Find the shapes
2 Hidden pictures	1.5–2.5	Describe and compare what we see.	3Ld.01 3Sc.06 3So.01 3Rd.02 3Wc.02 3Us.03	Learner's Book Lesson 4.2 Workbook Lesson 4.2 **Digital Classroom:** Grammar presentation – Subject and object pronouns
3 That's impossible!	1.0–2.25	Use our imaginations and describe ourselves.	3Ld.04 3Lo.01 3Sc.02 3Rd.01 3Uv.06	Learner's Book Lesson 4.3 Workbook Lesson 4.3 **Digital Classroom:** Activity – Talking about people; Activity – Adverbs of frequency
4 Experiments and results	1.25–2.25	Do experiments and write about the results.	3Ld.02 3Sc.01 3Sc.03 3Sc.04 3Wc.01 3Wca.02 3Wor.01	Learner's Book Lesson 4.4 Workbook Lesson 4.4 ⬇ Sample answer for Unit 4 ⬇ Photocopiable 22 **Digital Classroom:** Activity – Questions!

(continued)

Lesson	Approximate number of learning hours	Outline of learning content	Learning objectives	Resources
5 Animal camouflage	1.5–2.75	Read and talk about animal camouflage.	3Ld.03 3Ld.04 3Sc.02 3So.01 3Rd.01	Learner's Book Lesson 4.5 Workbook Lesson 4.5 ⬇ Photocopiable 3 **Digital Classroom:** Activity – Hidden animals; Slideshow – Animal camouflage; Activity – Animal camouflage: matching
6 Project challenge	1.5–2.25	Make a camouflage frog or butterfly, or write an animal camouflage poem.	3Sc.05 3Sc.06 3Sc.07 3Rd.02 3Wca.02	Learner's Book Lesson 4.6 Workbook Lesson 4.6 ⬇ Photocopiable 2 ⬇ Photocopiable 23 ⬇ Photocopiable 24 ⬇ Photocopiable 25 ⬇ Differentiated worksheets 4A, B and C
7 What do you know now?	0.5–1.0	Self-assessment and reflection.		Learner's Book Lesson 4.7

Cross-unit resources
⬇ Unit 4 Audioscripts
⬇ End of Unit 4 test
⬇ Unit 4 Progress report
⬇ Unit 4 Wordlist

BACKGROUND KNOWLEDGE

What is an optical illusion?

An optical illusion is an image that we see in a different way to how it really is. The image tricks our eyes into seeing things that aren't really as they appear.

Some optical illusion images trick us into seeing something different from the images that make it up (such as a duck image that is actually a rabbit image), like the images that learners see in Lesson 4.2. Other optical illusions force the eye to see so much light, movement, colour, dimension and size that it confuses the brain, such as the snake image in Lesson 4.3.

Animal camouflage

Camouflage is a defence mechanism that some animals use to blend in with their surroundings and hide, to protect themselves from predators. Different creatures have different types of camouflage – depending on their skin, fur, feathers, etc., as well as the surroundings that they want to hide in.

Some birds, like some species of owl, have feathers that look just like the bark of trees so that their potential prey doesn't see them. Some fish look almost exactly like the seafloor so they blend in perfectly. Other animals have different camouflage depending on the seasons, for example the Arctic fox has dark fur in summer, and then white fur in winter to blend in with the snow.

TEACHING SKILLS FOCUS

Assessment for learning

Assessment for learning (AFL) is an approach to teaching and learning where the information collected (for example, during assessments) is used to determine where learners are in their attainment, and how to achieve learning goals. As a result, teachers can adjust their teaching strategies and learners can adjust their learning strategies.

There are a number of classroom strategies that have proven to be particularly effective in promoting formative assessment practice.

a **Questioning:** This should be used as a pedagogical tool to allow teachers to find out what students know, understand and are able to do.

b **Effective teacher feedback:** This should focus on success criteria, and will tell learners what they have achieved, where they need to improve, and suggest ways in which improvement can be achieved.

c **Peer feedback:** Using established success criteria, learners tell each other what they have achieved, whether improvement is needed and where, and suggest ways in which improvement can be achieved.

d **Student self-assessment:** This incorporates self-monitoring, self-assessment and self-evaluation, and encourages learners to be responsible for their own learning.

e **Formative use of summative assessment**

The following assessment for learning activities can be introduced in this unit at different points:

- **Exit tickets** (see Unit 2.2, Plenary ideas)
- **Think-Pair-Share:** At the end of an activity or lesson, learners reflect individually and then share with a partner – ask them to think of three things they have learned, what they found easy/interesting, something they found difficult, and a question they still have not found the answer to, or something related to the lesson they would like to learn in the future.

- **Traffic lights:** Give each learner a set of three cards: red, yellow and green (red = *I don't understand*, yellow = *I understand some of it*, green = *I understand everything*). At different points during a lesson, you can ask learners to choose a card and put it on their desk to show how much they have understood.

- **K-W-L-VN:** This is an adaptation of the K-W-L chart. At the beginning of a lesson, learners make a four-column table and label the columns: K (what they know or they think they know), W (what they want to know), L (what they have learned) and VN (very new information they have learned and had never thought of before). They brainstorm and fill in the first two columns at the beginning of the lesson, and then return to fill in the third and fourth columns at the end.

Your challenge

In each unit of the Learner's Book, opportunities to introduce assessment for learning are highlighted.

Look through Unit 4 and use the activities above to introduce more opportunities for assessing learners in this way. As you continue with the following units, tick off the relevant points where you can introduce these and other strategies. How much time do these activities take? Is it possible to do them regularly in class?

Reflection

How useful was the information that you collected for planning the next lesson? How well did learners understand the aim of these activities? Are there any drawbacks?

4.1 Think about it: Optical illusions

LEARNING PLAN

Learning objectives	Learning intentions	Success criteria
3Ld.01	• **Listening:** Listen and read, follow instructions; listen and understand a song.	• Learners can discuss optical illusions.
3Sc.06, 3Sc.07, 3So.01	• **Speaking:** Sing a song; talk about optical illusions and imaginary things; ask and answer questions; discuss results of experiments.	• Learners can sing a song. • Learners can conduct experiments.
3Rd.02	• **Reading:** Read and understand instructions. • **Vocabulary:** shapes and colours; *optical illusion, square, circle, triangle, rectangle, cube, shape, straight, side, corner, top, bottom, dot, back-to-back, twirl*	• Learners can discuss the results of experiments.

21st-century skills

Critical thinking opportunity: Compare and contrast; conduct experiments and discuss results; understand metaphor in a poem.

Communication: Contribute in lessons by asking questions, attempting responses and explaining understanding; share thoughts with others to help further develop ideas and solve problems.

Learning to learn: Complete tasks in class as required; join in with learning activities with other children.

Materials: Learner's Book pages 61–63; Workbook pages 44–45; photos of optical illusions; rulers; sheets of card; chopstick or a long pencil; sticky tape; crayons or pencils of different colours; **Photocopiable 20, 21**

Starter ideas

Getting started (10–20 minutes)

• Show learners some pictures of optical illusions. You can search for free pictures on the internet.

• Ask learners to describe what they see. How sure are they of what their eyes are seeing?

• Ask if they have ever seen the light effect of heat on the road or on sand in summer. Do they know the name for that? Elicit ideas from the class.

• Focus on the photos in the book and discuss the questions.

Answers
a–c Learner's own answers.
The light effect of heat on the road or on sand in summer is called a heat haze.

› **Digital Classroom:** Use the slideshow 'Photo tricks' to explore the subject of photography and perspective. The i button will explain how to use the slideshow.

Sing along! *Clouds* (10–15 minutes)

• If there are clouds in the sky, you could go to the schoolyard with the class and look for images in the clouds.

• Tell the class you are going to listen to a song. Give each learner a copy of **Photocopiable 20**: Sing along! *Clouds*.

• Play the song at least twice. Ask the class what it is about. Elicit answers, i.e. clouds, but they are metaphorically compared to sheep.

> **Critical thinking opportunity:** Ask learners why they think the clouds are compared to sheep, for example because they are white and 'woolly'.

- As an extension task, you could ask learners to draw a picture to illustrate the poem.

Audioscript: Track 25

Learner's Book page 61

Clouds

White sheep, white sheep,

On a blue hill,

When the wind stops,

You all stand still.

When the wind blows,

You walk away slow.

White sheep, white sheep,

Where do you go?

Main teaching ideas

> **Digital Classroom:** Use the video 'Optical illusions' to explore the subject of optical illusions. The i button will explain how to use the video.

1 Talk about the pictures (10–15 minutes)

- Focus on the pictures. Ask learners to describe what they see. Supply additional vocabulary as needed.

> **Critical thinking opportunity:** The activities in this lesson involve learners in solving problems; they have to do an experiment, observe what happens, analyse and draw conclusions.

- Ask learners to look at the pictures in turn and follow the instructions. You may ask the class to work in pairs.

- You could model the first activity. Then learners do the experiments and discuss the results with their partner.

- When they have finished, have an open class discussion. Introduce the idea of an 'optical illusion'.

> **Critical thinking opportunity:** Discuss the word 'optical': it means something to do with our eyes, something we see. Discuss 'illusion': it means a

trick. Therefore, an 'optical illusion' is a picture that tricks our eyes.

Answers

A Lines a and b are the same length.

B The yellow circles are the same size.

C The blue and orange lines are the same length.

2 Vocabulary: shapes (5–10 minutes)

- Focus on the pictures. Say the words and ask the class to say them after you.

- Tell the class that they are now going to listen to an audio. They listen and point to each shape they hear. They say the shape word themselves.

- For the second part of the audio, the class listen to the descriptions and have to point to the correct shape.

- Play the audio a few times. Stop after each sentence and ask the class which shape it is.

- Elicit the answers from the class. Ask learners what helped them to understand.

Audioscript: Track 26

Learner's Book page 63

Listen, point and say.

Square. A pink square.

Circle. A silver circle.

Triangle. A gold triangle.

Rectangle. A turquoise rectangle.

Cube. A brown cube.

Listen and point to the matching shape.

1 This shape has three straight sides and three corners.

2 This shape has four straight sides and four corners. Two sides are long and two sides are short.

3 This shape has four straight sides and four corners. All four sides are exactly the same.

4 This shape is round. It doesn't have any corners.

5 You can pick up this shape. It has a top, a bottom, and four sides. It is like a box.

Answers
1 triangle, 2 rectangle, 3 square, 4 circle, 5 cube

> **Digital Classroom:** Use the activity 'Find the shapes' to revise shapes and colours vocabulary. The i button will explain how to use the activity.

3 Talk and discover! (10–15 minutes)

- Ask the class to work in pairs or small groups. Learners look at the pictures, read the questions and discuss the answers. Have them make notes as they discuss.

- When they have finished, have an open class discussion.

Answers
Left image: You can see a white cube in this picture. It is not really there. Your eyes are tricking you into thinking the white lines join together.
Right image: It looks like there are black dots in the white circles. You cannot count them as they disappear when you look at them. The black dots are not really there – they are an optical illusion.

4 Make an optical illusion toy (15–25 minutes)

- Tell the class that they are going to do an experiment.

- Read the instructions and allow time for the class to draw and tape the pictures.

- A chopstick or drinking straw could be used instead of a pencil. The paper should be cut into two squares or two circles, of approximately 7 cm in height.

- You may wish to do the activity together with learners.

> **Critical thinking opportunity:** Ask the class to describe what happens when they twirl the pencil, and to explain why they think this happens. Supply additional vocabulary as necessary.

Answers
The bird appears to be in the cage. It is an optical illusion that blends the two images together as they spin so fast.

Workbook

Learners do Activities 1–4 on pages 44–45.

Plenary ideas
Consolidation (15–25 minutes)

- Give learners a sheet of paper and ask them to draw a picture using only the shapes they have learned about in this lesson.

- When they have finished, they show the picture to the class and describe the shapes they have used.

- Hand out copies of **Photocopiable 21** and ask learners to complete the challenge in pairs.

Homework ideas

- Learners look for pictures and other optical illusions and bring them to class on the next day.

- **Home–school link:** Learners show their families the optical illusions in the book, and have them answer the questions.

4.2 Art: Hidden pictures

LEARNING PLAN

Learning objectives	Learning intentions	Success criteria
3Ld.01	• **Listening:** Listen and read; listen and follow instructions.	• Learners can speak about what they can see.
3Sc.06, 3So.01	• **Speaking:** Speak about optical illusions; speak about what they can see.	• Learners can speak about optical illusions.
3Rd.02	• **Reading:** Read and understand instructions.	• Learners can use commas in a sentence with a list.
3Wc.02	• **Writing:** Use commas in a sentence with a list; write sentences.	• Learners can write about what they can see.
3Us.03	• **Language focus:** direct object pronouns: *him, her, it, them, me, I can see …*	
	• **Vocabulary:** *moustache, glasses, beard*	

21st-century skills

Collaboration: Listen attentively while other students are contributing; respectfully wait for their turn to speak.

Communication: Use simple techniques to start, maintain and close conversations of various lengths.

Learning to learn: Participate sensibly and positively in learning activities in class.

Materials: Learner's Book pages 64–65; Workbook pages 46–47; pictures of people and scenes (optional); pictures of Genghis Khan

Starter ideas

I can see … (5–10 minutes)

- If learners have brought pictures of optical illusions, ask the class to say what they see or think they see.

- Ask the class to look out of the window and say what they can see. Alternatively, bring pictures of people and scenes, and ask learners to describe them using *I can see … .*

Main teaching ideas

1 Listen and point to the picture (10–15 minutes)

- Focus on the picture. Tell learners that they are going to listen and point to each element as they hear it.

- Play the audio and encourage learners to listen and point.

- Then ask learners to read the sentences with a partner.

Audioscript: Track 27

See Learner's Book page 64

Answers

Learners point to each element in the image as they hear it mentioned in the audio.

Language detective: Pronouns (5–10 minutes)

- Focus on the Language detective box. Ask learners to pay attention to the words in red in Activity 1 – they are all pronouns.
- Explain what a pronoun is, and ask learners what they notice about 'them'.
- Compare the use of pronouns in English and in the learners' own language.
- Learners respond to the questions about pronouns in the Language detective box.

Answers

We use pronouns so that we do not have to reuse the noun. Pronouns are short, whereas nouns can be long. *Them* can refer to boys, girls or things.

> **Digital Classroom:** Use the grammar presentation 'Subject and object pronouns' to revise subject and object pronouns. The i button will explain how to use the grammar presentation.

2 Talk and play a partner game: Me too! (5–10 minutes)

- As a class, play the pronoun game. Say something or someone you can see and encourage the class to answer – making sure their answer matches the pronouns used. For example, *'I can see some pencils.' 'I can see* ***them*** *too!'*
- Divide the class into pairs and ask them to play the game. If necessary, learners may use the pictures you brought to the class or the picture in Activity 1 in the Learner's Book.

> **Assessment ideas:** Circulate, listening to the learners' interactions. Supply additional vocabulary if necessary. Take notes of mistakes for remedial work.

Answers

Learner's own answers.

3 Talk (10–15 minutes)

- Focus on the pictures in the Learner's Book and tell learners that they can see them in two ways.
- Tell them to work with a partner. They look and ask each other the questions.
- As a class, discuss what images they have seen first.

> **Assessment ideas:** Circulate, listening to learners' interactions and their use of the past simple to answer the questions. Take notes of mistakes for remedial work.

Answers

Learner's own answers.

4 Read and find: Picture hunt (15–20 minutes)

- Focus on the drawing on the left-hand side of the page and read the instructions.
- Ask learners to work in pairs and try to find the faces. Tell them to use the expressions listed in the activity.
- When they have finished, ask pairs to report to the class.

Answers

Learner's own answers.

Writing tip (5 minutes)

- Before learners start Activity 5, read about the use of the comma in the Writing tip as a class.

5 Write (25–30 minutes)

- Read the information about the painting with the class.
- Ask learners to look at the painting carefully and write what they see, beginning as shown.
- When they have finished, ask volunteers to read what they have written. Do learners all see the same things in the picture? Encourage them to compare and contrast their descriptions using *I can see … .*

> **Assessment ideas:** Ask learners to check if they have used commas correctly.

Answers

Learner's own answers.

> **Workbook**
>
> Learners do Activities 1–4 on pages 46–47.

Plenary ideas

Consolidation (10–15 minutes)

> **Assessment ideas:** As a class, ask learners to discuss what they have found interesting in the first two lessons of the unit. Ask: *What was the most difficult thing to do?*

Homework ideas

- Ask learners to search the internet and find more optical illusions that involve finding two (or more) images.

- **Home–school link:** Learners show their family the pictures in Activities 4 and 5, and ask them what they can see.

4.3 Talk about it: That's impossible!

LEARNING PLAN

Learning objectives	Learning intentions	Success criteria
3Ld.04, 3Lo.01 3Sc.02 3Rd.01 3Uv.06	• **Listening:** Listen to conversations; listen to descriptions of situations. • **Speaking:** Act out and guess opposite words; describe self. • **Reading:** Read instructions and questions. • **Language focus:** adverbs of frequency: *always, usually, often, sometimes, never* • **Vocabulary:** prefixes: *un-, im-; impossible, possible, unkind, unhappy, untidy, impatient, impolite;* parts of the body: *finger, eye, brain*	• Learners can listen to descriptions of situations. • Learners can describe behaviours. • Learners can describe themselves. • Learners can act out and guess opposite words. • Learners can discuss being patient, polite and mature.

21st-century skills

Critical thinking opportunity: Explain why things happen; make predictions and estimations from given information.

Communication: Contribute in lessons by asking questions, attempting responses and explaining understanding.

Values: Learn about being patient, polite and mature.

Materials: Learner's Book pages 66–67; Workbook pages 48–49; photos of flying fish, squid or other animals doing unusual things

Common misconceptions

Misconception	How to identify	How to overcome
Learners quite often omit the object pronouns, for example: *My favourite meal is pizza. I eat (**it**) twice a week. My mother bought (**it**) for me. I was so excited and enjoyed (**it**) very much.*	Write an incorrect sentence. Point at *I eat* and say: *I eat … what? What's missing here? My mother bought … What did she buy? What did I enjoy?* Elicit the answers.	Ask learners to read the sentences and ask the same kind of question to the subject, and check if they need to put in the pronoun.
Learners sometimes use the personal pronoun instead of the objective pronoun, for example: *I bought a computer game and a blue t-shirt. I bought **they** because they were very cheap and nice. Can you give **they** to me?*	Write the incorrect sentence and provide both options, for example: *I bought **they / them** because they were very cheap and nice.* Ask the class to choose the correct form. Ask: *What did I buy? Are you talking about who bought something or are you talking about what you bought?* Elicit answers and have learners choose the correct form.	Ask learners to write a two-column table with the personal pronouns on the left and the objective pronouns on the right. Every time they do an activity, encourage them to ask the questions, for example: *Who is doing / did this? What did (I) (buy)?* Have them check with the table.

Starter ideas

Optical illusions and impossible things (10–20 minutes)

- If learners have looked for optical illusions that involve finding two (or more) images, ask them to share these with the class. Ask learners what they can see.

- To generate interest in the topic of impossible events or things, ask the class to do some impossible things, such as climb up the walls or fly around the room.

- Ask about things that are seemingly impossible, for example: *Can fish fly? Can birds swim under water?* Elicit ideas.

Main teaching ideas

1 Talk about it (5–15 minutes)

- Ask the class to read the sentences in the Learner's Book. Ask if it is possible for an a horse to fly or a cat to sing.

- Elicit more examples of impossible things, for example: an invisible car; water that flows uphill; people that live under water; a tree with pink leaves.

- You may wish to show photos of flying fish and other animals doing unusual things such as flying squid or puffins swimming under water. You could also show photos from suitable webpages, for example Science Focus, or the YouTube video '17 Animals That Can Do Impossible Things'.

Answers
Learner's own answers.

2 Try this! (5–10 minutes)

- Ask learners to look at the picture of the pencils and count the tops.

- Then they count the bottoms. How many are there?

- Tell them to try to follow the length of one pencil from top to bottom.

- Elicit reactions.

> **Critical thinking opportunity:** Ask learners to try and explain what happens, for example the bottom of the last pencil fades away but the eyes trick the brain and make it 'see' the bottom.

Answers
There are five tops. There are six bottoms.

3 Talk. Look at the picture of the snake (5–10 minutes)

- Ask learners to focus on the picture of the snake. In pairs, they read the instructions and try to answer the question.

- Tell them to use their finger to trace the body of the snake from the tail to the head.

- Discuss responses as a class.

Answers

The snail's head and tail do not match – it is an optical illusion.

4 Word study: Act it out! (10–15 minutes)

- Learners read about negative prefixes. Read the explanations with the class.

- Ask learners to read the pairs of words aloud.

- Ask learners to work with a partner. They choose one of the pairs of words to act out. Can the class guess the words they are acting out?

- As an extension, ask the class to think of other words they know that they can add negative prefixes to, e.g. *un-* interesting, able, comfortable, helpful, friendly, fair; *im-* possible, polite, patient.

Answers

Learner's own answers.

> **Digital Classroom:** Use the activity 'Talking about people' to revise adjectives with *un-* and *im-* prefixes. The i button will explain how to use the activity.

5 Vocabulary and values (10–20 minutes)

- Focus on the different situations depicted in the pictures.

- Elicit answers from the class about what is happening in the situations. Encourage learners to try to answer the questions.

- Tell the class that they are going to listen to people speaking about the situations.

- Play the audio, stopping after each situation. Discuss the answers with the class.

- Elicit more examples of these behaviours from the class.

> **Critical thinking opportunity:** You may wish to discuss other behaviours and ask learners to give examples, such as *tidy/untidy, kind/unkind, helpful/unhelpful, fair/unfair*, etc. Ask learners to add these words to the opposites list. The examples may vary from culture to culture, so it is important to consider whether the examples accurately reflect behavioural norms in learners' own setting. You can choose alternative examples/situations if they would be more appropriate.

Audioscript: Track 28

Learner's Book page 67

Listen and look. Answer the questions.

Patient / impatient

You are waiting for a bus. A **patient** person waits quietly and feels calm. An **impatient** person doesn't like waiting and feels angry.

Look at the picture. Which person is **impatient**?

Polite / impolite

You are walking and you bump into an old lady.

A **polite** person says, 'Sorry!' An **impolite** person doesn't say anything.

Look at the second picture. Is the girl **polite** or **impolite**?

Answers

The boy in the white shirt is impatient. The girl is polite because she says sorry.

> **Digital Classroom:** Use the activity 'Adverbs of frequency' to revise adverbs of frequency. The i button will explain how to use the activity.

Language detective (5–10 minutes)

- Revise the meaning and pronunciation of *always, usually, sometimes* and *never*.

- Focus on and explain the bar chart: 100% shaded = always; approximately 75% = usually; approximately 40% = sometimes; 0% = never.

- Draw attention to and check word order with the verb *to be*: *I am + usually + patient*.

- Give some examples and elicit examples from the class.

6 Listen to the children (5–15 minutes)

- Tell the class that they are going to listen to children describing themselves using the adjectives from this lesson.

- Explain that adjectives are words we use to describe people, things, places, etc. Ask learners to think of some examples of adjectives.

- Tell learners that the children are also using the words *always*, *usually*, *often*, *sometimes* and *never* to show how frequent things are.

- Play the recording. Learners listen to the conversation.

- Have the class work in small groups and hold their own conversations. Group members describe themselves using the adjectives in Activities 4 and 5, and the words in the Language detective box.

Audioscript: Track 29

Learner's Book page 67

Speaker 1:	Are you happy or unhappy?
Speaker 2:	I'm usually happy.
Speaker 1:	Me too.
Speaker 3:	I'm often happy, but sometimes I'm unhappy.
Speaker 1:	How about lucky or unlucky?
Speaker 3:	I'm always unlucky.
Speaker 2:	No, you're not. You're just sometimes unlucky.
Speaker 3:	No, I am never lucky.
Speaker 2:	Oh, come on. Never? Never ever?
Speaker 3:	Well, OK ... I'm almost never lucky.

Answers

Learner's own answers.

> **Workbook**
>
> Learners do Activities 1–3 on pages 48–49.

Plenary ideas

Consolidation (10–15 minutes)

> **Assessment ideas:** Do a 3-2-1 activity: ask learners to say three interesting things they have found in the lesson, two things they have learned, and one question they still have about the lesson. Can the rest of the class help them answer their question?

Homework ideas

- Learners search the internet for images similar to the ones they have seen in this lesson. Tell them to print the images and write two questions about each picture. They bring the pictures to the class the next day.

- **Home–school link:** Learners show their family the pictures of the snake and the pencils, and ask them what they see.

4.4 Write about it: Experiments and results

LEARNING PLAN

Learning objectives	Learning intentions	Success criteria
3Ld.02 3Sc.01, 3Sc.03, 3Sc.04 3Wc.01, 3Wca.02, 3Wor.01	• **Listening:** Listen and follow instructions; follow aural instructions. • **Speaking:** Give opinions, give instructions; discuss results of experiments; ask and answer questions. • **Writing:** Use correct punctuation; write instructions; complete sentences. • **Language focus:** revision of use of question marks and imperatives • **Vocabulary:** *fingertips, brain, confused, right-handed, left-handed*	• Learners can listen and carry out instructions. • Learners can carry out experiments. • Learners can discuss experiments. • Learners can give opinions.

21st-century skills

Critical thinking opportunity: Compare and contrast information; conduct experiments and discuss results.

Collaboration: Keep to the instructions to complete the task.

Communication: Attempt responses and explain understanding.

Materials: Learner's Book pages 68–69; Workbook pages 50–51; Sample answer for Unit 4; **Photocopiable 22**

Starter ideas

Let's find out! (10–15 minutes)

- If learners have searched for images of optical illusions, ask them to share these with the class and ask questions about them.

- Ask the class: *How can our eyes trick us?* Ask learners to think of the optical illusions they have just shared with the class. Elicit ideas.

- Ask the class to look at the photos in the Learner's Book. What do they see? How are their eyes tricked by the photos on this page? Have their eyes ever tricked them in real life? Invite learners to describe the situations. You may also give your own examples, such as when it's very hot it can look as though there is water on the road surface.

- Explain that sometimes people can see pictures in clouds. What pictures can they see in the clouds in the book?

- You may also show other pictures of clouds and challenge learners to find images in them.

Main teaching ideas

1 Experiment 1: The jumping finger (10–15 minutes)

- Explain to the class that they are going to carry out an experiment to find out if one eye is stronger than the other.

- Play the audio and ask the class to follow in their books. If necessary, stop after each sentence to give learners more time.

> **Differentiation ideas:** With less confident groups, ask learners to read the instructions in the book and check they understand them. Model if necessary. You could also ask more confident learners to pair up with less confident learners and do the experiment together.

• Elicit the answers from the class. Compare their findings with the ideas they had before conducting the experiment.

> **Assessment ideas:** Ask learners what they need to remember to write when they ask a question, i.e. a question mark. Ask: *Where do you write the question mark?* Elicit answers. Then remind learners of how they give instructions. Ask them to circle the words that tell people what to do.

Audioscript: Track 30
See Learner's Book page 68

Answers
Your finger appears to move when you open and close different eyes.

> **Digital Classroom:** Use the activity 'Questions!' to revise question formation. The i button will explain how to use the activity.

2 Record the results (10–15 minutes)

• Tell the class that Kambiz also carried out this experiment.

• Focus on the explanations of what Kambiz found and recorded.

> **Critical thinking opportunity:** Ask learners to read Kambiz's notes and look at his drawings. They compare them with their own experience. Were their results similar to Kambiz's or were they different?

• Ask learners to draw and label pictures to show their own experiment results.

Answers
Learner's own answers.

Tell me why! (5–15 minutes)

• Ask learners how they can explain the result of their experiment. What happens when they change the fingers? Elicit explanations.

> **Differentiation ideas:** Less confident learners may find it difficult to explain the process in English, so allow them to use their L1 if necessary. Echo their

contributions in simple English and ask them to repeat after you. Write key vocabulary on the board for reference.

• Read the explanation with the class and compare it with their ideas. Were they correct?

3 Experiment 2: Right or left (15–20 minutes)

• Ask the class if they are left- or right-handed.

• Read the explanation. Ask: *Have you tried writing with your 'non-dominant' hand?* Ask learners to try. How difficult is it?

• Explain to the class that most people have a dominant eye, just like they have a dominant hand. Ask: *Which is your dominant eye?* Elicit ideas.

• Focus on the questions and tell the class that they are going to listen to the directions for the second experiment. They listen and write the missing words to complete the sentences.

> **Differentiation ideas:** You could ask less confident groups to look at the pictures before they listen. Discuss what they think the pictures show. This will help them understand the aural instructions. More confident learners could work in pairs or small groups and predict what the instructions will be. They can write a draft in pencil and then check how correct they were as they listen.

• Play the audio recording again and have learners complete the questions and answers. Hand out copies of **Photocopiable 23**. They listen to the audio and fill in the missing words to complete the directions.

• Check answers as a class. Then ask the class to do the experiment themselves.

• Ask: *Which eye did your hands go to – your left eye or your right eye?*

• See **Sample answer for Unit 4** for an example answer to this writing task.

Answers
Answers will vary. Note that two-thirds of people have right-eye dominance.

Audioscript: Track 31

Learner's Book page 69

Experiment 2: Right or left?

Question: Which eye is dominant?

1 Hold your arms in front of you.

2 Put your hands together. Make a hole, in a triangle shape.

3 Keep both eyes open. Look through the triangle.

4 Find something to stare at.

5 Keep looking at that object. Move your hands slowly to your face.

Check your writing (10–15 minutes)

- Ask the class to look at the 'Check your writing' questions and to check the sentences they have written.

- As a class, discuss how well they have done the activity. Have they forgotten anything? How could they remember next time?

4 Record the experiment results for your class (10–20 minutes)

- As a class, look at the graph in the Learner's Book. Explain that each coloured square is one child. The graph shows how many children in the class are left-eyed or right-eyed.

- Ask learners to answer the questions about the graph.

- Then draw a graph on the board like the one in the Learner's Book. Ask learners to copy it in their notebooks.

- Ask each learner to write their initials in a square in the correct row (depending on whether they are left-eyed or right-eyed) and colour in the square with their initials. You may need to explain what initials are, i.e. the first letter of their name and surname.

- Once the table is complete, read the graph and count how many children have a dominant right eye and how many have a dominant left eye.

Answers

Graph in Learner's Book: sixteen children have a dominant right eye; three children have a dominant left eye.

Learners fill in their own class chart and write the results.

Workbook

Learners do Activities 1 and 2 on pages 50–51.

Plenary ideas

Consolidation (10–15 minutes)

> **Assessment ideas:** Ask learners to discuss which they thought was the most interesting experiment. How interesting were the information and experiments in this lesson? Elicit ideas and have learners write a few sentences with their impressions in their learning log.

Homework ideas

- Learners look for other experiments that show we don't see things in the same way. They could visit suitable websites, e.g. Psych2Go, Wonderopolis, etc., and then share their findings with the class.

- **Home–school link:** Learners can ask their family to do these experiments at home.

4.5 Read and respond: Animal camouflage

LEARNING PLAN

Learning objectives	Learning intentions	Success criteria
3Ld.03, 3Ld.04	• **Listening:** Contrast and compare pronunciation: British versus American English.	• Learners can read an informational text about animal camouflage.
3Sc.02, 3So.01	• **Speaking:** Speak about animal camouflage; speak about a poem; recite a poem.	• Learners can speak about animal camouflage.
3Rd.01	• **Reading:** Read an information text about animal camouflage; distinguish between British and American English spelling; understand the meaning of words from context.	• Learners can recite a poem. • Learners can discuss a poem. • Learners can contrast and compare British versus American English pronunciation and spelling.
	• **Vocabulary:** *pinto, blotch, camouflage, hide, pattern, bark, antennae, blend, hard, fur, stripes, creep, meal*	

21st-century skills

Critical thinking opportunity: Compare and contrast information; understand cause and effect.

Collaboration: Respond positively to what others say about the topic and the group task they are doing; add to what others are saying by contributing further ideas and examples.

Materials: Learner's Book pages 70–73; Workbook pages 52–53; photos of animals that live in the desert, in the jungle and in the Arctic; large sheet of poster paper; **Photocopiable 3**

Starter ideas

Animals in disguise. (5–10 minutes)

⟩ **Critical thinking opportunity:** Remind learners of animals that live in the desert. Ask: *What colour are they? What colour is the land around them? Is there any relationship between these two facts?*

Ask learners to think about the animals that live in the jungle or in places where there is a lot of snow. What differences do they find? Why do these animals have those colours? Elicit ideas.

Main teaching ideas

1 Talk about it (5–10 minutes)

• Ask learners to look at the pictures on the pages and decide if it is easy to see the animals. Ask them to explain their answer.

• Ask: *What do you think the words 'animal camouflage' mean?* Elicit ideas.

⟩ **Critical thinking opportunity:** Ask what learners know about animal camouflage. Help them to find the relation between the colour of the animals and the environment where they live.

• Encourage learners to elaborate on their ideas, and add extra vocabulary as necessary.

⟩ **Assessment ideas:** With the class, create a K-W-L-VN poster. Learners can create individual K-W-L charts using **Photocopiable 3**. In the K column, learners write what they know or think they know about animal camouflage. In the W column, they write questions they would like to find answers for. Tell them they will fill in the other columns at the end of the lesson.

2 Read and listen (5–15 minutes)

- Tell the class to look again at the pictures and find the animals. What animals are camouflaged in these images? Elicit answers.

- Learners may initially find it difficult to see the insects in the pictures. If they find the butterfly, they could then read about the stick insect and look again to see if they can find it in the picture.

- Tell them they are going to listen and read about the animals and insects in the pictures.

- Play the audio at least twice.

> **Differentiation ideas:** With less confident groups, you could stop after each section and ask a few comprehension questions, for example: *Are the horses in the first picture real? What does 'pinto' mean?* With more confident groups, you could ask them to summarise each section in their own words.

Audioscript: Track 32

See Learner's Book pages 70–71

3 Word study (10–15 minutes)

- Ask the class to find the blue words in the story and read the sentences aloud.

- They then look at the words and match them to the correct definition.

- Check answers as a class.

> **Critical thinking opportunity:** Ask learners to re-read the text and find other words they don't know the meaning of. Encourage them to guess the meaning from the context. Ask learners if they know another different meaning for 'bark': to make a sound like a dog.

> **Differentiation ideas:** Ask more confident learners to write a definition for the new words they have found. Less confident learners may look up the meanings in a dictionary.

Answers

hide – c: be in a place where nobody can see you
hard – e: difficult, not easy
bark – d: the outside part of a tree or branch
blend – a: mix two things together so they become one thing
meal – f: food, for example dinner or lunch
fur – b: the hair that covers an animal

4 Write. Work with a partner. Talk about and write the answers to these questions (15–25 minutes)

- Ask learners to work with a partner. They read and discuss the questions. Then they write down their answers.

- Check answers as a class.

> **Differentiation ideas:** Ask less confident learners to read the text again before they discuss and write the answers.

> **Assessment ideas:** Circulate, asking learners questions about their work. Take notes of mistakes for future remedial use.

CROSS-CURRICULAR LINK

Science
You may wish to visit suitable websites with the class and find out about forms of camouflage and other animals that use it. Suitable examples include Bored Panda, K5 Computerlab and National Geographic.

Answers
Suggested answers:
a Some animals use camouflage to hide and stay safe. Some animals use camouflage to hunt and catch other animals.
b A place that is yellow, for example a yellow flower or leaf.
c birds
d Yes it is. It can hide on branches and leaves. Its body is the same colour as bark and its long legs and antennae look like sticks.
e It needs to hide in the grass so that it can catch other animals and eat them.
f Brown in summer and white in winter

> **Digital Classroom:** Use the activity 'Hidden animals' to reinforce comprehension of camouflage. The i button will explain how to use the activity.

5 Pronunciation (10–25 minutes)

- You might want to use this as extension material as this is beyond the requirements of the Cambridge Primary English as a Second Language curriculum framework.

- Ask learners where people speak English besides the UK. Find the places on the map.

- Explain that in the USA, for example, people speak English, but their pronunciation is different.

- Read the explanations with the class and tell them to listen to the audio.

- Play the audio at least twice. Then ask the class to repeat trying to imitate each accent.

CROSS-CURRICULAR LINK

Social science

Ask learners if people in different regions of their country speak their language in the same way. Are there any differences? Elicit answers. Explain that accents differ not just between countries with the same language but also between provinces or regions within the same country.

You may wish to visit suitable websites and find out about the accents of English around the world and also the different accents spoken in the learners' country. Examples include English with Lucy and International Dialects of English Archive.

Audioscript: Track 33
See Learner's Book page 72

Answers
Learners practise their pronunciationThe poets are American.

Language focus (5–15 minutes)

- Focus on the examples in the Language focus box. Ask the class to find the differences in the spelling.

- Then tell learners to turn to Activity 6 and decide if the poem is written in American or British English. What makes them think so?

- You may direct learners to suitable webpages where they can find more examples for the different spellings and vocabulary of British and American English, such as Learning English and British Council.

6 Read and listen (5–10 minutes)

- Ask learners to look at the camouflage picture and find an animal hiding on the bark of the tree.

- Talk about the title of the poem. Point out that we sometimes add -*ish* to certain adjectives to mean 'quite', e.g. *tallish* = quite tall.

- Tell learners they are going to read and listen to the poem and fill in the last word of the poem.

- Play the audio at least twice. Elicit the answer from the class.

Audioscript: Track 34
See Learner's Book page 73

Answers
A frog is hiding in the picture. The last word of the poem is 'meal'.

> **Digital Classroom:** Use the slideshow 'Animal camouflage' to reinforce the topic of animal camouflage. The i button will explain how to use the slideshow.

> **Digital Classroom:** Use the activity 'Animal camouflage: matching' to revise animal vocabulary and reinforce comprehension of the passage *Hidden Animals*. The i button will explain how to use the activity.

7 Talk (10–20 minutes)

- Ask learners to read the poem again. Then they read and answer the questions.

- Encourage them to look for clues in the poem and justify their opinions.

> **Critical thinking opportunity:** If learners need prompting, ask which word the missing word will rhyme with, i.e. *feel*. What word can they think of that rhymes with feel, and will fit with the meaning here?

CROSS-CURRICULAR LINK

Science

This poem is about the grey tree frog. There are many varieties of tree frogs. You may wish to ask the class to look for photographs and information about tree frogs and ask related questions, for example: *Where do they live? How do they camouflage themselves? What colour are they?* Learners can find information in suitable websites, such as The National Wildlife Federation.

Answers

a   the frog
b   Learner's own answers.
c   It could be a snake or a bird (foxes don't usually eat frogs or climb trees!). The word 'strikes' suggests a snake.
d   The snake eats it. (But other answers are possible if learners can justify them.)
e   meal
f   tree – me, bark – dark, hear – near, yikes – strikes, feel – (meal)

Workbook

Learners do Activities 1–3 on pages 52–53.

Plenary ideas

Consolidation (10–20 minutes)

> **Assessment ideas:** Bring the K-W-L-VN poster to the board and have learners take out their individual charts (**Photocopiable 3**). With the class, revisit what learners have written in the K and W columns. What questions have they found the answer to? Have them write the information on the L column. Then ask them what totally new or very new information they have learned. Ask them to write it in the VN (Very New) column.

Homework ideas

- Learners look for information in books or on selected websites about one of the animals they have learned about in this lesson or other animals that have good camouflage skills. They write a few sentences about the animals' ability and add some photographs.

- **Home–school link:** Learners teach the poem *Grayish, Greenish* to their family. Can their family guess what the missing word is?

4.6 Project challenge

LEARNING PLAN

Learning objectives	Learning intentions	Success criteria
3Sc.05, 3Sc.06, 3Sc.07	• **Speaking:** Discuss a project; discuss steps of a project; organise work; present their project to the class.	• Learners can read and understand instructions.
3Rd.02	• **Reading:** Read and understand instructions.	• Learners can give instructions. • Learners can plan a project.
3Wca.02	• **Writing:** Write sentences. • **Language focus:** Unit 4 review • **Vocabulary:** Unit 4 review	• Learners can make a camouflage frog or butterfly. • Learners can write an animal camouflage poem.

21st-century skills

Creative thinking: Design new items based on a model.

Communication: Share their thoughts with others to help further develop ideas and solve problems.

Learning to learn: Listen and respond positively to feedback and understand why a correction was given; learn from mistakes and feedback.

Materials: Learner's Book pages 74–75; Workbook pages 54–55; Project A: drawing supplies, scissors; Project B: drawing supplies, sheets of paper; **Photocopiable 2**, **23**, **24**, **25**; End of Unit 4 test; **Differentiated worksheets 4A, B and C**

Starter ideas

Looking back (15–20 minutes)

* Ask the class to choose a lesson from this unit they liked a lot. Ask them to explain why they liked it, and to write a short summary.

* Hand out copies of **Photocopiable 24** and carry out the task as a class or in groups.

> **Assessment ideas:** Divide the class into two teams and play Definition Bingo to revise new vocabulary and useful phrases. This game will give you the opportunity to assess how much learners remember from previous lessons. Definition Bingo is played like normal Bingo, but using definitions instead of words. Choose words from this unit that you would like learners to revise. Write definitions for these words on slips of paper and put them in a box or a bag. Write the words on the board. Learners draw a six-square grid, choose six words from the list and write them in their grid. Pull the slips of paper out of the box one at a time and read the definition. Learners cross out the corresponding word. The first one to complete a line or the whole card calls out *Bingo*!

Main teaching ideas

Learners choose an end-of-unit project to work on. Look at the examples in the pictures and help learners to choose. Provide materials.

Project A: Make a camouflage frog or butterfly (60–90 minutes)

* Read the directions on page 74 of the Learner's Book.

* Give out drawing supplies and a copy of **Photocopiable 23**.

* Learners look around the classroom and decide where they want their animal to hide.

* They colour their frog or butterfly according to the place where they are going to hide it.

- When they have finished, the groups hide the frogs and butterflies.

- The rest of the class must close their eyes while the groups hide the camouflage animals.

- The class looks for the animals. Set a time limit of two minutes.

- When the time is up, ask the class: *How many animals did you find in two minutes? Which animals were not found? What made those animals hard to find?*

- Each group writes about what they did. They write sentences in the simple past, and attach the camouflage frog or butterfly to the writing.

- Tell them to use the sentence openings in the book.

- **Writing tip:** When group members have finished writing their draft, ask them to exchange their text with their partners and give each other feedback. Partners check writing and spelling and help each other correct any mistakes, using **Photocopiable 2**: Peer editing checklist.

- Learners write the final draft.

> **Assessment ideas:** You may wish to video-record groups as they work, so they can then use copies of the recordings to assess what they have done and how they have worked. The copies can then be shared with the family and filed in their portfolios. You may also display the slideshows or the scrapbooks during an open day for families to see.

Project B: Write an animal camouflage poem (60–90 minutes)

- Ask learners to work individually. They write a poem about animal camouflage.

- Learners find a photo of a camouflaged animal, either online or in this unit. They can also draw a picture of their camouflaged animal.

- Encourage learners to do some research about their animal.

- Tell them to use the questions in the activity to help them to write the poem. This will help them organise their ideas.

- They can use the poem on Learner's Book page 75 as a model.

- **Writing tip:** When group learners have finished writing their draft, ask them to exchange their text with a partner and give each other feedback.

Partners check writing and spelling and help each other correct any mistakes, using **Photocopiable 2**: Peer editing checklist.

- Learners then write the final draft.

- **Share your work:** Everybody who wrote a poem can put their camouflaged animal photo or drawing on the board. They read their poem aloud and the class has to find the matching picture.

> **Assessment ideas:** You may wish to video-record groups as they work, so that they can then use copies of the recordings to assess what they have done and how they have worked. The copies can then be shared with the family and filed in their portfolios. You may also display the slideshows or the scrapbooks during an open day for families to see.

> **Assessment ideas:** When learners have finished, give them a copy of **Photocopiable 25** and read the instructions as a class. Ask learners to work independently and think about their work on the project. They reflect and answer the questions. Ask them to tick off the aims they have achieved. Insist on the importance of giving honest answers.

Workbook

Learners do the Check your progress quiz on pages 54–55.

Plenary ideas

Reflect on your learning (5–10 minutes)

- Draw learners' attention to the 'Reflect on your learning' questions in the Learner's Book.

- Learners answer the questions to reflect on their project work.

Consolidation (10–15 minutes)

- Ask learners to reflect on and discuss what they liked most about Unit 4; encourage them to explain why. This may also be a good opportunity for them to think about what aspects of the unit they have found most difficult and why.

- You may wish to keep a record of learners' comments, to see how they progress over time.

> **Assessment ideas: Portfolio opportunity:** If you have been filing learners' work for Unit 4, you may find it useful to put all the work of this unit together. You could ask learners to make a cover for their Unit 4 work, decorating it with an image that represents what they have learned.

Homework ideas

- Hand out copies of **Differentiated worksheets 4A, B and C** depending on each learner's ability, and ask them to complete the activities at home.

- Learners draw a picture of what they have liked most about this unit.

- **Home–school link:** Learners show their family their projects.

4.7 What do you know now?

How can our eyes trick us? (30–40 minutes)

- Learners work in pairs. They work together through all the tasks set in this section.

- They write the answers in their notebooks. You may ask them to have a special section in their notebooks where they record the answers.

Answers

1 Suggested answer: An optical illusion is an image that we see in a different way to how it really is. The image tricks our eyes into seeing things that aren't really as they appear.

2–4 Learner's own answers.

Look what I can do! (15 minutes)

- Review the five *I can …* statements on page 76 of the Learner's Book. Learners demonstrate what they can do.

- Learners colour in the faces to show which things they can do.

- Encourage them to be honest in their answers.

> **Workbook**
>
> Learners answer the Reflection questions on page 55.

>5 Inventions

Unit plan

Lesson	Approximate number of learning hours	Outline of learning content	Learning objectives	Resources
1 Can inventions help the planet?	1.5–2.5	Talk about why we invent things for the environment, and give opinions about inventions.	3Ld.04 3Sc.06 3So.01 3Rd.01 3Ro.01 3Wca.02	Learner's Book Lesson 5.1 Workbook Lesson 5.1 ⬇ Photocopiable 26 **Digital Classroom:** Video – Inventions to help the planet; Activity – Word families
2 Great inventors	1.75–2.75	Read and talk about what the inventors wanted to do.	3Ld.04 3Sc.02 3So.01 3Sor.02 3Rd.03 3Wca.03 3Wca.04	Learner's Book Lesson 5.2 Workbook Lesson 5.2 ⬇ Photocopiable 27 **Digital Classroom:** Grammar presentation – Verbs with *to*
3 The plastic problem	1.0–2.0	Listen and talk about young inventors helping the planet.	3Ld.03 3Lo.01 3Sc.03 3Sc.05 3Rd.01 3Us.04	Learner's Book Lesson 5.3 Workbook Lesson 5.3 ⬇ Photocopiable 28 **Digital Classroom:** Activity – The engineer
4 Planning an invention	1.5–2.25	Write plans for an invention.	3Sc.07 3Sor.01 3Rd.02 3Wca.01 3Wor.02 3Wc.02 3Us.04	Learner's Book Lesson 5.4 Workbook Lesson 5.4 ⬇ Sample answer for Unit 5 ⬇ Photocopiable 1 ⬇ Photocopiable 2 ⬇ Photocopiable 29 **Digital Classroom:** Animation and activity sheet – Our Kitchen-o-Mat and Our School-o-Mat
5 *Jenny, Lenny and the Jumperoo*	1.75–3.0	Read and perform a long poem.	3Lo.01 3So.01 3Sor.02 3Rd.01 3Rd.03 3Ro.01	Learner's Book Lesson 5.5 Workbook Lesson 5.5 **Digital Classroom:** Activity – *Jenny, Lenny and the Jumperoo*

(continued)

Lesson	Approximate number of learning hours	Outline of learning content	Learning objectives	Resources
6 Project challenge	1.5–2.5	Make a book of inventions or a poster about an inventor who helps the planet.	3Sc.04 3Sc.05 3Rd.02 3Wca.02 3Wca.03 3Wca.05 3Wc.01	Learner's Book Lesson 5.6 Workbook Lesson 5.6 ⬇ Photocopiable 30 ⬇ Differentiated worksheets 5A, B and C
7 What do you know now?	0.75–1.0	Self-assessment and reflection.		Learner's Book Lesson 5.7

Cross-unit resources

⬇ Unit 5 Audioscripts

⬇ End of Unit 5 test

⬇ Progress test 2

⬇ Unit 5 Progress report

⬇ Unit 5 Wordlist

BACKGROUND KNOWLEDGE

Inventions

- In this unit, learners read about inventions.
- The 10 most important inventions of all time include:
  - the World Wide Web by Tim Berners-Lee in 1989
  - the light bulb by Thomas Edison in 1879
  - the telephone by Alexander Graham Bell in 1876
  - the refrigerator by William Cullen in 1835
  - Braille by Louis Braille in 1829
  - the thermometer by Santorio Santorio in 1593
  - the microscope by Hans and Zacharias Janssen in 1590
  - the printing press by Johannes Gutenberg in 1440
  - paper by Cai Lun in (approx.) 100 CE
  - the wheel by unknown (first records in Mesopotamia) around 3500 BCE.

DNA

DNA is the abbreviation of deoxyribonucleic acid. It is material that is found in every human and animal cell, and contains the instructions needed for the living thing to develop, survive and reproduce. DNA was discovered in 1869, but it was not until much later that people knew what it looked like and were able to take a picture of it. In 1953, James Watson and Francis Crick, helped by the research done by biophysicists Rosalind Franklin and Maurice Wilkins, found that DNA has a spiral made of two strands wound around each other.

TEACHING SKILLS FOCUS

Differentiation: supporting more confident learners

Differentiation helps teachers to cater for the needs of learners who have different abilities and are at levels of readiness in diverse conditions. This therefore gives learners the best chance to succeed. Generally speaking, teachers tend to associate differentiation with low-achieving or less confident learners, and with shy or unmotivated learners. However, differentiation should also cover more confident learners as well.

More confident learners may not only be the ones who get high grades in all subjects or finish sooner than

CONTINUED

the rest. Sometimes, higher achieving learners may be those who do not finish their work on time because they are never sure it is perfect enough, or learners who stop paying attention or misbehave because they are bored.

Here are some ideas for how to work with more confident learners:

- Find out in what areas of learning these learners are more confident or have higher abilities.
- Provide extension and enrichment of the activities, possibly linking the assignment to their area of interest or giving them authentic problems.
- Give learners opportunities to work together. Working with peers of similar capacities is both stimulating and challenging.
- Make sure that activities are content-rich.

- Encourage learners to take on new challenges.
- Use flexible timing with time-based activities.
- Allow learners to create their own extensions to existing activities.

Your challenge

In each unit of the Learner's Book, opportunities to introduce differentiation are highlighted. Look through Unit 5 and highlight opportunities for introducing some of the differentiation ideas above. How can you differentiate the activities further?

Reflection

How well did the ideas work out? How did learners react? Were they engaged and challenged enough?

5.1 Think about it: Can inventions help the planet?

LEARNING PLAN

Learning objectives	Learning intentions	Success criteria
3Ld.04	• **Listening:** Listen and identify opinions; listen for specific information.	• Learners can sing a song.
3Sc.06, 3So.01	• **Speaking:** Sing a song; state and support opinions; discuss environmental problems caused by plastics and inventions that offer solutions; describe inventions and what they do; ask and answer questions.	• Learners can state and support opinions. • Learners can discuss environmental problems caused by plastics and
3Rd.01, 3Ro.01	• **Reading:** Read about plastic homes.	inventions that offer solutions.
3Wca.02	• **Writing:** Take notes; fill in a table.	• Learners can describe inventions.
	• **Language focus:** phrases of expressing opinion: *I think, I don't think, I agree, I disagree.*	
	• **Vocabulary:** *invent, inventor, cute, useful, grow, plant holders, keep away, bugs;* word families: *inventor, invent, invention;* descriptive words	

21st-century skills

Critical thinking opportunity: Understand that new things are invented to solve a problem; understand cause and effect.

Collaboration: Demonstrate how to interrupt politely and at appropriate moments in group talk; respond positively to what others say about the topic and the group task they are doing.

Learning to learn: Search for information on a specific topic when doing a project; take basic notes about key information while reading and listening.

Materials: Learner's Book pages 77–79; Workbook pages 56–57; pictures of inventions, e.g. plane, car, light bulb, printing press; **Photocopiable 26**

Starter ideas

Getting started (10–20 minutes)

- Show some pictures of inventions. Ask the class if they know the names of any of them. Supply any words as needed. Elicit the word 'invention' and ask the class to explain in their own words what an invention is.

- Ask: *What do we call a person who invents something?* Elicit the word 'inventor'. Do learners know the names of inventors, for example Edison, Da Vinci, Pasteur, etc.?

- Ask the class: *Where do inventions come from?* Some suggestions may include science labs, the inventor's brain, an 'accident', etc.

- Focus on the photo on page 77 and ask the class where the children are and what they are doing, for example in a lab, doing experiments, inventing things, etc.

- Explain that we don't *make* an experiment but instead we *do* an experiment. This is a common mistake with learners whose first language has the same verb for both *do* and *make*.

- Focus on questions a–c on page 77 of the Learner's Book and discuss answers as a class.

- Ask learners: *What is 'imagination'?* Encourage them to come up with ideas, for example thinking about new things, creating new things, thinking about new ideas, etc.

- Encourage learners to think about games they play. Do they impersonate characters? Do they invent dialogues or new endings to stories? Do they imagine how things might be different or new solutions to problems? Encourage the class to express themselves.

Answers
Learner's own answers.

> **Digital Classroom:** Use the video 'Inventions to help the planet' to explore the subject of inventions to help the planet. The i button will explain how to use the video.

🎧 35 Sing along! *Imagination* (10–15 minutes)

- Tell the class you are going to listen to a song about imagination.

- Give each learner a copy of **Photocopiable 26**: Sing along! *Imagination*. Play the song at least twice. Ask the class what it is about. Elicit answers.

- Sing the song and encourage learners to join in.

> **Critical thinking opportunity:** Ask questions about the song's lyrics, such as: What could you pretend your bed could be? What could you imagine your chair could be? What other 'impossible,' pretend things does the song mention?

- You could extend the activity by asking some more questions, for example: *Can you see into your imagination? Close your eyes and go into it – what can you see there? What can you hear? Can you smell something? What is it? What can you feel in your imagination?* Then ask learners to share their ideas with the class.

Audioscript: Track 35

Learner's Book page 77

Imagination

Sometimes when I'm feeling low
I know I can use my imagination.
Come on now imagine with me, together we'll play happily
When we use our imagination.
Let's pretend this bed is a boat.
Let's pretend that chair is a rocket ship!
We can go anywhere we want
When we use our imagination
We can fly to the moon
Set sail on the ocean blue
We can be anything we want to be
When we use our imagination!
Clap your hands, sing along with me
It's so fun to see what we can imagine
Come on now imagine with me, together we'll play happily
When we use our imagination.
Let's take a ride on our flying horse!
We headed to an underwater course
Look a tunnel on the ocean floor
Now we're back to my front door!
Hey there's a chipmunk waving from a tree
Want to come to my party?
When we arrive what do we see?

It's a chipmunk tea party!
When we use our imagination we have so much fun
Come on imagine with me.
Come on now imagine with me, together
we'll play happily
When we use our imagination.
Come on!
We can do anything we want to do
That's right!
We can be anything we want to be
When we use our imagination!
We can do anything we want to do
You got it!
We can be anything we want to be
When we use our imagination!

Main teaching ideas

1 Talk about the pictures (10–15 minutes)

- Focus on pictures a–c. Explain that they are all inventions made by children. Ask learners to think about what each invention is made of, and what they do.

- Discuss each image one at a time and elicit ideas.

CROSS-CURRICULAR LINK

Environmental science

The inventions are all made of plastic bottles. Encourage the class to think how useful this re-use of plastic bottles is, and why. Have them consider the negative impact of plastic bottles on the environment, for example how many bottles are thrown away each year (38 billion water bottles in the USA alone!), how they affect the oceans, animals, etc.

Answers
a a toy frog made out of plastic
b pencil holder made out of plastic
c planter made out of plastic

---

2 Listen to the children talk about their inventions (5–15 minutes)

- Tell learners that they are going to listen to the children talking about their inventions in the pictures. As they listen, ask them to think about the questions in the table.

- Play the recording at least twice. Learners write the inventions and complete the table.

- Copy the table on the board and check answers as a class.

> **Differentiation ideas:** With less confident groups, you could play each description twice and then pause before playing the next one, to allow time for learners to write the answers. More confident learners may take advantage of the extra listening opportunity to make notes of other interesting details, such as which materials were used, how the invention works, etc.

Audioscript: Track 36

Learner's Book page 78

Maya:	For Earth day, our teacher asked us to invent things out of plastic bottles. I'm not an inventor and I couldn't think of anything so I made a frog. It is a toy frog and it doesn't really do anything, but it is cute! I look at it and it makes me happy. That's important, isn't it?
Jamal:	I wanted to invent a useful thing. So I thought about what we need. We need food that grows near us. Then I thought, if we grow plants in plastic bottles, the water will stay in. The bottles keep the bugs away. So my invention is a planter.
Indigo:	Well, I can never find my pencils, so I invented plastic pencil holders. I made them funny so that I remember to put my pencils away!

Answers

Invention:	a	b	c
What is it?	A toy	A planter	A pencil holder
What does it do?	It's cute and you can play with it.	Grows plants that you can eat.	Holds pencils and helps you keep tidy.
Why did they make it?	Because the teacher told them to.	To grow plants and help the environment.	To find pencils and keep tidy.

3 Vocabulary: Word families (10–20 minutes)

> **Critical thinking opportunity:** Focus on the mind map and the words inside each circle. Ask learners to look at the labels of each mind map and the example word in each, and explain each of the word types – 'do' words are action words, 'thing' words are objects and 'person' words are types of people.

- Ask learners to write each of the words from the box into the correct mind map.

- Draw learners' attention again to the words in the box and ask: *Which words are from the same word families?*

- Learners work in pairs and write sentences that use the words in the same word family, for example 'A collector collects things for their collection.' Then ask pairs to share their sentences with the class.

> **Differentiation ideas:** With less confident groups, you could give an example or a sentence starter for them to then complete. More confident learners can think of other words and make new word families.

Answers
do: *collect, create, direct, invent*
thing: *collection, creation, direction, invention*
person: *collector, creator, director, inventor*
Learner's own answers.

> **Digital Classroom:** Use the activity 'Word families' to revise word formation of noun, verb and person. The i button will explain how to use the activity.

4 Listen to the teacher and children discuss the inventions (5–15 minutes)

- Tell the class that they are going to listen to children discuss the inventions from Activity 1 with their teacher.

- Focus on the Word box. Check that learners understand the meaning of each word/phrase. If they do not, ask them to look up the words in the dictionary. Ask them to listen for these words and phrases in the discussion.

- Play the recording once. Ask learners to put up their hands every time they hear one of the words/phrases and then repeat the sentence.

- Divide the class into pairs and play the recording again. Ask learners to discuss and complete the table based on the discussion in the audio.

- Check the table as a class.

> **Differentiation ideas:** With less confident groups of learners, you may wish to share the transcript with them so they not only check their answers but also contextualise any new vocabulary they might encounter.

> **Critical thinking opportunity:** When learners have finished, ask them to work in small groups and discuss which plastic bottle project they like best. Encourage them to explain why.

- Ask the class to use their imagination – can learners think of other uses for plastic bottles to give them a 'second life'? Elicit ideas.

Audioscript: Track 37

Learner's Book page 79

Teacher: What do you think of the plastic bottle projects, Milly?

Milly:	Hmmm, I think the frog toy is silly. It's a bad idea and it doesn't help the environment.
Jamie:	Well it keeps the bottle out of the rubbish.
Nas:	Yes, and it's cute. It makes people think about plastic bottles in a fun way.
Milly:	What? One bottle? That's not helpful.
Jamie:	I think everything helps a little.
Teacher:	Well, what do you think of the planters, Milly?
Milly:	They're a good idea. They're really useful. The plants help the environment and give us things to eat.
Nas:	(yawn) But they're boring for kids.
Milly:	I don't think they're boring.
Nas:	Look. If you don't make things interesting, kids won't pay attention.
Jamie:	Yeah. I agree. We're tired of being told boring things about the environment.
Nas:	That's why the pencil holders are the best. They're fun. They keep pencils tidy and they remind you not to use bottles. Chi-ching! Result!
Milly:	But they don't help the environment as much as the planters do.

Answers
Learner's own answers.

5 Read the text about the plastic bottle house (10–15 minutes)

- Ask learners to read about the plastic bottle house. These houses are made in Nigeria using recycled plastic bottles, which are filled with sand to make walls.

- Ask the class to work in pairs and discuss how the plastic bottle house is like the children's projects.

- Draw learners' attention to the last line of the text – 'Many small actions can make a difference' – and ask them to think about what it means. Can they give more examples?

- Allow learners a few minutes to think about and discuss their responses. Then have an open class discussion.

Answers
The plastic bottle house is like the children's projects, as the house uses recycled plastic bottles.
The last line in the text means that you don't have to do something really big to make a difference. Small things like recycling some plastic bottles can make a difference – especially if lots of people do small actions.

6 Let's find out! (15–25 minutes)

- Ask learners to visit suitable websites, such as the BBC, Critical Cactus, Made for minds, etc., or look for information in books and learn more about plastic bottle houses.

- Ask learners to explain why these houses are good for the environment.

- You may wish to ask learners to do this activity in small groups. Then they can report their findings to the class.

Answers
Learner's own answers.

Workbook
Learners do Activities 1–4 on pages 56–57.

Plenary ideas

Consolidation (10–15 minutes)

Ask learners to think of something they would like to invent. What does it do? Ask learners to tell the class about it.

Homework ideas:

- Learners write a few sentences describing the invention they thought about in the plenary in class. They draw a picture of it.

- **Home–school link:** Learners tell their family about the inventions they read about. They think of something they can make to re-use plastic bottles. They can draw a picture or make the actual object.

5.2 History of inventions: Great inventors

LEARNING PLAN		
Learning objectives	**Learning intentions**	**Success criteria**
3Ld.04 3Sc.02, 3So.01, 3Sor.02 3Rd.01 3Wca.04	• **Listening:** Listen for information and detail. • **Speaking:** Speak about inventions; discuss what the inventors wanted to do; talk about women inventors. • **Reading:** Read about what the inventors wanted to do. • **Writing:** Take notes, complete sentences. • **Language focus:** use *by* and *with* to indicate 'agent' and 'instrument' • **Vocabulary:** *design, heat, DNA, molecule, cell, particles; jobs, word building*	• Learners can learn about some important inventors and inventions. • Learners can speak about important inventors and inventions. • Learners can talk about women inventors. • Learners can discuss the role of women in science. • Learners can calculate how long ago things happened.

21st-century skills

Critical thinking opportunity: Understand that new things are invented to solve a problem; identify problems and solutions; understand cause and effect.

Communication: Use simple techniques to start, maintain and close conversations of various lengths.

Values: Explore equality between men and women.

Materials: Learner's Book pages 80–81; Workbook pages 58–59; realia or photos of a vinyl record and a cassette; pictures of the following: the internet, light bulb, telephone, refrigerator, braille, thermometer, microscope, printing press, paper, wheel, a solar house, a DNA helix and a mobile/cell phone; pictures of Alexander Graham Bell, Thomas Edison and Galileo; dictionaries; list of Nobel Prize winners (optional); **Photocopiable 27**

Starter ideas

What is this? (10–15 minutes)

- To generate interest in the topic of the history of inventions, ask the class what they use to listen to music. Elicit some answers, for example CD player, computer, MP3 player, etc.
- Show a vinyl record and a cassette (or pictures of these items) and ask the class to guess what they are. Elicit ideas. Ask if they have ever seen or listened to music using one of these objects.

Main teaching ideas

1 Talk about inventors (10–15 minutes)

- Show pictures of Alexander Graham Bell, Thomas Edison and/or Galileo. Ask learners if they know who they are and what they invented. Elicit ideas.
- Focus on the photos and ask learners to match them to the inventor. Ask: *Who invented the telescope?* Have them answer, for example, *The telescope was invented by …*
- Can they think of other inventors? Elicit ideas.

> **Critical thinking opportunity:** see Cross-curricular link below.

- You may wish to write the names of the inventors on the board and ask the class to try to match them to the invention, for example: *… was invented by ….*

Science

Show pictures of the following: the internet, a light bulb, a telephone, a refrigerator, braille, a thermometer, a microscope, a printing press, paper, a wheel. Tell the class that these are considered to be the ten most important inventions of all time. Ask: *Why do you think they are so important? What did people do before these things were invented? Which of these things do learners think had been invented when their parents went to school?* Elicit ideas from the class.

Answers

The telephone was invented by Alexander Graham Bell. The lightbulb was invented by Thomas Edison. The telescope was invented by Galileo.
Learner's own answers.

2 Read and listen about these inventors, and Key word: science (10–15 minutes)

- Show photos of a solar house, a DNA helix and a mobile/cell phone. Ask the class if they know what each of these items are. Elicit answers and help with vocabulary.

  〉 **Critical thinking opportunity:** Ask the class what they think these objects have in common. Elicit ideas, and then explain that they were all invented or discovered by women.

- Focus on the photos of the three scientists. Explain that these three women invented or discovered remarkable things. Draw learners' attention to the picture of Shirley Jackson with US President Obama. Ask: *Why do you think one of the ladies is with President Obama?* Elicit ideas.

- Tell the class that they are now going to learn about these women and why they are important.

- Before playing the recording, point out the key word box to the class. Do learners know what 'DNA' means? Elicit ideas.

- Have learners look up the word in the dictionary and discuss the meaning. Explain further to help learners understand. (See Background knowledge, page 116, for a suggested definition.)

- Ask them to write the definition in their notebooks.

- Play the recording about famous scientists while learners follow in their books. Hand out copies of **Photocopiable 27** and ask learners to complete it in pairs.

Answers

Learners read and listen about female inventors.

Reading tip (5–10 minutes)

- Focus on the Reading tip, and read it with the class.

- Tell the class that they are going to find many words related to science in this unit, and they will sometimes need to look up words in the dictionary to understand.

- You may wish to have learners start a vocabulary bank for this unit in their notebooks where they can write the new words, a definition and add a drawing or graphs if necessary.

Language detective (5–10 minutes)

- Focus on the explanation in the box.

- Have learners give more examples about themselves, using the word 'to'. For example, *I want to go to the party. I hope to help protect the planet.*

〉 **Digital Classroom:** Use the grammar presentation 'Verbs with *to*' to revise sentences where one verb is followed by a second verb with *to*. The i button will explain how to use the grammar presentation.

3 Talk about it (5–10 minutes)

- Remind learners of the three women scientists and their discoveries. Ask: *Why did they make their inventions?* Encourage learners to read the text again to elicit ideas.

- Then ask learners to complete the sentences.

Answers
Suggestions include:
Shirley Jackson wanted to *study small particles*.
Rosalind Franklin wanted to *discover more about our bodies*.
Mária Telkes wanted to *use the sun to heat houses*.

4 Talk with your friends (15–30 minutes)

- You could do this activity as a Think-Pair-Share activity. Learners work individually through the questions, make notes of their ideas and then pair up with a partner. They then discuss their ideas and get together with another pair to share their ideas. They compare and discuss their answers before having an open class discussion.

- Ask the class to look at the images of inventions and inventors from Activities 1 and 2. Ask: *What is the difference between them?* (The inventors in Activity 1 are all men, and the inventors in Activity 2 are all women.)

- Work through the remaining questions as a class, in groups or as a Think-Pair-Share activity.

> **Critical thinking opportunity** and **Values: Gender equality:**

Ask learners if they know women who invent things today. You may wish to have learners look for information about modern women inventors. They can look it up in books or on suitable websites, such as the list of inventions and discoveries by women on Wikipedia, 'Women in Innovation' on the website Inside Outside, the website A Mighty Girl, etc. Ensure that discussion of women inventors is in no way discriminatory by focusing on the rights women were denied in the past.

Ask the girls in the class if any of them is thinking of becoming a scientist or an inventor when they grow up. If some of them would like to, ask them why and what they want / hope / expect to do in their professional career. Elicit ideas.

> **Differentiation ideas:** This discussion may prove challenging, especially for less confident groups. Allow occasional use of L1. Then echo learners'

contributions in simple English, provide help with additional vocabulary and have them repeat their contributions in English after you. You may also wish to write some of their ideas on the board and ask them to copy them in their notebooks.

Answers
a Activity 1 inventors are all men; activity 2 inventors are all women.
b Learner's own answers.

5 Find the dates (15–20 minutes)

- Focus on the information about the three scientists/inventors in Activity 2. Ask learners to find the dates in the texts and calculate how long ago each was. (See Cross-curricular link below.)

- As an extension, remind learners of the ten most important inventions they discussed at the beginning of the lesson. Have them find the years when they were invented and work out how long ago each was.

CROSS-CURRICULAR LINK

Maths

Ask learners what they need to do in order to work out how long ago, i.e. they subtract the years mentioned from the current year. For example Rosalind Franklin invented a way of photographing DNA in 1952. The current year is, for example, 2021. 2021 – 1952 = 69 years.

> **Differentiation ideas:** With less confident learners, you could do the operations in groups or as a class.

Answers
Mária Telkes invented her sun house in 1948.
Rosalind Franklin discovered a way to photograph DNA in 1952.
Shirley Jackson discovered particles in 1973.
Learner's own answers.

6 Picture dictionary: Different jobs for different people (10–15 minutes)

- Ask learners to look at the puzzle and find the different job words. They write the jobs out in full by filling in the missing words.

- Learners can look at the Jobs page in the Picture dictionary (page 170) for help.

> **Critical thinking opportunity:** Ask learners to look at the words for jobs in the Picture dictionary. What do they notice about them? How do we make words for jobs? Help them notice the suffixes used for making 'job words': *-er, -ist, -or, -ian*.

Answers

inventor, architect, scientist, engineer

Workbook

Learners do Activities 1–3 on pages 58–59.

Plenary ideas

Consolidation (15–20 minutes)

> **Assessment ideas:** Ask learners to say three things they have learned in this lesson, two things they have found interesting and one thing they still have questions about.

CROSS-CURRICULAR LINK

Maths and history

Learners work in small groups and create a timeline with all the discoveries and inventions they have learned about in the lesson.

Homework ideas

- Learners choose one invention or discovery, look for information (online and/or in books) and write a fact file about it.

- **Home–school link:** Learners tell their family about the inventions and inventors they have read about in class. They can ask about inventors and scientists in their country. If a parent is a scientist or an inventor, you may consider inviting them to talk to the children in class.

5.3 Talk about it: The plastic problem

LEARNING PLAN

Learning objectives	Learning intentions	Success criteria
3Ld.03, 3Lo.01	• **Listening:** Identify rhyming words; listen and understand a poem; listen and identify opinions.	• Learners can listen and identify the opinions of speakers.
3Sc.03, 3Sc.05	• **Speaking:** Giving opinions; giving reasons for opinions; discuss environmental problems caused by plastics and inventions that offer solutions; recite a poem; ask and answer questions.	• Learners can recite a poem with correct intonation and rhythm.
3Rd.01	• **Reading:** Read a poem.	• Learners can discuss environmental problems caused by plastics and inventions that offer solutions.
3Us.04	• **Language focus:** wh- questions, *because* • **Vocabulary:** *break down, microbe, I agree … because …, solve, well spent, develop, plain, disagree, device, snoring, soaring, assignment*; phrases of expressing opinion: *I think, I don't think, I agree, I disagree*	• Learners can give opinions and reasons for them.

21st-century skills

Learning to learn: Answer *who, where, what, why* and *how* questions after listening to a sentence or short paragraph.

Social responsibilities: Understand there is a need to share and protect resources.

Values: Respect the opinion of others and interact with respect.

Materials: Learner's Book pages 82–83; Workbook pages 60–61; sticky notes; index notes; sticky tack; **Photocopiable 28**

LANGUAGE BACKGROUND

Wh- questions

Wh- questions are used to ask for information. They are *what, when, where, who, which, whose* and *why*. Although *how* does not begin with *wh-*, it is also included in this group. These questions cannot be answered with *Yes* or *No* answers, for example *Where do you live? How did he find the house? Who is she?*

Wh- questions are formed with *wh-* + an auxiliary verb (*be, do* or *have*) + subject + main verb. For example: *Where is he? What was she doing at midday? When did he come back?*

These questions can also include the use of a modal verb: *wh-* + a modal verb + subject + main verb. For example: *Who can help me? What do we have to do? Where should they go?*

Because

We use *because* to give reasons for something that has happened. For example: *Why didn't he call earlier?* **Because** *he didn't have your telephone number.*

We can also use *because* to give reasons for our opinions. For example: *I think this project helps the planet the most* **because** *it helps save water.*

Common misconceptions

Misconception	How to identify	How to overcome
Learners often use a gerund or an infinitive without *to* after a verb when an infinitive with *to* is needed. For example: *I hope see you on Saturday.* *I'd like have a pen-friend in another country.*	Write an incorrect sentence and the correct version of the sentence. Ask learners to identify the difference between the two. Ask which the correct one is. Elicit answers and encourage learners to explain why they think this.	With the class, review which verbs are followed by infinitive with *to*. Brainstorm a list of verbs and examples. You may ask learners to make a poster and write the verbs in colour. You could keep this poster visible for them to use as reference.
It's quite common for learners to use *want + to + -ing*. It seems that they think *want to* is a chunk but don't necessarily follow it with the correct form of the verb. For example: *I want to painting my bedroom.* *I want to going to a good concert with you.*	Write an incorrect sentence and the correct version of the same sentence. Ask learners to identify the difference between the two. Ask which the correct one is. Elicit answers and invite learners to explain why.	Remind learners that *want* is always followed by a verb with *to*. Have them give examples and write them in their notebooks. Ask them to write *want to + infinitive* in colour. When they are writing sentences, ask them to highlight *want* and then write the correct form.

Starter ideas

What is it for? (10–20 minutes)

- If learners have done the homework activity, ask them to share their fact file with the class and explain what inventions they researched.

- Ask learners to think back on the inventions they learned about in Lessons 5.1 and 5.2, and the inventions they have researched. What problems did these inventions solve?

Main teaching ideas

1 Read about problems and finding solutions (10–20 minutes)

- Tell the class that they are going to read about a serious problem that affects us all. Focus on the introductory text and ask learners to read it. Ask: *What problem does it refer to?* (There is too much plastic in the world.)

- Remind learners of the children's inventions in Lesson 5.1. Ask: *What was the purpose of those projects?* (to give plastic bottles a 'second life' and use them again).

- Ask learners to continue reading and look at what the young inventors are doing. Then they match the problems to the solutions.

- Focus on possible unfamiliar vocabulary, e.g. break down, microbe, etc. Ask: *What do these words mean?* Ask learners to look them up in the dictionary and (if relevant) add them to the science words bank they started at the beginning of the unit.

- Discuss the answers as a class.

Answers
problem 1: c, problem 2: a, problem 3: b

2 Listen and discuss in small groups (10–15 minutes)

- Ask learners to listen to two girls discussing the inventions. Tell them to listen and say if they agree or disagree.

- Play the recording twice.

- Ask learners to discuss their ideas. Tell them to use the expressions in the speech bubble when talking about their ideas and opinions.

> **Differentiation ideas:** With less confident groups, you may model a response first by giving your opinions. You may also have learners think and write their opinion before saying it aloud.

Audioscript: Track 39

Learner's Book page 82

Emma:	Which invention do you like best?
Sara:	I think Boyan's invention is best because plastic is a big problem in the ocean.
Emma:	I disagree. I think that more people can use Lucy's invention every day.
Sara:	I agree that Lucy's invention is good but we need to stop sea pollution now.

Answers
Learner's own answers.

- Ask learners to work in small groups and decide which project they think helps the planet most.

- Ask learners to make notes of their answers.

- Focus on the examples in the Speaking tip box. Remind learners of ways in which they can give opinions to share their ideas.

- **Values:** Tell learners to always remember to be polite, and to give opinions clearly and calmly. Highlight the importance of respecting different opinions and taking turns to speak.

- You may wish to brainstorm ways of sounding polite, for example: *I'm sorry but …, I don't think I can agree with that*, etc.

- After a few minutes, ask groups to appoint a spokesperson and share their ideas with the class.

> **Critical thinking opportunity:** See Cross-curricular link below.

CROSS-CURRICULAR LINK

Environmental science

Ask learners to discuss what other solutions there might be to the problem of plastic pollution. You may ask learners to look for information and ideas in suitable websites, for example Oceanic Society, National Geographic, The Ocean Clean-up or Greenpeace. Ask them to make notes and share their ideas with the class.

Answers
Learner's own answers.

3 Read and listen to the poem (5–10 minutes)

- Ask the class who invents things, for example inventors, scientists. Do they think other people can invent things? Elicit ideas.

- Focus on the activity and explain that engineers also invent things.

- Tell the class they are going to read and listen to a poem about engineers.

- Play the recording and encourage learners to read along as they listen.

- Ask learners to underline words they don't understand. Then discuss the meanings of the words they underlined as a class.

Audioscript: Track 40

See Learner's Book page 83.

Answers
Learners read and listen to the poem.

4 Talk about the poem (5–15 minutes)

- As a class, discuss the questions. Ask: *What does an engineer make?* Elicit ideas.

- Can learners think of jobs or other people who invent things, for example computer scientists, clothes designers, cooks, farmers, dads, mums, etc.?

- Encourage the class to think what these people can invent or have invented, for example new ways of cooking food, new food products, video games, computer programmes we use every day, etc.

- Ask learners if they invent things. What have they invented? What is it used for? Elicit ideas and answers.

Answers
Learner's own answers.

5 Listen again (10–15 minutes)

- Ask learners to read the poem *The Engineer* again and find rhyming words in the poem.

- Play the recording of the poem again and ask learners to check if they were right.

- Then ask learners to read the poem out loud, stressing the rhythm and the rhyming words.

Answers
hear – engineer, invent – spent, you – too, brain – plain, device – twice, soaring – snoring, invention – intention

---

Workbook

Learners do Activities 1–3 on pages 60–61.

> **Digital Classroom:** Use the activity 'The engineer' to practise identifying words that rhyme. The i button will explain how to use the activity.

Plenary ideas

Consolidation (10–15 minutes)

As a fun plenary for this lesson, hand out copies of **Photocopiable 28** and make paper helicopters as a class.

> **Assessment ideas:** Learners use sticky notes or index cards to create exit tickets and evaluate their learning. Write the questions below on the board and ask learners to answer them.

- What have I learned?

- What have I found easy?

- What have I found difficult?

When they have finished, they put their sticky notes on the board or on a large sheet of paper. They then read each other's responses and comment on them.

Homework ideas

- Learners write a few sentences about other solutions they can think of to the problem of plastics.

- **Home–school link:** Learners tell their family about the three inventions and inventors. Which invention do family members think is the best?

5.4 Write about it: Planning an invention

LEARNING PLAN

Learning objectives	Learning intentions	Success criteria
3Sc.07, 3Sor.01 3Rd.02 3Wca.01, 3Wor.02, 3Wc.02 3Us.04	• **Speaking:** State and support opinions; describe inventions and what they do; ask and answer questions. • **Reading:** Read and understand instructions; read descriptions of inventions. • **Writing:** Complete a form; draw and write an explanation of own invention; use correct spelling and punctuation; use simple connectives. • **Language focus:** *because*	• Learners can read and understand instructions. • Learners can complete a form about inventions. • Learners can state and support opinions. • Learners can draw and write an explanation of their own invention.

21st-century skills
Critical thinking opportunity: Describe objects and activities according to key features; identify cause and effect; articulate preferences and justify choices. **Collaboration:** Take part in tasks by interacting with others and stay on task; communicate own knowledge of a topic; ask others questions about a topic. **Communication:** Contribute in lessons by asking questions, attempting responses and explaining understanding; share their thoughts with others to help further develop ideas and solve problems.

Materials: Learner's Book pages 84–85; Workbook pages 62–63; writing and drawing materials, sheets of paper; reference books; internet access; Sample answer for Unit 5; **Photocopiable 1, 2, 29**

Starter ideas

What can I do? (10–20 minutes)

- If learners have done the homework activity, ask them to share their ideas for solutions to the problem of plastics with the class.

- Then divide the class into groups and ask them to discuss the idea they like the most. Have them explain their choices, and agree and disagree politely.

- When they have finished, each group shares their conclusions with the class.

Main teaching ideas

1 Talk about these inventions by children (5–10 minutes)

- Have learners work in small groups. They look at the drawings and discuss what each invention does.

- Then they match each drawing with its name.
- Have them use: *I think … .*

Answers
a a walking house, **b** a vacuum cleaner ride,
c a rainwater drink machine

2 Read and write (5–10 minutes)

- Ask learners to look at the invention form. A child who has invented something has filled it in.

- Draw the class's attention to the '3 Explain your invention' section and explain that the questions are missing. Ask learners to write in the missing questions. They can use the words in the box to help.

- Check answers as a class.

> **Critical thinking opportunity:** Ask learners what they think of this invention. Encourage them to explain their opinions using 'because', for example: *I think it's … because …*

Answers

Suggestions include: What is it? What problem does it solve?/Why did you invent it? How does it work? Who is it for?

3 Write: Make your own invention, and Language focus (45–60 minutes)

- Tell the class to imagine that they are going to make their own invention. They are going to fill in a form about their invention. Hand out copies of **Photocopiable 29** for learners to use.

- **Step 1:** Explain to the class that most inventions are created to fix or solve a problem in the world or to make something easier. Once you think of a problem, you can then think of an invention that solves the problem. Working individually, ask learners to brainstorm possible problems in the world, using the prompts listed in the Learner's Book. Then ask learners to choose one problem and imagine a solution – an invention that solves the problem. They can look for ideas in books or online, draw pictures for ideas or ask classmates for ideas. Explain to learners that their invention can be a funny invention, a useful invention, a serious invention – whatever they like. They just need to be able to explain how their invention solves a problem.

> **Differentiation ideas:** With less confident learners, you may wish to do the brainstorming of problems and possible solutions as a class or in small groups. Write contributions on the board and then learners can choose from there. You can also consider having more and less confident learners do the brainstorming activity together in pairs.

- **Step 2:** Ask learners to complete the form to write about their invention. Learners can use **Photocopiable 29** to draw a large picture of their invention and label the parts. Have them re-read the example form for the emergency eye cover from Activity 2 and use it as an example.

- Read through the Language focus box as a class. Remind learners of *Why? … because …* questions and answers. Give a few examples, and encourage learners to ask and answer questions with *Why?*

- **Step 3:** When they have finished, ask learners what they need to look for to in order to make sure everything is correct. Focus on the

questions. Ask learners to think of the answers while they are reading their text aloud. Do they need to change, correct or add anything? Have them check their handwriting. Is it easy to understand? Remind learners of their Writer's checklist (**Photocopiable 1**). Ask them to get their copy and use it to check their work.

- **Step 4:** Ask learners to use the questions to check spelling and punctuation. Check and correct grammar if necessary.

> **Assessment ideas:** Ask learners to exchange their work with a partner. Using **Photocopiable 2**, the Peer editing checklist, they read each other's work and make comments on the clarity of the description. Ask: *Is there anything that needs to be changed or corrected?* When learners receive their work back, they make the necessary adaptations and share it with the class.

- See **Sample answer for Unit 5** for an example answer to this writing task.

Answers

Learners plan, write and check their invention plans.

Workbook

Learners do Activities 1 and 2 on pages 62–63.

> **Digital Classroom:** Use the animation 'Our Kitchen-o-Mat and Our School-o-Mat' and the activity sheet to reinforce the topics of invention and problem-solving. The i button will explain how to use the animation and activity sheet.

Plenary ideas

Consolidation (20–30 minutes)

- When learners have finished their invention plan, have them present it to the class.

- Learners give their opinions of the inventions.

- Then they can organise an exhibition for other classes to see the invention plans.

Homework ideas

- Learners prepare an advertisement to present their invention to another class. If possible, they record it to present to the class.

- **Home–school link:** Learners share their inventions with their family. They can ask for advice on how to improve it if necessary.

5.5 Read and respond: *Jenny, Lenny and the Jumperoo*

LEARNING PLAN

Learning objectives	Learning intentions	Success criteria
3Lo.01	• **Listening:** Listen to a poem; listen for specific information.	• Learners can read and understand a poem.
3So.01, 3Sor.02	• **Speaking:** Give and justify opinions; explain the meaning of words; discuss the value of learning from failure; recite a poem.	• Learners can give and justify opinions. • Learners can discuss the value of learning from failure.
3Rd.01, 3Rd.03, 3Ro.01	• **Reading:** Read a funny long poem; use context clues to guess the meaning of unfamiliar words and phrases.	• Learners can recite part of a poem.
	• **Vocabulary:** *wires, pliers;* opposites words; rhyming words; *invention, plastic, constructed, pollution*	• Learners can use context clues to guess the meaning of unfamiliar words and phrases.

21st-century skills

Critical thinking opportunity: Articulate preferences and justify choices; describe problems to a situation given in a story.

Learning to learn: Show awareness of own progress in learning English.

Values: Take care of our planet, learn from our failures, work together.

Materials: Learner's Book pages 86–89; Workbook pages 64–65

Starter ideas

Vote for my invention! (15–20 minutes)

- If learners have done the homework activity, ask them to present their invention advertisement to the class.
- Learners vote for the best advertisement.
- If learners have recorded their advertisements, have them upload them to the class blog.

Main teaching ideas

1 Talk about it (5–10 minutes)

- Tell the class that they are going to read a poem that includes a number of new words and phrases. Explain that we do not always understand all of the words when we read something, and we need to figure them out.

> **Critical thinking opportunity:** Ask the class what they can do when they come across new words that they do not know. Elicit a few ideas, e.g. look them up in a dictionary, use the context to guess the meaning. Tell learners to think of other ways as they read the poem.

2 Read and listen (5–10 minutes)

- Tell learners to read and listen to the poem.
- Play the recording at least twice. Learners follow in their books.

Audioscript: Track 41

See Learner's Book pages 86–88.

> **Digital Classroom:** Use the activity '*Jenny, Lenny and the Jumperoo*' to reinforce comprehension of the poem. The i button will explain how to use the activity.

3 Talk about the poem with your partner (10–15 minutes)

- Do this activity as a Think-Pair-Share activity. Focus on the questions – learners work individually through them, making notes of their ideas, and then pair up with a partner. They then discuss their ideas with their partner before getting together with another pair to share ideas.

- Encourage learners to make notes of their ideas through their discussions.

Answers

a Lenny and Jenny are twins – they look similar but they act very different.

b Gran tells them to go outside because they are arguing.

c They find lots of litter and pollution outside.

d Jenny plans inventions on her tablet. Lenny helps to make the inventions with his tools.

e The Super Bag Shred shredded the plastic into smaller pieces, which was worse because these then got into the animals. The Super Bag Melter created smoke and pollution.

f They learn to work together without fighting. The last sentence shows this.

4 Talk. What do you think of the poem? (10–15 minutes)

- Ask learners to look at the list of adjectives. Clarify the meaning of the words if necessary.

- Ask learners to describe what they think of the poem using some of these adjectives and the suggested structure to justify their opinions: *I think the poem is … because …*

- Allow a few minutes for learners to think of their answers, and then discuss answers as a class.

- **Values:** Remind the class of the importance of respecting turn-taking and each other's opinions. Also encourage them to use polite forms of disagreement.

Answers

Learner's own answers. Suggested answer: the poem is funny, and positive because it shows that it is always good to try.

5 Values: Take care of our planet (10–20 minutes)

- Focus on sentence in the Learner's Book: *Lenny and Jenny took action to help take care of our planet.* Ask learners what they think it means. Ask: *How did they take action? What did they do and how did their actions help the planet?*

- Divide the class into pairs and ask them to write down three simple things they can do to help the planet. Encourage them to justify their ideas.

> **Critical thinking opportunity:** You may wish to start a discussion on the value of doing small things together to make a big difference; for example, if we all do a 'small' thing like not dropping litter, the planet would be a much cleaner and safer place.

- Support learners by providing additional vocabulary as needed.

> **Differentiation ideas:** This may be a difficult topic for learners to express themselves in English. Allow for some use of L1 if necessary. Echo their contributions in English and have them repeat after you. Write useful language on the board and have learners copy in their notebooks.

Answers

Learner's own answers.

6 Vocabulary (20–40 minutes)

- Ask learners to re-read the poem and find the words in purple. In pairs or small groups, ask learners to discuss the meanings of these words.

> **Critical thinking opportunity:** Remind learners of their discussion from the beginning of the lesson about the strategies they can use to understand new words in a text (for example the pictures).

- Allow a few minutes for learners to re-read and discuss the new words. Then discuss the meanings as a class.

> **Differentiation ideas:** If you notice that less confident learners are having difficulties explaining the words in English, allow some use of L1. Echo the explanations in simple English, have learners repeat after you and write the meanings in their notebooks. Encourage more confident groups to write definitions for the words.

- Tell the class that this poem also has many special words that sound like their meanings.

- Have them look for the words in blue in the text. Then play the poem audio again. Ask: *What impression does the sound of the words give?* Elicit ideas from the class. Learners can then look up the words in a dictionary, write the meaning in their notebooks and add a picture of what the words evoke in them.

Answers

Purple words: wires, pliers, shred, welder, tip, tools.
Blue words: bop, Cough! Cough!, sniffed, Slam! Bang! Twizzle! Crash! Ding!

7   Talk (15–25 minutes)

- Ask learners to work in groups. They choose a stanza from the poem and listen to it again.

- Then they practise saying it out loud, like on the audio.

- When they feel confident enough, they perform their stanza for the class.

Workbook

Learners do Activities 1–4 on pages 64–65.

You might want to use Activities 2 and 3 as extension material as they are beyond the requirements of the Cambridge Primary English as a Second Language curriculum framework.

Plenary ideas

Consolidation (10–15 minutes)

> **Assessment ideas:** Ask learners to draw a face to show how they feel about their performance in this lesson: smiley face = ready to move on, neutral face = fairly satisfied, sad face = not very happy, need to improve. Then they write a sentence or two about this in their learning log.

Homework ideas

- Learners look for three or four new words in books at home, or words in their local environment. They write them on index cards and draw pictures for each of them on separate cards. Then they bring them to class the next day.

- **Home–school link:** Learners read the poem to their family. They can discuss how to make the most out of failure.

5.6 Project challenge

Learning objectives	Learning intentions	Success criteria
3Sc.04, 3Sc.05	• **Speaking:** Discuss a project, discuss steps of a project, organise work, present their project to the class.	• Learners can read and understand instructions.
3Rd.02	• **Reading:** Read and understand instructions, read and choose relevant information for a project.	• Learners can give instructions. • Learners can plan a project. • Learners can make an inventions book.
3Wca.02, 3Wca.03, 3Wca.05, 3Wc.01	• **Writing:** Write descriptions of inventions, write about inventors, use correct spelling and punctuation, use science vocabulary. • **Language focus:** Unit 5 review • **Vocabulary:** Unit 5 review	• Learners can make a poster about an inventor. • Learners can present their projects.

21st-century skills

Creative thinking: Design new items based on a model.

Collaboration: Respect the importance of doing a fair share of group work; keep to the instructions to complete the task; invite others to give their opinions during the task.

Learning to learn: Listen and respond positively to feedback and understand why a correction was given; learn from mistakes and feedback.

Materials: Learner's Book pages 90–91; Workbook pages 66–67; Project A: drawing supplies, sheets of paper, card, staples or string to bind the book; Project B: drawing supplies, sheets of paper, card, photos of famous inventors who have helped the planet (optional); **Photocopiable 30**; End of Unit 5 test; **Differentiated worksheets 5A, B and C**

Starter ideas

Looking back (15–25 minutes)

• Ask the class to choose a lesson from Unit 5 that they liked a lot. Ask them to explain why they liked it.

• Ask learners to sing *Imagination* as a class (audio track 35).

• If learners have done the homework activity from the previous lesson, have them work in small groups. Ask them to place all the word cards and picture cards they have made on the table upside down. They take it in turns to pick up a word card, read it and then choose the picture to match. If they make a correct match, they can keep both cards.

Main teaching ideas

Learners choose an end-of-unit project to work on. Explain the projects, look at the samples together and help them to choose. Provide materials.

Project A: Make a book of inventions (60–90 minutes)

• Read the directions in the Learner's Book. Give out drawing and writing supplies.

• Learners work in a group. Each group member chooses an invention and looks for information about it. If possible, have them look for inventions that are good for our planet or that help the environment.

- They could use the questions in the Learner's Book to select and organise the information they find.

- They draw a picture of their invention and write the information they have found.

- They make the book covers with hard card and string or staples. They decorate the book covers.

- They present the project to the class.

- Ask the class to decide which invention they like best. Have them explain their opinions.

> **Assessment ideas:** You could video-record groups as they work so that they can then use copies of the recordings to assess what they have done and how they have worked. The copies can then be shared with their family and filed in their portfolios.

Project B: Make a poster about an inventor who helps the planet (60–90 minutes)

- Read the directions in the Learner's Book. Give out drawing and writing supplies.

- Learners work in a group. Each group should choose an inventor who helps the planet. It can be someone from this unit, or another person they find out about.

- Hand out source material that you have found prior to the lesson where learners can look for information about their chosen inventor. Ask them to use the questions in the Learner's Book to select and organise the information they find.

- Using the information they have found, they design their poster. Tell them they can use photos or draw pictures. Encourage them to arrange the information in an interesting way.

- They show the poster to the class, talk about the inventor and answer questions.

- When they have finished, ask the class to decide which inventor is doing the most interesting/ useful things.

> **Assessment ideas:** You may wish to video-record groups as they work so that they can then use copies of the recordings to assess what they have done and how they have worked. The copies can then be shared with the family and filed in their portfolios.

> **Assessment ideas:** When learners have finished working on the projects, give them a copy of **Photocopiable 30**

and read the instructions as a class. Ask learners to work independently and think about their work on their project. They reflect and answer the questions. Ask them to tick off the aims they have achieved. Insist on the importance of giving honest answers.

> **Workbook**
>
> Learners do the Check your progress quiz on pages 66–67.

Plenary ideas

Reflect on your learning (5–10 minutes)

- Draw learners' attention to the 'Reflect on your learning' questions in the Learner's Book.

- Learners answer the questions to reflect on their project work.

Consolidation (10–15 minutes)

- Ask learners to reflect on and discuss what they liked most about this unit; encourage them to explain why. This may also be a good opportunity for them to think about what aspects of the unit they have found most difficult and why.

- You may wish to keep a record of their comments to see how they progress over time.

> **Assessment ideas: Portfolio opportunity:** If you have been filing learners' work for Unit 5, you may find it useful to put all the work of this unit together. You could ask learners to make a cover for their Unit 5 work, decorating it with an image that represents what they have learned.

Homework ideas

- Learners draw a picture of what they have liked most about this unit.

- **Home–school link:** Learners show their family their projects.

- Hand out copies of **Differentiated worksheets 5A, B and C** depending on each learner's ability, and ask them to complete the activities at home.

5.7 What do you know now?

How can inventions help the planet? (30–40 minutes)

- Learners work in pairs. They work together through all the tasks set in this section.

- They write the answers in their notebooks. You may ask them to have a special section in their notebooks where they record the answers.

- Whenever their opinion is requested, encourage them to be honest in their answers.

Answers

1–6 Learner's own answers.

Look what I can do! (15 minutes)

- Review the *I can* … statements on page 92 of the Learner's Book. Learners demonstrate what they can do.

- Learners colour in the faces to show which things they can do.

- Encourage them to be honest in their answers.

Workbook

Learners answer the Reflection questions on page 67.

> 6 Dinosaurs

Unit plan

Lesson	Approximate number of learning hours	Outline of learning content	Learning objectives	Resources
1 In the time of dinosaurs	1.75–3.5	Learn about dinosaur fossils and when dinosaurs lived.	3Ld.01 3Sc.02 3So.01 3Rd.01 3Ug.04 3Uv.01	Learner's Book Lesson 6.1 Workbook Lesson 6.1 ⤓ Photocopiable 3 ⤓ Photocopiable 31 ⤓ Photocopiable 32 **Digital Classroom:** Video – Working with dinosaurs; Activity – How long ago?
2 Dinosaur Q & A	1.0–1.5	Ask and answer questions about dinosaurs.	3Ld.03 3Sc.06 3Sc.07 3Rd.01 3Rd.03 3Wca.05 3Ug.04 3Ug.08	Learner's Book Lesson 6.2 Workbook Lesson 6.2 ⤓ Photocopiable 33 **Digital Classroom:** Activity – What could dinosaurs do?; Grammar presentation – Could and couldn't
3 Dinosaur discoveries	1.5–2.75	Discuss new dinosaur discoveries.	3Ld.04 3So.01 3Sor.01 3Sor.02 3Wca.01 3Wca.03 3Ug.04 3Us.01	Learner's Book Lesson 6.3 Workbook Lesson 6.3 **Digital Classroom:** Video – Dinosaurs in the films; Activity – As easy as can be; Activity – There aren't any dinosaurs
4 Dinosaur fantasies	1.0–1.75	Write a fantasy story about a pet dinosaur.	3Rd.02 3Wca.04 3Wca.05 3Wor.01 3Wor.02 3Wc.02 3Wc.03	Learner's Book Lesson 6.4 Workbook Lesson 6.4 ⤓ Sample answer for Unit 6 ⤓ Photocopiable 1 ⤓ Photocopiable 2 ⤓ Photocopiable 34 **Digital Classroom:** Activity – My pet dinosaur
5 Baby dinosaurs	1.5–2.0	Read and talk about dinosaur babies.	3Ld.03 3Sc.03 3Sc.07 3Rd.01 3Rd.03	Learner's Book Lesson 6.5 Workbook Lesson 6.5 ⤓ Photocopiable 3 **Digital Classroom:** Activity – A good scientist

(continued)

Lesson	Approximate number of learning hours	Outline of learning content	Learning objectives	Resources
6 Project challenge	1.5–2.5	Make a dinosaur mural or write a report on a dinosaur.	3Sc.04 3Sc.05 3Rd.02 3Wca.02 3Wca.03 3Wc.01	Learner's Book Lesson 6.6 Workbook Lesson 6.6 ⬇ Photocopiable 1 ⬇ Photocopiable 35 ⬇ Differentiated worksheets 6A, B and C
7 What do you know now?	0.75–1.0	Self-assessment and reflection.		Learner's Book Lesson 6.7

Cross-unit resources
⬇ Unit 6 Audioscripts
⬇ End of Unit 6 test
⬇ Unit 6 Progress report
⬇ Unit 6 Wordlist

BACKGROUND KNOWLEDGE

Making fossils

In Lesson 6.1, learners read about fossils. You can have them make their own fossils.

- **Materials:** 1 cup of salt, 2 cups of flour, $\frac{3}{4}$ cup of water, small dinosaur toys.

- **Method:** Mix the salt, flour and water together in a bowl until you get soft dough. Take small handfuls and shape into small 'biscuit'-sized rounds then press the dinosaur toy into the dough. Bake in an oven at 200 °C for 45–60 minutes until the fossils are dry. (Thicker fossils may take up to 3 hours.)

Egg fossils

In Lesson 6.5, learners read about dinosaur egg fossils. Dinosaur eggs are rarely discovered intact because, like any egg, they were quite fragile. The first dinosaur egg fossils were found in France by Jean-Jacques Poech in 1859, and at first, everyone thought they were just giant bird eggs. In 2011, an egg was found in Antarctica and scientists believe that it belonged to a now-extinct giant marine reptile.

TEACHING SKILLS FOCUS

Language awareness

For many learners around the world, English is an additional language. For some, it might be their second or third language; others might be learning all or some of their school subjects through English; regardless, for all of them English is a vehicle for learning. It is therefore our responsibility to make sure that their knowledge and awareness of English is not an obstacle to learning. Teachers can achieve this by becoming more aware of language, i.e. understanding the difficulties and challenges learners face when learning the language, why these difficulties occur and how to overcome them.

Awareness-raising activities help learners to become more mindful of language so that they improve their understanding. These activities do not necessarily have to be just using the language itself – in fact, these activities are often the first step in all language learning.

CONTINUED

Your challenge

Awareness-raising activities and techniques are particularly useful, as learners will be able to process new content according to their own level of competence, and respond to it in different ways.

Use the following awareness-raising techniques to help learners process new content:

- Provide enough scaffolding.
- Think aloud, and describe what you are doing when modelling an answer.
- Use visuals, gestures and body language to convey ideas.
- Repeat or reformulate ideas using specific examples.
- Give learners 'thinking time', i.e. enough time to process information and respond to it.

- Introduce activities that help learners 'notice' and expand vocabulary.
- Introduce activities that help learners 'notice' grammar.
- Give learners opportunities to use the language themselves.

In each unit of the Learner's Book, opportunities to introduce awareness-rising techniques are highlighted. Look through Unit 6 and highlight opportunities for introducing the techniques above.

Reflection

Are you giving learners enough thinking time? Which technique has proved the most successful with less confident learners? Do you need to make any adaptations?

6.1 Think about it: In the time of dinosaurs

LEARNING PLAN

Learning objectives	Learning intentions	Success criteria
3Ld.01	• **Listening:** Listen to a song; listen to dinosaur facts; listen and follow instructions.	• Learners can sing a song about dinosaurs.
3Sc.02, 3So.01	• **Speaking:** Speak about dinosaurs; practise topic vocabulary; speak about the passing of time; talk about prior knowledge of dinosaurs.	• Learners can listen to and understand a talk about dinosaur facts.
3Rd.01	• **Reading:** Use context clues to guess word meaning; read and say large numbers.	• Learners can talk about the passing of time.
3Ug.04, 3Uv.01	• **Language focus:** past simple, ... *years ago*	• Learners can say and read large numbers.
	• **Vocabulary:** large numbers; *dinosaur, fossil, mud, sand, bones, teeth, footprints, tracks, tail, nest*	• Learners can talk about dinosaurs.

21st-century skills

Critical thinking opportunity: Understand the passing of time; draw inferences.

Communication: Try to use alternative words or expressions; if they are not understood, ask for clarification when they have difficulties in understanding what others have said.

Learning to learn: Demonstrate ability to think about how well they are learning English.

Materials: Learner's Book pages 93–95; Workbook pages 68–69; pictures or a video of dinosaurs, e.g. National Geographic videos, Planet dinosaur BBC; map of the world; large sheets of poster paper; exit tickets or sticky notes; **Photocopiable 3**, **31**, **32**

Starter ideas

Getting started (15–25 minutes)

- Show learners pictures or a video of dinosaurs, for example National Geographic or Planet dinosaur BBC. Ask learners if they know the names of the animals. Write the contributions on one side of the board.

- Ask: *What do you know about dinosaurs?*

- Ask learners to work in small groups. Give them a copy of **Photocopiable 3**: K-W-L ('know', 'would like to know', 'learned') chart. Ask learners to write what they know (or think they know) about dinosaurs in the first (K) column. In the second column, they write what they would like to know about dinosaurs in the form of questions.

> **Critical thinking opportunity:** Invite learners to look at the fossilised dinosaur bone on Learner's Book page 93 and to guess what part of the dinosaur's body the bone came from, i.e. the thigh bone (femur). Ask: *How big do you think this dinosaur was? How can you tell?* (by comparing the size of the bone to the person sitting next to it).

- Learners respond to Getting started questions a–c in the Learner's Book.

CROSS-CURRICULAR LINK

Science

Focus on the photo of the palaeontologist in the Learner's Book. Ask the class to read the caption. Ask: *What is he doing? What's his job?* Elicit *palaeontologist* and *fossil*. Explain that a palaeontologist is a scientist who studies the fossilised remains of organisms, e.g. animals, plants, insects and humans, and palaeontology is the science that studies life as it existed millions of years ago.

Answers

Learner's own answers.

> **Digital Classroom:** Use the video 'Working with dinosaurs' to explore the subject of jobs for people who like dinosaurs. The i button will explain how to use the video.

Sing along! *Fossils* (10–15 minutes)

- Tell the class they are going to listen to a song. Give each learner a copy of **Photocopiable 31**: Sing along! *Fossils*.

- Play the song at least twice and ask learners to identify familiar words.

- Ask the class what the song is about. Elicit answers, e.g. dinosaurs, fossils.

- Sing the song and encourage learners to join in.

Audioscript: Track 42

Learner's Book page 93

Fossils

Dinosaurs lived so long ago,

What were they like?

How do we know?

Look at fossils, yes, fossils

To learn about dinosaurs.

Where did they live and what did they eat?

What was their size? How big were their teeth?

Look at fossils, yes, fossils

To learn about dinosaurs.

Footprints, teeth and eggs and bones,

Hardened for years and turned into stone.

Look at fossils, yes, fossils

To learn about dinosaurs.

Main teaching ideas

1 Write (10–15 minutes)

- Ask the class to open the Learner's Book to page 94. Focus on the article and encourage learners to describe the animals in the pictures. Elicit a few ideas.

- Then ask learners to look at the two headings – they are both questions. Working with a partner, ask them to answer the questions. They write down their ideas.

- Ask learners to share their ideas with the class. Have they all come up with the same answers? Encourage them to discuss any differences.

Answers
Learner's own answers.

2 Listen and read the article (5–15 minutes)

- Tell the class that they are now going to listen and read the article.

- Play the audio at least twice.

- Ask learners if the answers they wrote match the information in the article. Discuss the differences.

> **Audioscript:** Track 43
>
> See Learner's Book page 94.

Answers
Learner's own answers.

3 Listen to the audio again (10–20 minutes)

- Ask learners to work in pairs and read the sentences in their Learner's Book. Play the audio and have learners decide whether each sentence is true or false.

- Play the audio again while learners listen and check their answers.

- As a class, discuss the answers and ask learners to correct the false statements.

> **Differentiation ideas:** As an extension, ask learners to write two or three sentences to add to the exercise with their partner. When they have finished, they pass their sentences on to another pair to decide if they are true or false. More confident learners could decide without looking again at the text. Less confident learners may re-read the text before deciding.

Answers
a   True.
b   False – Some dinosaurs / not all dinosaurs were huge.
c   False – Some dinosaurs / not all dinosaurs ate meat.
d   False – Early humans did not hunt dinosaurs (because humans were not around when dinosaurs were alive).

4 Vocabulary: Very big numbers! (5–15 minutes)

- Numbers over 1000 are beyond the requirements of the Cambridge Primary English as a Second Language curriculum framework.

- Focus on the numbers. Ask learners to try and read them.

- Tell the class that they are going to listen to the numbers and sentences.

- Play the recording once and ask learners to just listen.

- Then play it again and have learners repeat each number. Check for correct pronunciation.

> **Audioscript:** Track 44
>
> Learner's Book page 95
>
> One thousand.
>
> One hundred thousand.
>
> One million.
>
> One hundred million.
>
> Two hundred and twenty million years ago.
>
> The first dinosaurs appeared two hundred and twenty million years ago.
>
> That's a long time ago!

Answers
Learners say the numbers and the sentences.

Try this! (5–10 minutes)

- Ask learners to work in pairs. Each learner writes down a number bigger than 100 and smaller than 1,000.

- They take it in turns to say the number to their partner, who writes it down.

- Then they check that their numbers match.
- If they don't match, ask learners to repeat the number, trying to improve the pronunciation.

Answers
Learner's own answers.

Language tip (10–20 minutes)

- For more practice with big numbers, ask learners to turn to the Picture dictionary Numbers page (page 162 in the Learners' Book) and review numbers.
- You may wish to revisit some of the content from Unit 5, for example: *How long ago did Galileo live? How long ago was the printing press invented?*
- Play the Secret number game with **Photocopiable 32**: Number chart. Learners guess a secret number (1–100) by asking questions such as: *Is it more than …? / Is it less than …?*
- They cross out numbers on the 100 number chart to narrow down possibilities and then arrive at the secret number.
- Learners should use a pencil to mark the numbers on their number charts so that they can erase and use the same number chart for a second game.

5 Let's find out! (10–15 minutes)

> **Critical thinking opportunity:** It may be difficult for young learners to have an accurate notion of the passing of time when speaking about millions of years. This activity will help them make concrete associations to understand the magnitude of the passing of time.

- Before listening, revise the names of the different parts of the arm: *shoulder, elbow, wrist, fingers.*
- Ask learners to hold out their arms and point to the different parts as you say them, in jumbled order. Practise reading the numbers in the diagram labels.
- Ask the class why no human has ever seen a living dinosaur. Remind them of the information they listened to in Activity 2, i.e. dinosaurs lived millions of years ago.
- Tell learners that they are going to listen to some instructions to measure how long ago dinosaurs lived.

- Ask them to get ready and play the audio at least twice. Model as they listen so that they can follow the instructions confidently.

> **Critical thinking opportunity:** After listening, ask: *What happened at each different time? For how many millions of years did dinosaurs live on Earth?* Learners work out how many years dinosaurs lived on Earth.

- Discuss with the class if they think humans will live on Earth as long as the dinosaurs did. Encourage them to explain their answers.

CROSS-CURRICULAR LINK

Maths

You may wish to show learners how these numbers would be written in digits. You could also point out that in the UK and USA the numbers would be written using commas rather than points (350,000,000).

Audioscript: Track 45

Learner's Book page 95

Hold out your left arm. Your arm will be a timeline. It represents 350 million years on Earth.

First, put your right finger on your left shoulder. This is 350 million years ago. This is when the first animals appeared on the land.

Now, slowly move your finger along your left arm. Stop at your elbow. This is 220 million years ago. This is when the first dinosaurs appeared. They lived for a very long time.

Now, move your finger slowly along your arm again. Stop at your wrist. This is 65 million years ago. This is when the last dinosaurs died.

Move your finger again, up to the fingernail of your longest finger. This is 100 thousand years ago. This is when the first humans appeared.

Answers
Learners listen and follow the instructions.

> **Digital Classroom:** Use the activity 'How long ago?' to reinforce relative times and the form … *years ago.* The i button will explain how to use the activity.

6   Read. Which photo shows a body fossil? Which body shows a trace fossil? (10–35 minutes)

- Focus on the photos. Ask the class about the kind of fossil shown. Elicit some ideas before reading the text.

- Ask the class to read the text about fossils. Then they match the photos to the correct description.

- Ask the class what kind of fossil they think would be most interesting to study. Encourage them to justify their answers.

- Read the text again and discuss the meaning of new words. Encourage the class to use the pictures and the context to work out the meaning.

- Ask learners to explain what a fossil is in their own words, for example it is a bone of a very old animal, a plant or a trace of a plant, or an animal footprint that has turned into stone. Help with vocabulary if necessary. You could visit suitable websites, for example Sciencing, Britannica or National Geographic, and show other images of fossils.

> **Critical thinking opportunity:** Ask learners: *What can scientists learn from fossils? What information does a fossil give scientists about life millions of years ago?* Elicit ideas.

CROSS-CURRICULAR LINK

Arts and crafts

Consider having an arts and crafts lesson and ask the class to make their own fossils. You could search on the internet for an easy way of making fossils in class (see also the suggestion in the Background knowledge for this unit, on page 139). After learners have made their fossils, they write a description of the fossil on a file card. You can make a 'fossil museum' corner and place the cards next to each fossil.

Answers
Photo A is a trace fossil. Photo B is a body fossil.

Workbook

Learners do Activities 1– 4 on pages 68–69.

You might want to use Activity 3 as extension material as this is beyond the requirements of the Cambridge Primary English as a Second Language curriculum framework.

Numbers over 1000 are beyond the requirements of the Cambridge Primary English as a Second Language curriculum framework.

Plenary ideas

Consolidation (15–20 minutes)

- Play the audio for Activity 2 (track 43) again. As a class, learners make a table and fill it in with the information they have heard about dinosaurs.

- Encourage them to decide what headings and information to include, e.g. food, size, body parts.

- You could encourage learners to add more headings and fill the information in their tables as they cover the different lessons.

> **Assessment ideas:** Give each learner a set of exit tickets or sticky notes with the following stems: *One thing I must remember about today's lesson is …; Today I have learned that …; I still find it difficult …*

- Ask learners to fill in the exit tickets. They share them on a notice board. Can they think of ways in which they can help each other overcome their difficulties?

Homework ideas

- Learners look for information in books and find out about dinosaurs in their country. They choose one, draw or print a picture, and write the name and how long ago it lived.

- **Home–school link:** Learners tell their family what they have learned about dinosaurs and fossils.

6.2 Science: Dinosaur Q & A

LEARNING PLAN

Learning objectives	Learning intentions	Success criteria
3Ld.03 3Sc.06, 3Sc.07 3Rd.01, 3Rd.03 3Wca.05 3Ug.04, 3Ug.08	• **Listening:** Listen for information. • **Speaking:** Describe and compare dinosaurs; talk about dinosaurs from pictures; ask and answer questions; describe what dinosaurs could do. • **Reading:** Read for information; use context clues to guess word meaning. • **Writing:** Write about what dinosaurs could and couldn't do. • **Language focus:** past simple; *ago, can, can't, could, couldn't* • **Vocabulary:** *meat-eating, grab, meal, balance, weapon, swing, hiss, roar, honk, plant-eating*	• Learners can listen and read information about dinosaurs. • Learners can ask and answer questions about dinosaurs. • Learners can talk about what dinosaurs could do. • Learners can write sentences about dinosaurs.

21st-century skills

Critical thinking opportunity: Compare and contrast; make assumptions and then check for facts from the text.

Communication: Use simple techniques to start, maintain and close conversations of various lengths.

Learning to learn: Participate sensibly and positively in learning activities in class.

Materials: Learner's Book pages 96–97; Workbook pages 70–71; large sheet of poster paper; **Photocopiable 33**

Starter ideas

Dinosaur time! (10–15 minutes)

• Remind the class of the facts they learned about dinosaurs in Lesson 1. On a large sheet of poster paper, they make a mind map with the facts they have learned. Write 'DINOSAURS' in the middle and have them put in the information they remember around it.

• If they have done the homework activity, ask learners to share the information they have found about the dinosaurs from Lesson 1. They add it to the mind map.

Main teaching ideas

1   Talk with a partner (10–15 minutes)

• Ask learners what 'Q & A' stands for (question and answer).

• Ask the class to look at the pictures of the dinosaurs and discuss with a partner which dinosaur could do the things listed.

• Check that the meaning of the sentences is clear to all learners before starting the activity.

• Learners discuss their answers. Tell them to make some notes of their ideas. You can also hand out copies of **Photocopiable 33**: Dinosaur hunter, for the learners to complete in pairs.

> **Assessment ideas:** Circulate, listening to learners' interactions. Make notes of mistakes for remedial work.

Answers

Learner's own answers. Model answer:
Which dinosaur could…

- eat leaves at the top of a tall tree? – *Apatosaurus*
- kill other dinosaurs with its teeth? – *Allosaurus*
- hit other dinosaurs with its tail? – *Ankylosaurus*
- make a noise with its head? – *Parasaurolophus*
- run very fast? – *Gallimimus*

2   Listen and read. (10–20 minutes)

- Remind learners of what 'Q & A' stands for, i.e. question and answer.
- Tell the class that they are going to listen to some information about the dinosaurs they see in the pictures.
- Read all the questions at the beginning of each section. Tell the class to keep their books shut. Ask them to predict the answers. You could write them on the board.
- Focus on the Key word box, and clarify the word 'predict'.
- Tell learners to open their books and direct their attention to the activity. Then tell them to listen and read the answers to check if they were right.

CROSS-CURRICULAR LINK

Science

When learners have finished the activity, ask them to look for information about other dinosaurs that could do the things they have read about. For example, T-rex and Velociraptors could walk on two legs and were meat-eating. They can visit suitable websites such as The Dinosaur Museum, Scholastic, The Dinosaur Race BBC, National Geographic or Live Science.

Audioscript: Track 46

See Learner's Book pages 96–97.

Answers

Learner's own answers.

> **Digital Classroom:** Use the activity 'What could dinosaurs do?' to reinforce comprehension of the text. The i button will explain how to use the activity.

Language detective: *could* as the past form of *can* (5–10 minutes)

- Focus on the meaning of *can/can't – could/couldn't*.
- Ask the class to find examples in the text of things that dinosaurs couldn't do.
- Ask learners to make up some questions beginning with *Could … ?* about the named dinosaurs. They work in pairs and ask their partner the questions. For example, '*Could Gallimimus run fast?*' *Yes, it could.* '*Could Allosaurus run on four legs?*' *No, it couldn't.*

> **Digital Classroom:** Use the grammar presentation 'Could and couldn't' to revise the past form of modal *can, could/couldn't*. The i button will explain how to use the grammar presentation.

3   Write. What could dinosaurs do? (10–15 minutes)

- Focus on the question – *What could dinosaurs do?* Ask learners to work as a group and together write five sentences.
- When they have finished, groups share their sentences with the class.

> **Differentiation ideas:** You could ask more confident groups to include sentences about other dinosaurs they have researched as well. Less confident learners could write questions about the dinosaurs they have researched in Activity 2, such as *What other dinosaurs could walk on two legs? How big was diplodocus?*

Answers

Learner's own answers.

Workbook

Learners do Activities 1, 2 and 3 on pages 70–71.

Plenary ideas

Consolidation (10–15 minutes)

> **Assessment ideas:** As a class, ask learners to add to the mind map they started at the beginning of the lesson. They include key or interesting information they have learned about dinosaurs.

- You may wish to show learners some short clips from BBC's series *Walking with Dinosaurs*, for example 'The smell of prey' on YouTube shows how some dinosaurs hunted and others used their tails as weapons.

Homework ideas

- Learners search for information about one of the dinosaurs mentioned in this lesson. They can visit suitable websites such as 'Meet some deadly dinos!' on National Geographic Kids or Nat Geo Kids Dinosaurs Playlist on YouTube. They can also look for books about dinosaurs, e.g. *Little Kids First Big Book of Dinosaurs* (National Geographic) or *DK's The Big Book of Dinosaurs*. They print or draw pictures and write three sentences about them.

- **Home–school link:** Learners ask their family the questions in *Dinosaur Q & A*. Then they can read the information together.

6.3 Talk about it: Dinosaur discoveries

LEARNING PLAN

Learning objectives	Learning intentions	Success criteria
3Ld.04	• **Listening:** Listen for information; listen for detail; brainstorm ideas, listen and take notes.	• Learners can listen to and understand information from an audio presentation.
3So.01, 3Sor.01, 3Sor.02	• **Speaking:** Ask and answer questions; explain supporting evidence for dinosaur facts; discuss and share information about dinosaurs; retell information using own notes.	• Learners can retell information from an audio presentation using own notes.
3Wca.01, 3Wca.03	• **Writing:** Write notes based on aural presentation; use correct spelling.	• Learners can explain supporting evidence for dinosaur facts.
3Ug.04, 3Us.01	• **Language focus:** quantifiers: *some, all, many, a lot of*; revision of past tense	• Learners can retell information about dinosaurs from an audio presentation using own notes.
	• **Vocabulary:** *tail, necks, scales, lizard, feathers, powerful, microscope, nests, bones, tuck, wing*	• Learners can take notes.

21st-century skills

Critical thinking opportunity: Compare different types of information.

Collaboration: Be aware of when and how to take turns, and when and how to interrupt; take part in tasks by interacting with others.

Learning to learn: Take basic notes about key information while reading and listening.

Materials: Learner's Book pages 98–99; Workbook pages 72–73; map of the world; index cards; sticky notes; sticky tack; large sheet of poster paper

LANGUAGE BACKGROUND

Quantifiers

Quantifiers are words that say how much or how many we are talking about. The most important are: *some, any, no, each, every, either, neither, much, many, more, most; (a) little; (a) few; several, all, both, half*.

Some quantifiers are used with singular nouns, for example *each*, and some are used with plurals, for example *many* and *much* with uncountable nouns.

A lot of and *lots of* can both be used with plural countable nouns and with singular uncountable nouns for affirmative and negative sentences and for questions, for example: *A lot of dinosaurs had feathers.*

All means 'every one'. It is used most often as a determiner with either a countable noun or an uncountable noun after it, for example: *All dinosaurs were extinct 65 million years ago.*

Common misconceptions

Misconception	How to identify	How to overcome
Learners quite often use *can* instead of *could* when referring to past contexts. For example: *The weather was nice, so I can go everywhere. You are so unlucky, because you can't come to my party.*	Write an incorrect sentence on the board. Ask learners: *Does this sentence refer to the past or to the present?* Elicit the answer. Write *can* and *could* on the board. Ask learners: *Which one do we use when we speak about the present?* Elicit the answer. Point at the incorrect sentence and ask: *So, how do we correct this sentence?* Elicit the answer.	Before deciding whether to use *can* or *could*, ask learners to identify what time the sentence is referring to: is it an event in the present or an event in the past? Then they choose the correct modal.
Learners sometimes use *a* instead of *some*, especially before nouns that should be plural, such as shorts, trousers, jeans, clothes, etc., or uncountable nouns. For example: *I bought a new dress and a new shoe.* *I got a new clothes and a ring for my birthday.* *We drank a tea and spoke about you.*	Write the incorrect sentences on the board. Explain that *a* is used only with singular nouns and never with plural or uncountable nouns, and that *some* is used with plural nouns and uncountable nouns. Write some plural nouns, e.g. *shorts, trousers, jeans, clothes*, on the board. Ask: *Do these words refer to one thing or to more than one thing?* Elicit the answer. Ask: *Which word should we use, a or some?* Elicit the answer. Write some uncountable nouns, for example *water, tea, meat,* etc. Ask: *Can we count water / tea / meat?* Elicit the answer. Ask: *So, which one do we use a or some with?*	Before learners decide whether to use *a* or *some*, ask them to circle the noun and think: *Is it singular or plural? Can I count it or not?*

Starter ideas

Which dinosaur? (10–20 minutes)

• If learners have done the homework activity from the previous lesson, ask them to share the information they have found with the class. You could collect all the summaries and keep them to make a dinosaur album, or upload them to the class blog and make a dinosaur slide-share.

• Divide the class into two groups and have them take turns to ask and answer questions about the dinosaurs from Lesson 6.2, for example: *Which dinosaur could break the legs of its enemies with its tail? Which dinosaur could run very fast?* Each group gets a point for a correct answer.

Main teaching ideas

> **Digital Classroom:** Use the video 'Dinosaurs in the films' to explore how film-makers rely on the knowledge of scientists to make films about dinosaurs, and to introduce vocabulary and concepts in the lesson. The i button will explain how to use the video.

1 Listen and learn (5–10 minutes)

- Focus on the text and read it with the class.
- Ask them to look at picture 1 on Learner's Book page 99 and read the question. Ask: *What new things are scientists learning about dinosaurs?* Elicit some ideas from the class.
- Then tell the class to listen to the audio. Play the recording. Were their ideas correct?

Audioscript: Track 47

Learner's Book page 98

Dinosaur discoveries

1 What new things are scientists learning about dinosaurs?

This is a very exciting time for dinosaur study. Every year, scientists find fossils of many new dinosaurs – about 30 new dinosaurs every year! Scientists are using new technology to study dinosaur fossils. They learn more about the way dinosaurs moved and what dinosaurs ate. They are also discovering what colours dinosaurs were.

2 Write (10–20 minutes)

- Tell the class that writing notes is an important skill because it helps us to remember the facts we hear. It also helps us to remember our own ideas before a discussion.
- Ask learners to look at the sample notes that a learner took to answer the question they have just listened to.
- Ask them to listen to the audio again and write notes for two more facts.
- Play the recording again. Then elicit answers as a class.

> **Critical thinking opportunity:** As a class, discuss with learners how to take notes. Elicit ideas, for example don't write full sentences, write the most important words, draw small pictures, write numbers instead of words, use bullet points and arrows. You could create a mini-poster with these strategies and keep it on display for learners to remind themselves when taking notes.

> **Differentiation ideas:** With less confident learners, you may wish to share the audio transcript of this first question (track 47). Ask them to read it and then read the question. Then they decide which words are important and which are not. Ask them to underline the key information they need to be able to answer the question.

Answers

what dinosaurs ate; what colour dinosaurs were

3 Talk. Listen to a child use the sample notes to talk about facts she learned (5–10 minutes)

- Tell the class that they are going to listen to a child use the sample notes to talk about facts she has learned.
- Divide the class into pairs. When they have listened to the audio, each pair will say one more fact. Tell learners to use their notes and say their fact as a full sentence.
- Play the recording. Then elicit contributions from the class.

Audioscript: Track 48

Learner's Book page 98

Every year scientists find fossils of new dinosaurs.

They can find 30 new dinosaurs in a year!

Scientists learn more about how dinosaurs moved.

4 Listen and look (5–10 minutes)

- Ask learners to look at pictures 2–4 on Learner's Book page 99 and read each question in turn.
- Learners describe the pictures and predict what the answers to the questions might be.

- Tell them to listen to the rest of the audio *Dinosaur discoveries*. Play the recording once. Were their ideas right?

5 Listen and write. Choose one question to write notes about (10–15 minutes)

- Ask learners to work in pairs. Each learner chooses one question to write notes about (question 2, 3, or 4 from *Dinosaur discoveries*).

- They write down their question in their notebooks and listen to the audio again. Ask them to write down three (or more) facts about the question they have chosen.

- Play the recording (track 49) once again.

> **Differentiation ideas:** Less confident learners may need to have the recording played twice or three times. When they have finished, ask them how they took their notes, for example: *Did you use bullet points? Did you write the important words? What words did you leave out?* More confident learners may take notes of all three questions.

Answers
Learners choose and write facts.

Language focus, and 6 Talk. Share dinosaur information with your partner (15–20 minutes)

- Focus on the sentence openings and the structures in the Language focus box. Ask learners to give a few examples with these sentence openings.

- Explain that in English we sometimes use comparisons to describe things that are equal or similar in some way, for example: *Some dinosaurs were as heavy as 17 buses* (*as* + adjective/adverb + *as*).

- Can learners think of other comparisons? Provide adjectives, for example *strong, tall, fast, dangerous, small, big*, etc.

- Remind the class of the use of quantifiers: *no, some, any, many, much, a lot of.* Explain that these words tell the quantity of something without giving precise information.

- Provide some examples and ask learners to give a few of their own. They can look back on Lessons 1 and 2 and use the information to give examples, for example: *Dinosaurs could run fast. Some of them could run as fast as 70 km per hour. Allosaurus and T-Rex both walked on two legs / had very small front legs.*

- Still in pairs, ask learners to share dinosaur information with their partner using their notes to answer the question they chose in Activity 5. Encourage them to try to use full sentences and to use some of the words in the Language focus box

- Learners can also point to the pictures as they explain and describe things.

> **Differentiation ideas:** You could provide less confident groups with a copy of the transcript of their question.

They check that they have taken notes of all the important facts. They can also write down the sentences they are planning to say, so that they feel more confident at the moment of speaking.

> **Digital Classroom:** Use the activity 'As easy as can be' to reinforce use of the *as ... as* form. The i button will explain how to use the activity.

> **Digital Classroom:** Use the activity 'There aren't any dinosaurs' to revise quantifiers, e.g. *no, some, any, all, much, many*. The i button will explain how to use the activity.

7 Share information with your class (20–45 minutes)

- Ask learners to focus on the questions again and discuss them. Each learner can say one fact so that everyone has a chance to speak.

- Write down the information on the board as learners say it.

> **Differentiation ideas:** You may ask more confident volunteers to come to the board and write the information themselves.

- Tell the class to listen to the audio again (track 49) and to add any new information.

- Play the recording and give learners time to check and add any missing facts.

CROSS-CURRICULAR LINK

History

On one set of index cards, write the years of key dinosaur discoveries, for example 1676, 2007, 2014, 2020, etc. On another set of cards, write information about the discovery, for example *Titanosaurus was found in Argentina. Many dinosaurs had feathers.* Ask learners to match the years to the discoveries and make a poster of a timeline.

You may wish to show learners You Tube videos about important discoveries, for example 'Reaper of death' dinosaur discovered in Alberta (National Geographic), or 'Most Amazing Fossil Discoveries Ever' (Origins Explained). Ask learners to find out where most dinosaur fossils have been discovered, i.e. North America, China and Argentina. Have them look for information about important discoveries in these countries and locate the sites on a map of the world. You can also look for maps on the internet. Learners can write notes on sticky notes or index cards and stick them on the map.

Answers

Learners share the facts with their partner. Learners' notes can include some of the following:

2 *How big were the biggest dinosaurs?* As long as three buses; as heavy as 17 elephants.

3 *Did dinosaurs have feathers?* Many dinosaurs had feathers; most small dinosaurs had feathers while big dinosaurs had scales and feathers; scientists can now tell the colour of the feathers.

4 *How are birds and dinosaurs alike?* Birds are living dinosaurs; birds and dinosaurs both have feathers, nests and eggs; they have similar bones; they sleep the same way.

Workbook

Learners do Activities 1–3 on pages 72–73.

Plenary ideas

Consolidation (10–15 minutes)

> **Assessment ideas:** Give each learner an index card or a sticky note and ask them to complete sentences with their impressions of the lesson. For example: *I now understand how / why …; The thing I found the most exciting today is …; An important question to ask is …,* etc. When they have finished, put them up on the board for everyone to read.

Homework ideas

- Learners imagine that they have made an important dinosaur discovery in their own country. They write a short text about it and draw a picture.

- **Home–school link:** Learners ask the questions from *Dinosaur discoveries* to their family, and challenge them to answer. They can ask them about dinosaur discoveries in their country.

6.4 Write about it: Dinosaur fantasies

LEARNING PLAN

Learning objectives	Learning intentions	Success criteria
3Rd.02 3Wca.04, 3Wca.05, 3Wor.01, 3Wor.02, 3Wc.02, 3Wc.03	• **Reading:** Read and follow instructions. • **Writing:** Write sentences about a pet dinosaur; plan a story; brainstorm ideas; use correct spelling and punctuation; use simple connectors; use descriptive adjectives. • **Language focus:** modal form of *can*, *like* + infinitive; use of comparatives and superlatives to describe things • **Vocabulary:** descriptive adjectives	• Learners can read and follow instructions. • Learners can brainstorm ideas. • Learners can plan and write sentences/a paragraph about a pet dinosaur. • Learners can use correct spelling, punctuation and grammar.

21st-century skills

Learning to learn: Produce short texts through participating in guided or shared writing activities.

Social responsibilities: Know and use words relating to groups to which they belong (for example, family, friends, school class or sports team).

Values: Look after pets in responsible way.

Materials: Learner's Book pages 100–101; Workbook pages 74–75; drawing supplies; sheets of paper; Sample answer for Unit 6; **Photocopiable 1, 2, 34**

Starter ideas

What do you remember? (15–20 minutes)

- If learners have completed the homework activity from the previous lesson, ask them to share the information they have found with the class.

- You can then upload the information to the class blog or make a poster with their texts.

> **Assessment ideas:** Divide the class into four groups. Ask groups to write four sentences about dinosaurs using the information they have learned in Lessons 1–3. Some sentences should be true and some false. When they have finished, groups take it in turns to say the sentences and decide if they are true or false. Ask groups to correct the false sentences.

Main teaching ideas

1 Talk (5–10 minutes)

- Ask the class: *How many years ago did dinosaurs die? So, did dinosaurs and humans live at the same time?* Elicit the answer. You might want to use this as extension material as this is beyond the requirements of the Cambridge Primary English as a Second Language curriculum framework.

- Although dinosaurs and humans did not live at the same time, there are lots of fantasy stories and movies about people and dinosaurs living together. Ask learners to talk about some of the dinosaur stories they have read or seen. Learners may mention *Jurassic Park*, *Godzilla*, *Dinotopia*, *The Good Dinosaur* or *Dinosaur Tales*, among others.

- Ask them: *Were the dinosaurs friendly or dangerous? What did the people and dinosaurs do together?* Invite learners to retell the stories or films they have seen or read.

2 Listen to and read the poem (10–15 minutes)

- **Values:** Ask learners if they have a pet. What is it? What do they do with their pets? Do they play with them? Do they take them for walks? Who looks after the pet? Do they do it? Do their parents look after it? How do they look after their pet? Elicit answers.

- Tell the class that they are going to read and listen to a poem. Focus on the title of the poem – *Unfortunately*. Discuss the meaning of the word *unfortunately* (and *fortunately*).

- Ask learners to come up with some statements beginning with *Unfortunately …* and *Fortunately …* .

- Play the audio at least twice. Discuss the meaning of new words.

- Play the audio again and ask learners to repeat it.

- Encourage learners to memorise the poem and recite it to a partner.

> **Critical thinking opportunity:** Ask: *Would you like to have a pet dinosaur? Why? Would a dinosaur make a good pet? Why?*

Audioscript: Track 50

See Learner's Book page 100.

> **Digital Classroom:** Use the activity 'My pet dinosaur' to revise capital letters, full stops and exclamation marks. The i button will explain how to use the activity.

3 Write. Imagine you have a pet dinosaur (30–45 minutes)

- Tell learners to imagine they have a pet dinosaur. They are going to write a story about it.

- Ask them to think about the questions in the Learner's Book and use these to collect ideas for their story.

- **Step 1:** Have learners brainstorm ideas and write some in the mind map. Focus on the section *How it looks*. Remind the class to use descriptive adjectives. Brainstorm descriptive adjectives with the class and write them on the board for reference. Learners choose the ones they need for their dinosaur and write them in their mind map.

- **Step 2:** Tell learners that they are now going to write a story about their dinosaur using some of the ideas in their mind map. They can use the sample story as a model. Focus on the checklist and tell the class to make sure they include these features in their story.

> **Critical thinking opportunity:** As a class, read the sample story. Ask learners to find the features in the checklist in the sample.

- Allow plenty of time for learners to plan and write their story.

- **Step 3:** When they have finished their first draft, ask learners to read the checklist and revise their text, making changes if necessary.

- **Step 4:** Focus on the checklist and read it with the class. Learners then use it to review their work – they check and correct spelling and punctuation. Remind learners of their Writer's checklist (**Photocopiable 1**). Ask them to get their copy and use it to check their work.

> **Assessment ideas:** When they are happy with their text, ask learners to exchange it with a partner. Using **Photocopiable 2**, the Peer editing checklist, they read their partners' text and make comments. Have learners say at least two things they like about their partner's text and one thing they would improve. When learners get their text back, they act upon the feedback they have received and write a final version of their story on **Photocopiable 34**.

- Finally, they draw the picture of their pet dinosaur at the bottom of the **Photocopiable 34**.

- See **Sample answer for Unit 6** for an example answer to this writing task.

CROSS-CURRICULAR LINK

Science

(See Critical thinking opportunity for Activity 3 above.)

Answers
Learners plan, write and check a story about their pet dinosaur.

> **Workbook**
>
> Learners do Activities 1, 2 and 3 on pages 74–75.

Plenary ideas

Consolidation (5–15 minutes)

- When learners have finished their writing, ask them to read their text about the pet dinosaur to the class.

- You can collect all the texts and make a Pet dinosaur storybook, or upload the stories to the class blog.

> **Assessment ideas:** As a class, discuss with learners what they found the most difficult to do in this lesson. How can they overcome the difficulties? Can the class offer advice? Elicit ideas. Ask learners to write down ideas and reflections in their learning log.

Homework ideas

- Learners write a description of their family pet dinosaur.

- **Home–school link:** Learners read their dinosaur story to their family. They ask parents and siblings to imagine a dinosaur they would like to have as a pet. Then they draw a picture together.

6.5 Read and respond: Baby dinosaurs

LEARNING PLAN

Learning objectives	Learning intentions	Success criteria
3Ld.03	• **Listening:** Listen to dinosaur fossil discoveries.	• Learners can read and understand a text about dinosaur babies.
3Sc.03, 3Sc.07	• **Speaking:** Talk about dinosaur babies; activate prior knowledge.	• Learners can talk about dinosaur babies.
3Rd.01, 3Rd.03	• **Reading:** Read about dinosaur babies; understand meaning from context; read and decide if sentences are true or false.	• Learners can use context clues to guess word meaning.
	• **Vocabulary:** *expert, exciting, nest, worn down, hatch, clue, dirt, berries, steal, dangerous, bone bed, grown-up, deer, volcano, erupt, curious, patient, hard-working, willing to change mind*	• Learners can read and decide whether sentences are true or false.
		• Learners can discuss the qualities of a good scientist and relate to these personally.

21st-century skills

Critical thinking opportunity: Find supporting evidence for statements; draw inferences based on illustrations.

Communication: Contribute in lessons by asking questions, attempting responses and explaining understanding.

Values: Discuss qualities of a good scientist and relate to these personally.

Materials: Learner's Book pages 102–105; Workbook pages 76–77; photos of baby animals; **Photocopiable 3**

Starter ideas

Cute babies (5–10 minutes)

- Remind the class of baby animals they may know the names of.

- Encourage learners to compare them to the adult animals. Ask: *What is different and similar? What do their mothers do to look after them?* Elicit ideas from the class.

Main teaching ideas

1 Talk about it (5–15 minutes)

- Ask learners to think what dinosaur babies might look like. Ask questions such as: *How different or similar would they be from the adults? What would they eat? Did they have brothers and sisters? How did they get food? How do scientists know about baby dinosaurs?* Elicit ideas from the class.

  ⟩ **Critical thinking opportunity:** As preparation for the reading activity, get learners to use their background knowledge when scanning and previewing the text for general information.

- Ask learners to look at the illustrations. Are the baby dinosaurs similar to what they thought? What can they learn about baby dinosaurs from the pictures? Elicit ideas.

- What kind of text do they think this is: fiction or non-fiction? How can they tell without reading it? Remind learners how text features and illustration help them to predict the kind of text they are going to read.

Answers
Learner's own answers.

2 Read and listen (5–10 minutes)

- Tell learners that they are going to listen to an amazing discovery and follow in their books.

- Play the audio at least twice.

- Play the audio again. Stop after each paragraph and discuss the meaning of new words and phrases.

- Ask learners what they think about this discovery.

Audioscript: Track 51

See Learner's Book pages 102–104.

3 Word study (10–20 minutes)

- Ask the class to find the blue words in the text and read the sentences.

- Then they look at the words and match them to the correct definition.

- Check answers as a class.

- Ask learners to look for more words that are new to them in the text. Encourage them to guess the meaning from the context. Help if necessary by giving clues.

- Ask them to write the words in their notebooks and write a sentence or draw a picture to show their meaning.

CROSS-CURRICULAR LINK

Science

Explain that baby dinosaurs are called 'hatchlings' because they hatch from eggs like turtles and crocodiles do. Ask learners to look for information about when the first dinosaur eggs were discovered. Did scientists know what they were? You may wish to direct learners to suitable websites to find out more about baby dinosaurs, for example Dinosaur Eggs & Babies (on You Tube), National Geographic or the American Museum of Natural History.

Answers
a hatched, **b** dangerous, **c** steal, **d** clues

4 Read. Is each sentence true or false? (5–20 minutes)

- Ask learners to read the sentences and decide whether they are true or false.

- Tell them to read the text again for help.

- When they have finished, ask them to correct the false sentences.

> **Differentiation ideas:** Ask less confident learners to read the text again before deciding whether the sentences are true or false. More confident groups may work in small groups and write some more true and false sentences. Have them exchange their sentences with another group and decide if they are true or false. They correct the false sentences.

Answers

a true, **b** true, **c** true, **d** true, **e** true, **f** false – They think they died because a volcano erupted, killing all the dinosaurs in the area.

5 Talk (10–15 minutes)

- Ask learners to read the sentences. They discuss in pairs or small groups which clues they found for each fact.
- When they have finished, discuss responses as as class.

Answers

a The bones of an adult maiasaur were near the nest; the babies' teeth were worn down, so something was bringing them food to eat.
b Their teeth were worn down.
c The bones of meat-eating dinosaurs were found near the maiasaurs' nest.
d The bones of hundreds of maiasaurs were found together.

6 Values (10–15 minutes)

- Read the qualities of a good scientist with the class.
- Encourage learners to reflect on why it is necessary for scientists to have these qualities, for example, *patient* – because it may take a long time to find what they are looking for.
- In pairs, ask learners to discuss which of the qualities of a scientist they think they have. Encourage them to justify their answers.

- Learners then reflect on what they would like to study if they were scientists.
- Supply additional vocabulary as necessary.

Answers

Learner's own answers.

Workbook

Learners do Activities 1, 2 and 3 on page 76–77.

> **Digital Classroom:** Use the activity 'A good scientist' to revise personal qualities vocabulary. The i button will explain how to use the activity.

Plenary ideas

Consolidation (10–20 minutes)

- Ask learners to get the KWL charts they filled in at the beginning of Lesson 6.1 (**Photocopiable 3**).

> **Assessment ideas:** As a class, review the facts listed in the Know column and correct any errors.

- Review questions in the W (What I want to learn) column and add statements to the L column (what I have learned). Are there any questions that remain unanswered? Thinking back on the information they have learned, can learners predict what the answers might be?

Homework ideas

- Ask learners to choose one question in their KWL chart that has remained unanswered and to look for information to answer it.
- **Home–school link:** Learners read the text about baby dinosaurs to their family.

6.6 Project challenge

Learning objectives	Learning intentions	Success criteria
3Sc.04, 3Sc.05	• **Speaking:** Discuss a project; discuss steps of a project; organise work; present their project to the class.	• Learners can read and understand instructions.
3Rd.02	• **Reading:** Read and understand instructions; research and read information.	• Learners can give instructions.
3Wca.02, 3Wca.03, 3Wc.01	• **Writing:** Write sentences; write a report.	• Learners can plan a project.
	• **Language focus:** Unit 6 review	• Learners can make a dinosaur mural.
	• **Vocabulary:** Unit 6 review	• Learners can write a report about a dinosaur.
		• Learners can present their projects to the class.

21st-century skills

Creative thinking: Design new items based on a model.

Collaboration: Respect the importance of doing a fair share of group work; keep to the instructions to complete the task; invite others to give their opinions during the task.

Communication: Share their thoughts with others to help further develop ideas and solve problems.

Materials: Learner's Book pages 106–107; Workbook pages 78–79; Project A: drawing supplies, big sheets of paper; Project B: map of the world, writing and drawing supplies, sheets of paper; **Photocopiable 1, 35**; End of Unit 6 test; **Differentiated worksheets 6A, B and C**

Starter ideas

Looking back (15–20 minutes)

• Ask the class to choose a lesson from Unit 6 that they liked a lot. Ask them to explain why they liked it and to make a short summary.

• As a class, sing the song *Fossils* from the start of the unit (audio track 42).

> **Assessment ideas:** Divide the class into two teams and play a definition game to revise new vocabulary and useful phrases. Each group chooses five words from this unit and writes a definition. Learners take turns to read a definition and guess the word. The team with the most correct guesses is the winner. This game will give you the opportunity to assess how much learners remember from previous lessons.

Main teaching ideas

Learners choose an end-of-unit project to work on. Look at the examples in the pictures and help learners to choose. Provide materials.

Project A: Make a dinosaur mural (60–90 minutes)

• With the class, read the directions in the Learner's Book. Group members choose a dinosaur group (A or B) and do their research. Each learner can choose one dinosaur from their chosen group.

• Learners read the questions and use them as a guide to look for the information they need.

• They draw the picture scene. Remind them to make the size differences noticeable.

- They write each dinosaur's name by its picture and write a description on their mural. When learners have finished writing the description, ask them to get their Writer's checklist (**Photocopiable 1**) and use it to check their work.

- They present the project to the class.

> Assessment ideas: You may wish to video-record groups as they work so that they can then use copies of the recordings to assess what they have done and how they have worked. The copies can then be shared with the learner's family and filed in their portfolio. You may also display the murals during an open day for families to see.

Project B: Write a dinosaur report (60–90 minutes)

- Ask learners to research a dinosaur of their choice.

- They write a report using the questions as help to organise the information. When learners have finished writing the report, ask them to get their Writer's checklist (**Photocopiable 1**) and use it to check their work.

- Then they draw a picture of their chosen dinosaur.

- Learners teach the class about the dinosaur they researched. They show their report and the picture. They may even consider giving the class some homework!

> Assessment ideas: You may wish to video-record groups as they work so that they can then use copies of the recordings to assess what they have done and how they have worked. The copies can then be shared with the learner's family and filed in their portfolio. You may also display the reports during an open day for families to see.

> Assessment ideas: When learners have finished the projects, give them a copy of **Photocopiable 35** and read the information as a class. Ask them to work independently and think about their work on their project. They reflect and answer the questions. Ask them to tick off the aims they have achieved. Insist on the importance of giving honest answers.

> **Workbook**
>
> Learners do the Check your progress quiz on pages 78–79.

Plenary ideas

Reflect on your learning (5–10 minutes)

- Draw learners' attention to the 'Reflect on your learning' questions in the Learner's Book.

- Learners answer the questions to reflect on their project work.

Consolidation (10–15 minutes)

- Ask learners to reflect on and discuss what they liked most about Unit 6; encourage them to explain why. This may also be a good opportunity for them to think about which aspects of the unit they have found most difficult and why.

- You may wish to keep a record of learners' comments to see how they progress over time.

> Assessment ideas: **Portfolio opportunity:** If you have been filing learners' work for Unit 6, you may find it useful to put all the work of this unit together. You could ask learners to make a cover for their Unit 6 work, decorating it with an image that represents what they have learned.

Homework ideas

- Learners draw a picture of what they have liked most about this unit.

- **Home–school link:** Learners show their family their projects.

- Hand out copies of **Differentiated worksheets 6A, B and C** depending on each learner's ability, and ask them to complete the activities at home.

6.7 What do you know now?

What do you know about dinosaurs? (30–40 minutes)

- Learners work in pairs. They work together through all the tasks set in this section.

- They write the answers in their notebooks. You may ask them to have a special section in their notebooks where they record the answers.

Answers

Suggested answers:

1 Learner's own answers.
2 Scientists know about dinosaurs because they have found fossils of their bones, their nests and their footprints. They study these fossils to learn about dinosaurs and their lives.
3 Most meat-eating dinosaurs, like Allosaurus, walked on two legs. This left their 'hands' free to grab the animals they wanted to eat.
4 The largest dinosaurs were as tall as a four-storey building / as long as three buses / as heavy as 17 elephants. The smallest dinosaurs were as small as a chicken.
5–6 Learner's own answers.

Look what I can do! (15 minutes)

- Review the *I can* … statements on page 108 of the Learner's Book. Learners demonstrate what they can do.

- Learners colour in the faces to show which things they can do.

- Encourage them to be honest in their answers.

> **Workbook**
>
> Learners answer the Reflection questions on page 79.

Check your progress 2

Starter ideas

Revision of vocabulary

- **Materials:** picture cards of the vocabulary you want learners to review (optional)

- Play a game to revise the verbs and language of instructions of Units 4–6.

- **Mystery picture:** Ask a volunteer to come to the board and show them a picture, or whisper a word into their ear. The learner draws the picture on the board, and the first learner to guess what the picture is can come up to the board to draw the next one. This game can also be played in teams with a point system.

Main teaching ideas

Partner game: Ask me a question!

- **Use of English:** Questions: *Why...? What...? Where...? How many...? Which...? Do...? Can...? Are...?* Vocabulary: *trees, dinosaurs, glasses, houses, children, windmills, bottles, books, birds, frogs*

- **Materials (per pair):** a coin, two different game markers, eight cards or squares of paper

- **Preparation:** Have learners play in pairs. Learners decide which side of the coin (heads or tails) means '1 space' and which side of the coin means '2 spaces'. Each pair writes the following words on the eight cards – one per card: *Why...? What...? Where...? How many...? Which...? Do...? Can...? Are...?* They place the word cards face down.

- **How to play:** Each member of the pair takes turns to toss a coin. They move one or two spaces on the game track, depending on which side of the coin is up. Their partner draws a card and asks them a question about the picture on their space, using the question word on the card. If they cannot answer a question, they must go back to their original position, and their partner will try to answer the question. Then they put the card back on the table, face down. The first player to get to the end of the game track is the winner.

1 Picture hunt

- **Use of English:** present perfect, direct object pronouns

- **How to play:** Learners work in pairs. They read the list (Learner's Book page 110). They then take it in turns to look for people and things hidden in the painting. When one of them finds a person or a thing, they say: *'I've found her / him / it / them!'*

2 My favourite invention

- **How to play:** Remind learners of the inventions they learned about in Unit 5. Learners write two sentences to answer the questions in the Learner's Book (page 110). When they have finished, they share their sentences with the class. Did anyone else in the class choose the same invention? Did they like it for the same reason or for a different reason?

3 Dinosaurs could do many things

- **Use of English:** past simple, *could*

- **How to play:** Remind learners of what they learned about dinosaurs in Unit 6. Ask them to write three sentences about some things that dinosaurs could do. When they have finished, they share their sentences with a partner.

> 7 Puzzles and codes

Unit plan

Lesson	Approximate number of learning hours	Outline of learning content	Learning objectives	Resources
1 Stripes and spots	1.5– 2.25	Describe and compare objects.	3Ld.01 3Sc.02 3Sc.07 3Rd.02 3Wca.05 3Wc.01	Learner's Book Lesson 7.1 Workbook Lesson 7.1 [⬇] Photocopiable 36 **Digital Classroom:** Video and activity sheet – Puzzles; Slideshow and activity sheet – The Secret Notebook: A guessing game; Activity – What do you see?
2 Have you ever …?	2.0–3.0	Interview each other about things we have done.	3Ld.02 3Ld.03 3Sc.01 3Sc.03 3Rd.03 3Wca.04 3Ug.06	Learner's Book Lesson 7.2 Workbook Lesson 7.2 **Digital Classroom:** Grammar presentation – Present perfect; Activity – Do and done
3 *Prince Henry's Party*	1.0–1.5	Use clues to solve problems.	3Ld.01 3Ld.04 3Sc.03 3Sc.04 3Rd.02 3Wca.05 3Us.03	Learner's Book Lesson 7.3 Workbook Lesson 7.3 **Digital Classroom:** Activity – Lunch time
4 Secret messages	1.25–2.25	Write messages in secret codes.	3Ld.04 3Sc.06 3Sc.07 3Rd.01 3Wca.04 3Wor.01 3Ug.01	Learner's Book Lesson 7.4 Workbook Lesson 7.4 [⬇] Sample answer for Unit 7 [⬇] Photocopiable 37 [⬇] Photocopiable 38 [⬇] Differentiated worksheets 7A, B and C **Digital Classroom:** Activity – Caesar's code
5 *A fair solution*	1.75–3.0	Read and act out a tale about a clever solution to a problem.	3Ld.04 3So.01 3Sor.02 3Rd.03	Learner's Book Lesson 7.5 Workbook Lesson 7.5 **Digital Classroom:** Activity – A fair solution; Slideshow and activity sheet – Nasreddin and his fine coat

(continued)

Lesson	Approximate number of learning hours	Outline of learning content	Learning objectives	Resources
6 Project challenge	1.0–2.0	Write a secret message or a questionnaire.	3Sc.05 3Rd.02 3Wca.02 3Wca.03 3Wca.04 3Wc.01	Learner's Book Lesson 7.6 Workbook Lesson 7.6  Photocopiable 39  Photocopiable 40
7 What do you know now?	0.75–1.0	Self-assessment and reflection.		Learner's Book Lesson 7.7

Cross-unit resources

 Unit 7 Audioscripts

⬇ End of Unit 7 test

⬇ Unit 7 Progress report

⬇ Unit 7 Wordlist

BACKGROUND KNOWLEDGE

Julie Larios

In Lesson 7.2, learners read a poem by Julie Larios.

Julie Larios is an American poet, writer and educator, born in 1949. She lives in Seattle, Washington. She taught creative writing at the University of Washington for many years before returning full-time to writing. She enjoys creating lists of intriguing words with which she then composes poems. Her love for words started early, when she was in seventh grade and she won a literary competition. She has published many books of poetry for children, including *On the Stairs*, a counting book featuring two mice counting the stairs that they ascend, and *Yellow Elephant: A Bright Bestiary*, in which each poem describes an animal and its colours. You can learn more about her work in her online blog.

Julius Caesar

In Lesson 7.4, learners read about Julius Caesar.

Julius Caesar (born around 100 BC) was a Roman general who was elected consul, the highest office in the republic. He used his power to make important reforms in the Roman administration and government. He was also a master of military strategy, and between 58 and 50 BC he conquered Gaul (modern France and Belgium) up to the river Rhine. He is considered to be one of the greatest military commanders in military history. His name 'Caesar' was adopted as a synonym for 'Emperor' and was used throughout the Roman Empire.

Nasreddin

In Lesson 7.5, learners read a story about Nasreddin.

Nasreddin, also known as Nasreddin Hodja, was a satirist born in present-day Turkey in the 13th century. He is considered a philosopher and a wise man, famous for his funny stories and anecdotes. His stories are usually humorous and sometimes have a pedagogical nature. Over the years, they have become popular in different regions and many more have been added to the original collection. The themes in the stories have become part of the folklore of many countries and cultures, particularly in the Muslim world, as they deal with concepts that are timeless. The oldest Nasreddin story is found in a book called *Saltukname*, which was written in 1480.

TEACHING SKILLS FOCUS

Metacognition

It is important that a learner can respond to a particular learning situation in an appropriate way. A successful learner will develop a range of strategies from which they choose the most suitable to solve particular problems and then adapt them to the needs of a specific situation and assess their level of success. This awareness of one's thinking skills, the ability to understand their own learning and the thought processes associated with questioning the effectiveness of processes, as well as exploring and discovering new ways of learning, is called *metacognition*.

Metacognitive activities help learners to:

- identify what they already know
- explain what they have learned
- communicate their knowledge, skills and abilities
- set their own learning goals
- monitor their progress
- evaluate and revise their work
- identify and implement effective learning strategies
- transfer learning to different contexts.

Your challenge

Some ideas that will help learners to develop their metacognitive awareness include:

1 Activate prior knowledge.

2 Give explicit strategy instruction, for example explain how to use a flowchart or a mind map and how these will help learners to organise their ideas.

3 Model the strategy that you want learners to learn, and do a 'think-aloud' in simple English.

4 Provide opportunities for asking self-reflection questions, such as:

- *What resources do I need to do this task?*
- *What problems am I likely to encounter?*
- *How can I solve them?*
- *Have I managed to complete the task successfully?*
- *What do I need to do to improve the next time?*

5 Encourage learners to monitor their own work, for example:

- *Am I doing well?*
- *Do I need to change anything?*
- *Do I need extra resources to do this? If so, where can I find them?*

6 Provide opportunities for higher-order thinking by means of questions, for example: *Why? What now? Why do you say so? What would happen if …?*

Getting learners to think about how they learn and speak about their mental processes may seem too difficult at lower levels, mainly because learners are not used to doing such things and also because they do not have the necessary vocabulary. You may need to supply them with the vocabulary they need to talk about how they learn and how they can learn better.

In each unit of the Learner's Book, opportunities to introduce metacognitive strategies are highlighted. Look through Unit 7 and highlight opportunities for introducing the strategies above.

Reflection

How successful have the activities been? How can you provide more and better scaffolding? How can you help learners to recall the language they need to speak about the thinking process?

7.1 Think about it: Stripes and spots

LEARNING PLAN

Learning objectives	Learning intentions	Success criteria
3Ld.01	• **Listening:** Listen to a song; listen and follow instructions.	• Learners can listen to and sing a song.
3Sc.02, 3Sc.07	• **Speaking:** Sing a song; talk about differences; describe and compare objects; answer maths questions; use descriptive adjectives, including colour, pattern and size; describe and compare colour, pattern and size.	• Learners can listen to and follow instructions. • Learners can describe and compare flowers and bugs.
3Rd.02	• **Reading:** Read and understand instructions; read and understand maths questions.	• Learners can use descriptive adjectives in the correct order.
3Wca.05, 3Wc.01	• **Writing:** Write descriptions. • **Language focus:** adjective order • **Vocabulary:** *spot, without, bug, size*	• Learners can write a sequence of three instructions.

21st-century skills

Critical thinking opportunity: Compare and contrast patterns.

Communication: Contribute in lessons by asking questions, attempting responses and explaining understanding.

Learning to learn: Memorise and repeat key words and phrases.

Materials: Learner's Book pages 111–113; Workbook pages 80–81; photos of flowers and bugs of different colours and with spots and stripes; access to the internet; **Photocopiable 36**

Starter ideas

> **Digital Classroom:** Use the video and activity sheet 'Puzzles' to introduce the topic of puzzles and riddles. The i button will explain how to use the video and activity sheet.

Getting started (10–15 minutes)

- Focus on the photographs on Learner's Book page 111. Ask the class to describe what they see in the pictures. What are the children doing? Elicit the word *puzzle*.

- Ask the class: *What kinds of puzzles can we solve?* Elicit ideas.

- Ask the class if they like to solve puzzles. What sort of real-life puzzles have they solved? What

kinds of puzzle games do they enjoy playing, for example jigsaw puzzles, letter codes, maths puzzles, crosswords, Sudoku, etc.?

- If learners don't like puzzles, ask them to explain why.

Answers
Learner's own answers.

Sing along! *This is the song that never ends* (5–10 minutes)

- Tell the class they are going to listen to a song. Give each learner a copy of **Photocopiable 36**: Sing along! *This is the song that never ends*.

- Play the song at least twice and ask learners to identify familiar words.

- Ask the class what the song is about. Elicit answers (it is about a song that goes on and on and never ends).

- Sing the song and encourage learners to join in.

Audioscript: Track 52

Learner's Book page 111

This is the song that never ends
This is the song that never ends.
Yes, it goes on and on, my friend.
Some people started singing it, not knowing what it was,
And they'll continue singing it forever just because ...

This is the song that never ends.
Yes, it goes on and on, my friend.
Some people started singing it, not knowing what it was,
And they'll continue singing it forever just because ...

This is the song that never ends.
Yes, it goes on and on, my friend.

Stop, stop!

Some people started singing it, not knowing what it was,
And they'll continue singing it forever just because ...

This is the song that never ends.

Oh, please stop!

Yes, it goes on and on, my friend.
Some people started singing it, not knowing what it was,

NO-oooo!

And they'll continue singing it forever just because ...

This is the song that never ends.
Yes, it goes on and on, my friend ...

Main teaching ideas

〉 **Digital Classroom:** Use the slideshow and activity sheet 'The Secret Notebook: A guessing game' to reinforce listening skills. The i button will explain how to use the slideshow and activity sheet.

1   Talk about it (5–10 minutes)

*   Focus on the pictures. Discuss with the class how the flowers are different from each other.

*   Do the same with the bugs. Help with additional vocabulary if necessary.

Answers
Learner's own answers. Suggested answer: the flowers are different sizes, different shapes, some have spots or stripes and some are plain, some have bugs on. The bugs have wings or no wings, are different colours, have spots of no spots.

2   Listen. Find each flower (5–10 minutes)

*   Tell the class to listen to the descriptions and find each flower.

*   Play the audio at least twice. Ask learners to identify the flowers.

*   Learners discuss what helped them decide.

Audioscript: Track 53

Learner's Book page 112

Narrator:	Listen and find the flower.
Child 1:	Find a little flower with a brown centre.
Child 2:	Find a little flower with a brown centre and stripes.
Child 3:	Find a little flower with a brown centre and stripes and a bug on it without wings.
Narrator:	Have you found the flower?
Narrator:	Listen and find a different flower.
Child 1:	Find a big flower without a brown centre and without stripes.
Child 2:	Find a big flower without a brown centre and without stripes with a bug.
Child 3:	Find a big flower without a brown centre and without stripes with a bug on it with spots on its wings.
Narrator:	Have you found the flower?

Answers
Learners find the flowers and bugs as described in the audio. 1: Flower 7   2: Flower 3

3   Vocabulary. Describe one flower or a bug (10–15 minutes)

*   Learners take turns to describe a flower or a bug. Their partner identifies it in the picture.

- Tell them to read the questions and use them as models.
- Before they start, look at the pictures and the words that illustrate them. Check that learners understand them.

> **Assessment ideas:** Circulate, listening to learners' interactions. Make notes of mistakes for remedial work. Help with vocabulary if necessary.

Answers
Learner's own answers.

4 Solve the puzzle (5–10 minutes)

- Focus on the picture again and ask the class to work in pairs.
- Learners take it in turns to describe to their partner two flowers and two bugs that are exactly the same.

Answers
Flowers 2 and 12 are the same. Bugs 5 and 11 are the same. Learner's own descriptions.

5 Talk about the picture (10–15 minutes)

- Focus on the questions. Ask learners to look at the picture carefully and find the answers.
- Then ask them to write some more maths questions about the picture using these questions as examples.

Answers
How many bugs without spots are there? *Five*
Are there more big flowers or little flowers? *Little flowers; there are nine*
Are there more green bugs or red bugs? *Red*
Make up some more questions about the picture. *Learner's own answers.*

Language focus (10–15 minutes)

- Read the examples with the class.
- Write *Number*, *Size* and *Colour* as headings on the board and supply more examples.
- Ask learners to look at the photos in the book and elicit more examples.
- Display some more pictures of flowers and bugs and elicit more examples with the class.
- Write the adjectives in the correct column.
- Ask learners to copy the examples in their notebooks.

> **Critical thinking opportunity:** Ask learners: *Which animal has stripes?* (e.g. tiger, zebra) *Which animal has spots?* (e.g. leopard, some dogs such as Dalmatians, cheetahs, etc.).

- Ask the class to search the internet and find photographs of animals or plants. They can print some of the pictures (or if available, show them on an interactive whiteboard) and describe them to the class.

> **Digital Classroom:** Use the activity 'What do you see?' to revise the order of adjectives. The i button will explain how to use the activity.

6 Write an instruction for your class to follow (15–20 minutes)

- Ask the class to write a drawing instruction for the class.
- Tell learners to read the example and use it as a model.

> **Differentiation ideas:** More confident groups might benefit from adding more challenge, for example using *quite/very big*, or other size words such as *tall, long, tiny, huge*. They could also specify the colour of the spots and stripes.

- When learners have finished, play picture dictation. Learners take it in turns to read their instruction to their partners. The rest of the class draws and colours the picture according to instructions.

Workbook
Learners do Activities 1–4 on pages 80–81.

Plenary ideas
Consolidation (10–15 minutes)

- Shared class writing activity: Write a simple sentence, for example *Draw two snails.* Invite learners to add to the sentence, for example *Draw two very big greenish snails with tiny purple spots.* Encourage learners to make funny contributions.

Homework ideas

- Learners look for puzzles they like and bring them to the following class.
- **Home–school link:** Learners show the pictures in the book to their family. They ask them to spot the differences.

7.2 Geography: Have you ever …?

LEARNING PLAN

Learning objectives	Learning intentions	Success criteria
3Ld.02, 3Ld.03	• **Listening:** Listen to a poem; listen and understand new vocabulary.	• Learners can listen to and understand a poem.
3Sc.01, 3Sc.03	• **Speaking:** Ask and answer questions using the present perfect; speak about what you have and have not done; interview a partner; recite a poem.	• Learners can ask and answer questions using the present perfect.
3Rd.03	• **Reading:** Read a poem; read and understand new vocabulary using context.	• Learners can interview each other about things they have done.
3Wca.04	• **Writing:** Write sentences and questions using the present perfect; write about what you have never done.	• Learners can read and understand new vocabulary using context.
3Ug.06	• **Language focus:** present perfect; *Have you ever …?*; *I have never …*; irregular verbs	• Learners can write about what they have never done.
	• **Vocabulary:** *climb, travel, stay awake, touch, lost, strange, whisper, bravely, outside, toss, wild, waves, storm*	

21st-century skills

Critical thinking opportunity: Make inferences and draw conclusions.

Communication: Use simple techniques to start, maintain and close conversations of various lengths.

Learning to learn: Participate sensibly and positively in learning activities in class.

Materials: Learner's Book pages 114–115; Workbook pages 82–83; pictures of people doing sports; a set of coloured cards (one red, one yellow and one green) per learner

Starter ideas

Language support – present perfect for experiences (5–10 minutes)

- Remind learners of the form of the present perfect: the present tense of *have* + the past participle of a verb:
  *I **have finished** my homework. She **has travelled** to France a few times.*

- Remind learners that we use the present perfect to speak about actions that started in the past and continue in the present: *I have lived here for 14 years.*

- We also use the present perfect to speak about events that happened sometime during someone's life. We can use 'never' to make the sentences negative and 'ever' to ask questions.
  I have been to China. I haven't been to the cinema lately.
  I have never been to Africa. Have you ever seen a lion?

- We can also use the present perfect to talk about something that happened recently, even if there isn't a clear or visible result in the present.
  I have seen my friends. The president has visited some schools.

Have you ever …? (5–10 minutes)

- Show pictures of people climbing mountains, doing extreme sports, sailing, running, etc.

- Ask the class: *Have you ever climbed a mountain / sailed around the world / done karate, etc.?*

- Elicit answers from learners.

Main teaching ideas

1 Look and listen (5–10 minutes)

- Tell learners that they are going listen to Nadir speaking about things he and his friends have done.

- They listen, look at the information in the chart and point at the names.

- Play the audio at least twice.

Audioscript: Track 54

Learner's Book page 114

Hello, my name is Nadir. People in my class have done lots of different things. We made a chart of things we have done.

Selene has climbed a mountain. But it wasn't a very big mountain.

Adil and Nazneen have travelled to another country. They both went to England last year!

I have walked in a forest. My dad and I did that last year. The trees were really big!

No one in my class has ever touched an elephant! Have you ever touched an elephant?

Answers
Learner's own answers.

---

2 Talk. Interview your partner (5–15 minutes)

- Ask learners to work in pairs. They take turns to interview each other and ask and answer the questions on the chart.

- Encourage them to ask other questions as well, for example: *Have you ever played badminton? Have you ever touched a snake? Have you ever travelled to Malaysia?* Supply additional vocabulary as necessary.

- You may wish to write a few examples on the board.

> **Critical thinking opportunity:** Focus on the questions. Ask learners what they notice about them, i.e. the use of 'ever'. Ask learners to look at all the questions. Where do they put 'ever'? Elicit answers.

> **Differentiation ideas:** More confident learners may want to explain their answers by adding further information, so they would probably need to use the past simple rather than the present perfect (for example: *Yes, I have. I climbed Mount Takao when I was 7.*) If you feel it appropriate to learners' level of English, explain the difference briefly (the present perfect is used here to talk about experiences generally; the past simple is used when we go into specific detail – dates, etc.).

Answers
Learner's own answers.

Language detective: Contractions (10–15 minutes)

- Read the examples with the class. Add complete sentences as examples.

- Explain how the present perfect is formed, and how contractions work.

- Encourage learners to supply their own examples and write them on the board.

- Ask learners how they would complete the list with *you, he* and *we*. Ask volunteers to write these forms on the board.

- Have the class copy the examples into their notebooks.

> **Digital Classroom:** Use the grammar presentation 'Present perfect' to revise the present perfect: affirmative, negative and questions with regular verbs. The i button will explain how to use the grammar presentation.

3 Write something your partner has done and something your partner has never done (15–25 minutes)

- Ask learners about what they have discussed with their partners.

- Ask them to say something their partner has done and something their partner has never done. Elicit a few examples and write them on the board.

- Ask learners to write something their partner has done and something their partner has never done using the sentences on the board as models.

> **Critical thinking opportunity:** Focus on the sentence in the Learner's Book. Ask learners what they notice about the use of 'never'. Where do they put 'never'? Elicit answers. Ask learners to look at the questions in Activity 2. Do they use 'never' in questions? Focus on the verb and ask: *Are sentences with 'never' affirmative or negative? Why don't we use the negative form of the verb when we use 'never'?* Elicit answers from the class (they're negative; because 'never' is a negative word; we don't use two negatives in English).

> **Differentiation ideas:** Using the rule they wrote in Activity 2, ask more confident learners to write similar rules for the use of 'never'.

Answers
Learner's own answers.

4 Interview a different partner. (15–25 minutes)

> **Assessment ideas:** Remind the class of the form of verbs in the present perfect. Focus on the verbs they have used so far. Ask the class what they notice about them. Ask: *How do they end?* Elicit the answer: they end in –ed. Then ask: *Which verbs end in –ed?* Elicit the answer, i.e. regular verbs in the past.

- Tell the class that, just as with the past simple, some verbs are regular but others are irregular and more difficult to remember. If you had the class make the irregular verbs poster in Unit 3, display it and tell the class that you are going to add one more column for the verb forms they need to make the present perfect. If you haven't, it may be a good idea to make this poster as a class.

- Explain that the form of the verb we use to make the present perfect is called 'Past participle'. Write this on top of the third column.

- With the class, look for the verbs *see, be* and *ride* in the list. Ask learners to say the past tense of these verbs. Now ask them to read the sentences in the book. Ask: *What is the past participle of these verbs?* Elicit the answers.

- Ask a volunteer to write the past participles in the correct column.

- Focus on the questions. Ask the class to work in pairs and ask and answer these questions.

- Then make up new questions using the same verbs.

Answers
Learner's own answers.

> **Digital Classroom:** Use the activity 'Do and done' to revise irregular past participles. The i button will explain how to use the activity.

5 Write a sentence about something unusual that you have done (25–30 minutes)

- Ask learners to work individually and write a sentence about something unusual that they have done.

- You may wish to model a few examples about yourself and challenge learners to say whether they are true or not! For example: *I have ridden a unicorn. I have played Quidditch.*

- Ask learners to look at the present perfect verbs from the irregular verbs chart in the Picture dictionary (on pages 172–173 of the Learner's Book) and use one of them in their sentence.

- When they have finished, collect all the sentences. Read the sentences aloud and have the class guess who has written each sentence.

- If learners have written a mixture of true and imagined events, have the class guess whether the sentences are true or not.

Answers
Learner's own answers.

6 Read and listen to the poem. (25–30 minutes)

- Tell the class that they are going to read and listen to a poem. Focus on the pictures and ask them what they think the poem is about. Elicit some ideas.

- Play the audio a few times. Learners follow in their books. Ask them if they were right in their prediction.

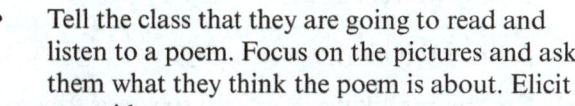

> **Critical thinking opportunity:** Encourage learners to use context clues and artwork to work out any unfamiliar words.

> **Differentiation ideas:** You may ask more confident learners to write a definition for the new words.

- Ask the class to practise reading the poem aloud with a partner.

Audioscript: Track 55

See Learner's Book page 115

Workbook

Learners do Activities 1–3 on pages 82–83.

Plenary ideas

Consolidation (10–15 minutes)

> **Assessment ideas:** As a class, discuss how learners feel they have performed in this lesson. Is there anything they still find confusing or difficult? You may wish to ask them to use Traffic Lights, i.e. red, yellow and green cards, to indicate how confident they are of today's work.

Homework ideas

- Learners write a few sentences about what their family members have done. Learners may also search the internet and find information about Julie Larios, the author of the poem. They may look for other poems to share with the class.

- **Home–school link:** Learners ask family members if they have ever done some of the things they read and spoke about in class.

7.3 Talk about it: *Prince Henry's Party*

LEARNING PLAN

Learning objectives	Learning intentions	Success criteria
3Ld.01, 3Ld.04 3Sc.03, 3Sc.04 3Rd.02 3Wca.05 3Us.03	• **Listening:** Listen to a story; listen to instructions. • **Speaking:** Role play a conversation; discuss a puzzle; act out a dialogue. • **Reading:** Read and solve puzzles and logic problems. • **Writing:** Write information in a table. • **Language focus:** indirect pronouns: *her, him, them, me* • **Vocabulary:** *plates, cups and cutlery, skates, scooters, skipping ropes, kites, toy airplanes, bicycles*	• Learners can listen and understand a story. • Learners can role play a conversation. • Learners can read and solve puzzles and logic problems. • Learners can fill a table with information. • Learners can use logic to solve puzzles.

21st-century skills

Critical thinking opportunity: Use logic to solve puzzles.

Creative thinking: Respond to songs, rhymes and poems in a variety of ways; act out the roles of various characters in games and drama.

Communication: Share their thoughts with others to help further develop ideas and solve problems.

Materials: Learner's Book pages 116–117; Workbook pages 84–85; sticky notes (optional)

BACKGROUND KNOWLEDGE

Adjective order

In English, when more than one adjective is used, they follow a specific order:

quantity or number – quality or opinion – size – age – shape – colour – nationality – origin – material – purpose or qualifier.

It is extremely unusual to use so many adjectives before a noun. However, this order should be respected regardless the number of adjectives; for example:

My mother has bought six small green bowls.

I've just seen six big black and white swans in the river.

Common misconceptions

Misconception	How to identify	How to overcome
Learners sometimes forget to include the indirect pronoun, for example: *My father gave this present.* *Sam and David gave a camera.*	Write the incorrect sentences on the board. Ask the class, for example: *My father gave the present? Who did he give the present to?* Elicit the answer, i.e. me. Ask: *Does this sentence say it? Where should we put it?* Write the missing pronoun in colour.	Tell the class to ask the question, for example: *Who did (my father, Tom, Samira, etc.) give / send etc. … to ?* Check that they have included the corresponding indirect pronoun.
Learners sometimes forget to use the preposition before an indirect pronoun, for example: *My best friend Carla gave it.* *I can write him once a week.*	Write the incorrect sentences on the board. Ask the class, for example: *Who did Carla give it **to**? Did she give it **to** me, **to** Ahmed? You can't write a person. You write a letter or a message or a tweet but not a person. What's missing here? Did you write **to** him?* Elicit answers. Stress **to** in order to highlight its importance.	Tell the class to ask the question, for example: *Who did (my father, Ahmed, they, etc.) give / send / write etc. … **to**?* Check that they have included the corresponding preposition.

Starter ideas

What have you done? (10–15 minutes)

- If learners have done the homework activity from the previous lesson, ask them to read what their family has done to the class.

- Remind the class of the poem in Lesson 2. Ask volunteers to recite it.

- If learners have looked for information about Julie Larios and poems by her, ask them to share what they found out with the class. You may wish to collect the poems and display them on a noticeboard for learners to read again when they wish.

Main teaching ideas

1 Read and talk: A puzzle story (5–10 minutes)

- Remind learners of puzzles they discussed in Lesson 1.

- Tell the class that *Prince Henry's Party* is a puzzle story, and that there are three parts to the puzzle. They are going to listen, read clues, talk to a partner and solve the puzzle together.

- First, they are going to listen and meet the characters. They listen and point to the picture as they hear each character described. Play the recording twice.

> **Differentiation ideas:** With less confident learners, it may be useful to give them sticky notes and ask them to write the names of the characters. Then they stick the notes next to the correct picture.

Audioscript: Track 56

Learner's Book page 116

Prince Henry is having a lunch party. Do you see him? He is wearing a crown.

Prince Henry has invited five guests to his party:

- His cousin, Lady Emily. Lady Emily is also wearing a crown. Do you see her?

- Maya. She is Lady Emily's best friend. She is wearing a blue dress.

- Jack and Zack. They are twin brothers, and they are both good friends with Prince Henry. Do you see them?

- Nora. She is Jack and Zack's sister. She is wearing a yellow dress.

There is one more important character in this story. Mr. Rabbit. He is Prince Henry's servant and yes, he is a rabbit. Do you see him?

Part 1: At the table, and Part 2: What's missing? (10–20 minutes)

- **Part 1:** Focus on the instructions. Ask learners to work with a partner. They read the clues and talk about who is sitting where. Copy the seating diagram on the board. Learners copy it in their notebooks or on a sheet of paper to make the seating plan with names.

- Then ask the class to work in pairs and act out their own conversation. They use the questions and answers as models and the items listed in the book.

> **Differentiation ideas:** Less confident learners may find having a copy of the transcript helpful. They can also write their lines before attempting the role play. More confident learners may decide to use other items besides the ones listed and extend the conversation further. Ask more confident pairs to do the role play for the whole class. You may wish to invite more people as guests, not just pairs, to take part in the role play.

- When they have all finished, discuss the solutions as a class.

Answers

Part 1: top (from left to right): Jack, Prince Henry, Nora; bottom (from left to right): Zack, Lady Emily, Maya

Part 2: Prince Henry – plate, Nora – knife, Jack – napkin, Zack – spoon, Lady Emily – cup, Maya – spoon

2 Listen, write and talk: Part 3: Mr Rabbit, you've forgotten something, and Language focus (10–20 minutes)

- Tell the class to listen to Prince Henry giving instructions to Mr Rabbit and complete the text with the missing words.

- Review indirect pronouns as necessary before doing the activity. Look at the Language focus box with learners. With the class look at the Language focus examples.

> **Assessment ideas:** Look at the sentences in Activity 2 and ask: *Sentence 1 says 'Please, give it to her'. Who is her? Why do we use him in sentence 2? Can we use him in sentence 3? Why?* Do the same with all the sentences.

- Play the audio at least twice. Learners complete the sentences. Then check answers as a class.

Audioscript: Track 57

Learner's Book page 117

Prince Henry:	Mr Rabbit, you've forgotten one plate, one cup, one napkin, one knife and two spoons.
Mr Rabbit:	I am very sorry, Prince Henry. I'll get them right away.
Prince Henry:	Thank you, Mr Rabbit. Nora is missing a knife. Please give it to her.
Mr Rabbit:	Here you are, Nora.
Nora:	Thank you, Mr Rabbit.
Mr Rabbit:	That's OK.
Prince Henry:	Jack is missing a napkin. Please give it to him.
Mr Rabbit:	Here is your napkin, Jack.

Jack:	Thank you very much.
Prince Henry:	Maya and Zack are each missing a spoon. Please give the spoons to them.
Mr Rabbit:	Here you are, Maya and Zack. My apologies.
Maya and Zack:	*(in unison)* No problem, Mr Rabbit.
Prince Henry:	Lady Emily is missing a cup. Please give it to her.
Mr Rabbit:	Here is your cup, Lady Emily.
Lady Emily:	Thank you, Mr Rabbit.
Prince Henry:	And I am missing a plate. Please give it to me.
Mr Rabbit:	Here you are, Prince Henry. Would you like anything else?
Prince Henry:	Yes, please. We would like lunch! Please bring us the menu.

Answers

Nora is missing a *knife*. Please give it to *her*.
Jack is missing a *napkin*. Please give it to *him*.
Maya and Zack are each missing a *spoon*. Please give the spoons to *them*.
Lady Emily is missing a *cup*. Please give it to *her*.
And I am missing a *plate*. Please give it to *me*.

〉 **Digital Classroom:** Use the activity 'Lunch time' to reinforce the use of object pronouns. The i button will explain how to use the activity.

Plenary ideas

Consolidation (15–25 minutes)

- Ask learners to think what they would like to eat and drink at the party.

- Brainstorm words for food and drink and write them on the board. Supply additional vocabulary if necessary.

- Learners improvise a free role play. As a class, make up a menu, taking suggestions from the learners. Learners can choose to play characters from the Prince Henry puzzle or just to be themselves.

- Briefly review suitable expressions for asking for and offering things: *I would like … / Please can I have …? Would you like …? What would you like …?*

- The role play could include asking Mr Rabbit for things he has forgotten to bring, as in Activity 2, therefore giving further oral practice of indirect pronouns.

〉 **Differentiation ideas:** With less confident groups, you may write a skeleton dialogue on the board with the key functional language needs and ask learners to complete it with the menu choices they would like to order.

Homework ideas

- **Home–school link:** Learners may challenge the family to solve the puzzle.

- Learners write a few sentences about how well the family has solved the problem.

7.4 Write about it: Secret messages

LEARNING PLAN

Learning objectives	Learning intentions	Success criteria
3Ld.04	• **Listening:** Listen to an informative text about codes.	• Learners can listen and read an informative text about codes.
3Sc.06, 3Sc.07	• **Speaking:** Talk about secret codes.	• Learners can talk about secret codes.
3Rd.01	• **Reading:** Read an information text; read about secret codes; read and guess the meaning of unfamiliar words from context; read and decode messages.	• Learners can read and decode messages.
3Wca.04, 3Wor.01	• **Writing:** Write coded messages; write questions using question marks.	• Learners can write questions using question marks.
3Ug.01	• **Language focus:** *Wh-* questions	• Learners can write coded messages.
	• **Vocabulary:** *ancient, deliver, message, emperor, army, enemy*	

21st-century skills

Critical thinking opportunity: Understand how codes work; encode and decode messages.

Creative thinking: Actively participate in investigative, exploratory and open-ended tasks; engage in activities with fantasy or mystery elements.

Communication: Use simple connectors such as *and, but* or *because* to link groups of words.

Materials: Learner's Book pages 118–119; Workbook pages 86–87; large sheets of poster paper; writing and drawing materials; access to the internet or history books; Sample answer for Unit 7; **Photocopiable 37, 38**; **Differentiated worksheets 7A, B and C**

Starter ideas

Keep it secret! (5–15 minutes)

*   Ask the class: *Why might you want to send a secret message? How would you make sure nobody understands it except the person you are sending it to?* Elicit ideas.

*   Ask: *What is a code? What are codes used for?* Elicit ideas.

*   Ask the class if they have ever written a message using a code. What code did they use? If they haven't, write a code message on the board. Use one of the systems in the lesson.

*   Challenge learners to decode the message. If they can't, leave the message on the board until the end of the lesson.

Main teaching ideas

1 Read and listen (15–25 minutes)

*   Tell the class that they are going to read and listen about a famous code.

*   Focus on the picture and ask the class to predict what the connection is with the title.

*   Ask them who they think Caesar is. Elicit ideas.

- Play the recording and ask the class to follow in their books.

- Discuss any new vocabulary with the class, for example *understand, ancient, enemy, messenger* (note similarity to the word 'message'), *delivered, decode* (note root word 'code'; you may also add 'encode').

CROSS-CURRICULAR LINK

History

When learners have finished Activity 1, ask, for example: *Who was Caesar? Why did he write code messages? Who delivered the messages? Why didn't he use the telephone or a computer?* You may wish to have learners find out about Julius Caesar and Ancient Rome, for example when he lived, how far the Roman Empire stretched, the most important events of his rule, etc. Learners can work in groups and do some research. Then they can make a poster using the information and pictures

---

Audioscript: Track 58

Learner's Book page 118.

> **Digital Classroom:** Use the activity 'Caesar's code' to reinforce comprehension of the text and the use of verbs in the past tense. The i button will explain how to use the activity.

2 Write: Caesar's letter code (10–20 minutes)

- Read Caesar's code together. Ask the class to work in small groups and try to decode the message.

- Allow plenty of time for learners to do this.

- When they have decoded the message, they do what the message orders.

> **Critical thinking opportunity:** Ask groups to explain how the message was encoded.

- As an extension activity, you could ask groups of learners to write coded messages using Caesar's code. They exchange the messages with other groups and carry out the orders or read the message to the class.

Answers

The secret instruction decoded is 'Stand on your left leg'.

---

3 Write: Number grid code (10–20 minutes)

- Read the description of the number code together. Ask the class to work in small groups and try to decode the message.

- Allow plenty of time for learners to do this.

- When they have decoded the message, they do what the message orders.

- As an extension activity, you could ask groups to write coded messages using the number code. They exchange the messages with other groups and carry out the orders or read the message to the class.

Answers

Rub your tummy. Sing a song.

---

4 Write and do (5–10 minutes)

- Ask learners to write the three secret instructions from Activities 2 and 3 in order.

- Tell them to use the sequencing words at the beginning of the sentences: '*First, …*', '*Next, …*' and '*Then, …*'.

- Then they read the sentences and do the actions.

Answers

First, stand on your left leg. Next, rub your tummy. Then, sing a song.

---

5 Write a message to your partner (10–20 minutes)

- Distribute **Photocopiable 37**. Ask learners to write a question using the code they like most and beginning with one of the question words.

- Remind them to use a question mark at the end.

- When they have finished writing their question, learners give the coded message to their partner and answer each other's question using the code they like best.

- Collect all the coded messages and make a class display, or ask learners to upload the messages to the class blog.

- See **Sample answer for Unit 7** for an example answer to this writing task.

Answers

Learner's own answers.

> **Workbook**
>
> Learners do Activities 1–4 on pages 86–87.

Plenary ideas

Consolidation (20–40 minutes)

- Remind learners of the code message you wrote on the board at the beginning of the lesson. Which code did you use? Can they decode it now after what they have learned? Challenge learners to decode the message.

- Ask learners to create their own secret code. Ask the class to imagine they are spies. Divide the class into small groups. Each group designs a code to send messages to group members.

- Enemy spies try to discover how the codes work and decode the messages.

> **Assessment ideas:** As a class, learners discuss which code they found the most difficult and which they found the most fun. Encourage them to explain why. Then ask them to write their opinions in their learning log using their favourite code.

Homework ideas

- Give learners a list of suitable websites or books they can find in the school library. Learners look for information about famous codes, such as Morse code, sliding scale or cryptograph. They write a few sentences and explain how they work on the following day.

- **Home–school link:** Distribute copies of **Photocopiable 38**. Learners challenge their family to decode messages.

- Hand out copies of **Differentiated worksheets 7A, B and C** depending on each learner's ability, and ask them to complete the activities at home.

7.5 Read and respond: *A fair solution*

LEARNING PLAN

Learning objectives	Learning intentions	Success criteria
3Ld.04 3So.01, 3Sor.02 3Rd.03	• **Listening:** Listen to a traditional tale. • **Speaking:** Discuss a story; act out a story; talk about fair and unfair situations; discuss problems and find solutions. • **Reading:** Read a traditional tale; use context clues to guess the meaning of unfamiliar words. • **Language focus:** Revision • **Vocabulary:** *expensive, delicious, hungry, tired, owner, yell, enjoy, demand, judge, clever, wise, sadly, coins, jingle*	• Learners can listen to and read a traditional tale. • Learners can discuss a traditional tale. • Learners can talk about fair and unfair situations. • Learners can discuss problems and find solutions. • Learners can use context clues to guess the meaning of unfamiliar words.

21st-century skills

Critical thinking opportunity: Infer characters' feelings.

Creative thinking: Act out the roles of various characters in games and drama.

Values: Learn about conflict resolution; learn about finding a fair solution.

Materials: Learner's Book pages 120–123; Workbook pages 88–89; map of the world; large sheet of paper; sticky notes

Starter ideas

Yummy food! (5–10 minutes)

• Remind the class of Prince Henry's party in Lesson 3. Ask them what food they would like to eat in that party. Help with vocabulary if necessary.

• Ask them what their favourite food is, and where they can buy the food they like.

• Elicit a few words for shops.

Reading tip (10–15 minutes)

• Read the text as a class.

• Pre-teach the concepts *problem* and *solution*. Ask learners if they have read a story about a problem. What was the solution to the problem?

• Also check understanding of *fair* and *unfair*. Elicit ideas of fair and unfair situations.

Main teaching ideas

1 Talk about it (5–10 minutes)

• Ask the class if they have ever been to a shop that has a delicious smell. Ask them about the shop, what it sold, etc.

• Add vocabulary as necessary.

2 Listen and read along (10–15 minutes)

• Tell learners that they are going to listen to and read a story. Ask them to look at the pictures and predict what the story is going to be about. Elicit ideas from the class.

• Play the audio at least twice. Ask the class if their ideas were correct.

Audioscript: Track 59

See Learner's Book page 120–122.

3 Talk (15–25 minutes)

- Learners read and answer the questions with a partner. They read the story again to find the answers. Then they get together with another pair and compare their answers and discuss any differences.

- Have an open class discussion of the answers.

- **Values:** Encourage learners to consider whether Nasreddin's solution was fair. What would they have done in the same situation? What is their opinion of the rich man? Was it fair to ask for money? Elicit opinions.

> **Differentiation ideas:** Less confident groups may write down their answers before discussing them with another pair and with the class. This will help them feel more confident at the moment of speaking. More confident learners could make a summary of the ideas put forward by the class.

Answers

a   The poor man, the rich restaurant owner and the judge (Nasreddin)
b   He smelled the food from the restaurant and imagined he was eating a delicious meal.
c   He said the poor man had to pay for the smell of the food.
d   Learner's own answers.
e   He shook the bag next to the rich man's ear and gave the money back to the poor man.
f   smell, sound, fair
g   Learner's own answers.
h   Learner's own answers.

> **Digital Classroom:** Use the activity 'A fair solution' to reinforce comprehension of the text. The i button will explain how to use the activity.

4 Vocabulary (10–15 minutes)

- Ask the class to look at the sentences. Focus on the words in blue and ask learners to find them in the text.

- Working individually, learners read the options and choose the best one. Then check answers as a class.

- Ask learners to re-read the story and underline any other unfamiliar words. Can they work out the meaning using the context? Encourage them to explain the meaning in their own words.

> **Critical thinking opportunity:** Ask the class to find more words that describe food, for example *lovely, wonderful*. Write the words on the board. Ask learners to add more words they can use. Can they find two words that describe Nasreddin? What do these words mean? Are they positive or negative words? Elicit answers (for example: he is clever and wise; he is intelligent and makes sensible/good decisions; they are positive words).

> **Assessment ideas:** Ask learners how easy or difficult the text is. What makes it difficult? What can they do to overcome the difficulties? (for example, look for words in a dictionary)

Answers
1a, 2b, 3a, 4b, 5b, 6a

5 Act it out! (25–40 minutes)

- Ask the class to work in groups of three. They read the story again and act it out.

- When groups feel confident enough, ask volunteers to act it out for the class. You could bring in some props for groups to use.

6 Values: Finding a fair solution (15–25 minutes)

- You could do this activity as a Think-Pair-Share activity. Individually, learners read each problem and reflect on the solutions. They can make notes of their ideas. Encourage them to justify their opinions.

- Learners pair up with a partner and discuss their opinions.

- After a few minutes, ask pairs to work with another pair, compare answers and discuss differences. Supply additional vocabulary as necessary.

- Finally, you could ask groups to appoint a spokesperson and share their ideas with the rest of the class.

Answers
Suggested answers:
a   Give half a biscuit to each child.
b   They could play with the ball together.
c   They could take turns: Leyla could work for half an hour then Osman could practise for half an hour. Leyla could wear ear plugs! Osman could go to another part of the house, far away from Leyla.

> **Workbook**
>
> Learners do Activities 1–4 on pages 88–89.
>
> You might want to use Activities 1 and 2 as extension material as they are beyond the requirements of the Cambridge Primary English as a Second Language curriculum framework.

> **Digital Classroom:** Use the slideshow and activity sheet 'Nasreddin and his fine coat' to tell another Nasreddin story. The i button will explain how to use the slideshow and activity sheet.

Plenary ideas

Reflection (10–20 minutes)

> **Assessment ideas:** Write the following on the board: *Today I learned that …; One thing I must remember is* … . Ask learners to copy and complete these sentence starters in their learning log.

Alternatively, give learners sticky notes and have them write their reflections there.

When they have finished, ask volunteers to share them with the class.

If they have used sticky notes, ask them to put them up on a large sheet of paper. Give the collated notes a title, for example *Today's reflections*, and keep it on display.

Homework ideas

- Learners look for information about Nasreddin and his stories in books or selected websites. They choose one and tell it to the class. What values does the story illustrate?

- **Home–school link:** Learners read the story to their family and discuss the questions together.

7.6 Project challenge

LEARNING PLAN

Learning objectives	Learning intentions	Success criteria
3Sc.05	• **Speaking:** Discuss a project; discuss steps of a project; organise work; present their project to the class.	• Learners can read and understand instructions.
3Rd.02	• **Reading:** Read and understand instructions; read and decode messages.	• Learners can give instructions. • Learners can plan a project.
3Wca.02, 3Wca.03, 3Wca.04, 3Wc.01	• **Writing:** Write sentences; write coded messages; write a questionnaire.	• Learners can write coded messages.
	• **Language focus:** Unit 7 review	• Learners can write a questionnaire about experiences.
	• **Vocabulary:** Unit 7 review	

21st-century skills

Creative thinking: Design new items based on a model.

Collaboration: Respect the importance of doing a fair share of group work; keep to the instructions to complete the task; invite others to give their opinions during the task.

Learning to learn: Listen and respond positively to feedback and understand why a correction was given; learn from mistakes and feedback.

Materials: Learner's Book pages 124–125; Workbook pages 90–91; Project A: writing supplies, sheets of paper; Project B: writing supplies, sheets of paper; **Photocopiable 39, 40**; End of Unit 7 test

Starter ideas

Looking back (5–10 minutes)

> **Assessment ideas:** Ask the class to choose the lesson they liked most in Unit 7, and to explain why. Ask: *What was the most difficult thing in this unit? Do you feel you have done well? What would you say is your strongest point? And your weakest?*

Main teaching ideas

Learners choose an end-of-unit project to work on. Look at the examples in the pictures and help learners to choose. Provide materials.

Project A: Write a secret message (45–90 minutes)

- Go through the instructions in the Learner's Book and clarify any doubts.

- **Step 1:** Distribute copies of **Photocopiable 39**. Ask learners to work in pairs or groups of three. Have them make up a new secret code. Tell them to get ideas from Caesar's letter code and the number grid code on pages 118–119. They can also create a symbol or simple drawing to represent each letter of the alphabet.

- **Step 2:** Learners think of three instructions using the new code. To do this, they can look at the Action verbs in the Picture dictionary (page 171).

- **Step 3:** Learners write the instructions using the new code. They check each other's work and see that the code works well.

- **Step 4:** When they have finished, they exchange photocopiables with another group of learners. Each group now uses the secret code grid they've received to decode the instructions and do the actions.

Project B: Write a questionnaire – 'Have you ever …?' (45–90 minutes)

- Ask learners to write a questionnaire, beginning as shown in the Learner's Book. Then they add four more items. Tell them to look at the list of irregular verbs on pages 172–173 for help.

- While they are compiling their questions, it may be worth pointing out that the questions should be realistic; for example, nobody will answer *yes* to a question such as: *Have you ever been to the Moon?*

- When they have finished, ask them to make a copy for each member of the group. Group members then circulate with their copy. They ask a classmate the first question. If they get a negative answer, they ask the next question. When they get a positive answer, they write the name on the line next to that item, and move on to find a new classmate to ask.

- Learners should try to get a name for every item on the questionnaire.

- When they have filled in the questionnaire, learners compare the answers with the group and take turns writing sentences about the classmates who have done each thing.

- Groups share the results with the class.

> **Assessment ideas:** When learners have finished their projects, give them a copy of **Photocopiable 40** and read the information as a class. Ask them to work independently and think about their work on their project. They reflect and answer the questions, ticking off the aims they have achieved. Insist on the importance of giving honest answers.

> **Workbook**
>
> Learners do the Check your progress quiz on pages 90–91.

Plenary ideas

Reflect on your learning (5–10 minutes)

- Draw learners' attention to the 'Reflect on your learning' questions in the Learner's Book.

- Learners answer the questions to reflect on their project work.

Consolidation (10–15 minutes)

- Ask learners to reflect on and discuss what they liked most about this unit, and encourage them to explain why. This may also be a good opportunity for them to think about what aspects of the unit they have found most difficult and why. You may wish to keep a record of their comments to see how they progress over time.

> **Assessment ideas: Portfolio opportunity:** If you have been filing learners' work for Unit 7, you may find it useful to put all the work of this unit together. You could ask learners to make a cover for their Unit 7 work, decorating it with an image that represents what they have learned.

Homework ideas

- Learners draw a picture of what they have liked most about this unit.

- **Home–school link:** Learners show their family their projects.

7.7 What do you know now?

What kind of puzzles can we solve? (30–40 minutes)

- Learners work in pairs. They work together through all the questions set in this section.

- They write the answers in their notebooks. You may ask them to have a special section in their notebooks where they record the answers.

Answers

Suggested answers:

1–3 Learner's own answers.

4 *it, her, give it to them*

Look what I can do! (15 minutes)

- Review the *I can* … statements on page 126 of the Learner's Book. Learners demonstrate what they can do.

- Learners colour in the faces to show which things they can do.

- Encourage them to be honest in their answers.

> **Workbook**
>
> Learners answer the Reflection questions on page 91.

> 8 My amazing body

Unit plan

Lesson	Approximate number of learning hours	Outline of learning content	Learning objectives	Resources
1 Inside our body	1.5–2.25	Identify parts of the human body.	3Ld.01 3Sc.02 3So.01 3Rd.01 3Wca.05 3Ug.02	Learner's Book Lesson 8.1 Workbook Lesson 8.1 ⬇ Photocopiable 3 ⬇ Photocopiable 41 ⬇ Photocopiable 42 **Digital Classroom:** Video – Exercise is good for you!; Activity – The body; Slideshow and activity sheet – Look inside a snake, a mouse and you!
2 Staying healthy	1.25–2.0	Learn about healthy eating and feeling unwell.	3Ld.02 3Ld.03 3Sor.02 3Wca.03 3Ug.07 3Us.02	Learner's Book Lesson 8.2 Workbook Lesson 8.2 ⬇ Photocopiable 3 **Digital Classroom:** Activity – It hurts
3 Healthy habits	1.5– 2.75	Talk about ways to take care of our bodies.	3Ld.04 3Sc.06 3Sc.07 3So.01 3Rd.02 3Rd.03 3Wca.04 3Wca.05 3Ug.07	Learner's Book Lesson 8.3 Workbook Lesson 8.3 ⬇ Photocopiable 3 ⬇ Photocopiable 43 **Digital Classroom:** Activity – Before or after?
4 A happy, healthy week	1.0–1.5	Write a plan for having a happy, healthy week.	3Ld.04 3Sc.07 3So.01 3Rd.02 3Wca.02 3Wca.03 3Wor.01 3Wor.02 3Ug.07	Learner's Book Lesson 8.4 Workbook Lesson 8.4 ⬇ Sample answer for Unit 8 ⬇ Photocopiable 1 ⬇ Photocopiable 44 ⬇ Differentiated worksheets 8A, B and C **Digital Classroom:** Grammar presentation – Will and won't

(continued)

Lesson	Approximate number of learning hours	Outline of learning content	Learning objectives	Resources
5 Taste, smell and your brain	1.75–3.0	Read about our tongue, nose and brain.	3Ld.04 3Lo.01 3Sc.01 3So.01 3Sor.02 3Rd.01 3Wca.04 3Wca.05	Learner's Book Lesson 8.5 Workbook Lesson 8.5 ⬇ Photocopiable 3 **Digital Classroom:** Activity – Taste and smell
6 Project challenge	1.5–2.5	Write a quiz or a book.	3Sc.04 3Sc.05 3Sc.06 3Rd.02 3Wca.04 3Wca.05	Learner's Book Lesson 8.6 Workbook Lesson 8.6 ⬇ Photocopiable 3 ⬇ Photocopiable 45
7 What do you know now?	0.75–1.0	Self-assessment and reflection.		Learner's Book Lesson 8.7

Cross-unit resources

 Unit 8 Audioscripts

 End of Unit 8 test

 Unit 8 Progress report

 Unit 8 Wordlist

BACKGROUND KNOWLEDGE

Proteins

In Lesson 8.3, learners read about proteins.

Proteins are nutrients that help to maintain body cells and tissues such as bones, skin and hair, etc. The two main sources of protein are animal products, for example meat, eggs and milk, and plant products such as nuts, soy and legumes.

Taste buds and the tongue

In Lesson 8.5, learners learn about how they taste foods using taste buds on their tongues, and that different areas of the tongue are sensitive to certain tastes.

In theory, there are areas of the tongue that are sensitive to four of the five tastes. In practice, however, many people taste sugar as equally sweet at the base area of the tongue and at the tip. For more information, you may wish to read the article 'The Taste Map of the Tongue You Learned in School Is All Wrong' in the online Smithsonian Magazine.

TEACHING SKILLS FOCUS

Skills for life

Skills for life (or life skills) are skills that we need in order to deal effectively with problems and issues we face in our everyday life. Training learners in life skills from an early age helps them to develop their self-confidence, their ability to deal with changes and challenges, as well as an understanding of their responsibilities as members of society.

These life skills include creativity, critical thinking, problem solving, decision making, communicating effectively, collaborating with others towards a common goal and social responsibility.

Critical thinking

There are many definitions of critical thinking, but in essence it is the ability to use our mind to achieve a goal by considering a particular issue from various perspectives, assessing and challenging assumptions, and exploring possible alternatives.

A critical thinker is someone who can:

- solve problems
- look for evidence and analyse it
- evaluate information
- make informed decisions
- formulate inferences
- try out and test new ideas.

Therefore, we should provide opportunities for learners to:

- engage in in-depth group discussions
- question their thinking processes
- evaluate their progress
- ask questions regularly
- reflect on their thinking
- do class projects that engage them in analysis, synthesis and evaluation
- consider different opinions and to justify their own.

Your challenge

One way to help learners develop critical thinking skills is by asking higher-order questions; these will engage them in applying, analysing, synthesising and evaluating information rather than just recalling facts. Use the following types of questions to help learners begin to develop critical thinking:

- Clarification questions, for example: *Why do you say that? What do we already know about this?*

- Questions that challenge assumptions, for example: *What else could we assume? You seem to be assuming ...*

- Questions that challenge evidence, for example: *Do you have an example of this? Why does this happen? Why is that happening? How do you know this? Show me ...*

- Opinion questions, for example: *How are ... and ... similar? What is another way to look at it? What alternative ways of looking at this are there? Why is ... necessary?*

- Questions about implications and consequences, for example: *What are the consequences of that? Then what would happen? What are the consequences of that assumption?*

- Questions about a question, for example: *Why do you think I asked this question? What else might I ask? What does ... mean?*

Opportunities to introduce critical thinking strategies are highlighted in each unit of the Learner's Book. Look through Unit 8 and highlight opportunities for introducing the techniques and questions above. Then think about the techniques that you could introduce, and how you can adapt them to your learners' abilities and level.

Reflection

How have learners responded to these critical thinking opportunities? What scaffolding is needed, if any? How else can you promote critical thinking in your lessons?

8.1 Think about it: Inside our body

LEARNING PLAN

Learning objectives	Learning intentions	Success criteria
3Ld.01	• **Listening:** Listen to a song; listen to body facts; listen to and follow instructions.	• Learners can talk about parts of the body.
3Sc.02, 3So.01	• **Speaking:** Speak about our body; sing a song about our body; practise topic vocabulary; speak about bones and muscles; talk about experiments; perform experiments on how exercise affects your heartbeat and breathing.	• Learners can listen to and understand a conversation about parts of the body. • Learners can sing a song about the body.
3Rd.01	• **Reading:** Use context clues to guess word meaning; read about bones and muscles; read and follow instructions.	• Learners can read and understand a set of instructions for an experiment.
3Wca.05	• **Writing:** Write facts about the heart and lungs; use correct spelling and punctuation.	• Learners can carry out an experiment and draw conclusions.
3Ug.02	• **Language focus:** imperatives • **Vocabulary:** parts of the human body: *body, skin, heart, lungs, bones, backbone, bend, twist, skull, brain, ribs, muscles, upper arm, pulse, breathe, breathing, apart, together*	

21st-century skills

Critical thinking opportunity: Conduct experiments and evaluate findings.

Collaboration: Take part in tasks by interacting with others and stay on task; communicate own knowledge of a topic.

Communication: Try to use alternative words or expressions if they are not understood; ask for clarification when they have difficulties in understanding what others have said.

Materials: Learner's Book pages 127–129; Workbook pages 92–93; large sheet of poster paper; pictures or photos of the human body, including images of a human skeleton, the muscular system and the organs; watch or clock with a second hand; **Photocopiable 3, 41, 42**

Starter ideas

> **Digital Classroom:** Use the video 'Exercise is good for you!' to introduce the topic of exercise and some of the exercise vocabulary in the unit. The i button will explain how to use the video.

Getting started (15–20 minutes)

- Ask the class if they do exercise. What sports do they do? Do they feel well after doing exercise? Discuss with the class why they think it is good (and necessary) to do sports.

- Focus on the picture on page 127 of the Learner's Book and ask learners what they see. Elicit ideas, for example children playing outdoors and doing exercise.

- Discuss with the class what they do to take care of their bodies. What are some good rules for staying healthy? How can we make our bodies stronger?

As a class, encourage learners to speak about the importance of being clean, eating well and sleeping at least eight hours a night, etc.

- Ask learners to work in small groups. Give them a copy of **Photocopiable 3**: K-W-L chart. Ask learners to write their ideas from the discussion in the *K (Know)* column: what they know (or they think they know) about healthy eating, a healthy lifestyle, etc. Then ask what they would like to know more about. They write this in the form of questions in the *W (Would like to know)* column. Tell them that they will go back to the table at the end of each lesson and write what they have learned in the *L (Learned)* column.

Answers
Learner's own answers.

Sing along! *Bones and muscles* (15–20 minutes)

- Tell the class you are going to listen to a songs. Give each learner a copy of **Photocopiable 41**: Sing along! *Bones and muscles*.

- Play the song at least twice. Ask the class what the song is about. Elicit answers.

- Sing the song and encourage learners to join in.

> **Differentiation ideas:** You could ask more confident learners to identify key science vocabulary, such as parts of the body. You may give less confident learners copies of the lyrics so that they can follow more easily.

CROSS-CURRICULAR LINK

Science

Revise the parts of the body with the class. Display a picture or a photo of the human body, and ask the class to identify parts of the body. Ask learners to identify the parts of the body mentioned in the song, for example *foot, ankle, shin, knee, thigh, hip, back, head, neck, shoulder*. If possible, display a picture of the human skeleton and identify the bones mentioned in the song. Tell the class to listen and touch the part of their body as you say it, for example *Touch your hip / neck*, etc.

Audioscript: Track 60

Learner's Book page 127

Bones and muscles

Chorus: Bones and muscles, and more bones.
Bones and muscles, and more bones.
Bones and muscles, and more bones.
Together, they help us move.

Verse: Well, the foot bone's connected to the ankle bone,
And the ankle bone's connected to the shin bone.
The shin bone's connected to the knee bone.
Together, they help us move.

Chorus: Bones and muscles, and more bones.
Bones and muscles, and more bones.
Bones and muscles, and more bones.
Together, they help us move.

Verse: Well, the knee bone's connected to the thigh bone,
And the thigh bone's connected to the hip bone.
The hip bone's connected to the back bone.
Together, they help us move.

Chorus: Bones and muscles, and more bones.
Bones and muscles, and more bones.
Bones and muscles, and more bones.
Together, they help us move.

Verse: Well, the back bone's connected to the shoulder bone,
And the shoulder bone's connected to the neck bone.
The neck bone's connected to the head bone.
Together, they help us move.

Chorus: Bones and muscles, and more bones.
Bones and muscles, and more bones.
Bones and muscles, and more bones.
Together, they help us move.

Main teaching ideas

1 Talk. What is inside our body, under our skin? (10–15 minutes)

- Ask the class what they think we have inside our bodies. Learners may mention the heart, blood, lungs, etc., for which you may need to supply and write the words in English. Ask learners what *skin* is and elicit an explanation. Help with additional vocabulary as necessary.

- It would also be useful to pre-teach or check learners' understanding of *breathe* and *breath*, as well as *fist*.
- Ask learners to turn to pages 128–129 of their Learner's Book. Focus on the pictures and the labels. Can they find the parts of the body they named?

Answers
Learner's own answers.

2 Listen and follow the instructions (5–10 minutes)

- Explain to the class that they are going to listen to a doctor speaking. Tell them to listen and put their hand up when they hear the words listed in the activity.
- Play the audio once. Stop when the class identifies the words.
- Ask learners to discuss the meaning of these words with a partner, and then as a class.
- Listen to the audio again as a class and follow the instructions.
- Play the audio at least twice.

Audioscript: Track 61

Learner's Book page 128

Hello. My name is Doctor Monroe. Today we're having a look inside the human body to learn about how our body works. Listen. *[Sound of a beating heart as heard through a stethoscope]*

What do you think that is? That's a heartbeat. Your heart beats day and night. It never, ever stops. You're not thinking about it but your heart is always working.

Your heart beats about 80 times every minute. When you run around and do exercise, it beats faster, like this. Whew! *[Sound of a noticeably faster heartbeat, as heard through a stethoscope]*

Your heart pumps blood all around your body through blood vessels. Look at the inside of your wrist. Do you see little blue lines there? Those are blood vessels. The blood in your blood vessels carries oxygen from the air you breathe and nourishment from the food you eat to all the cells in your body.

Now, take some deep breaths, like this. *[Doctor demonstrates taking a few deep breaths in and out]* When you breathe in, you fill your lungs with air. Your lungs are like two bags that get bigger when they fill with air. Air has oxygen in it. The blood vessels in the lungs pick up that oxygen. Your heart pumps the blood with oxygen to all parts of your body.

You breathe all the time – you breathe when you're awake and you breathe when you're asleep. When you run around and do exercise, you breathe faster, like this! *[Sound of doctor breathing harder and faster after running]*

Put your hand in a fist. Your heart is about the size of your fist. That's not very big, but your heart is a very important part of your body. You can take good care of your heart by eating good food, getting plenty of exercise and plenty of sleep.

3 Listen and write. (10–15 minutes)

- Play the audio again and ask the class to write two facts they have learned about the heart and the lungs.
- Then they share their facts with the class. Show a photo or picture of the human organs and identify the heart and the lungs. Can the class identify other organs? What do they do?

> **Differentiation ideas:** You may need to share the audio transcript with less confident groups, as the text is rich in new vocabulary. Have learners listen to the recording again while they read the script. Ask learners to underline or circle unfamiliar words and then discuss their meaning as a class.

CROSS-CURRICULAR LINK

Science

You may wish to gloss over the information about blood vessels in the audio or expand upon it, by talking about how blood 'vessels' (like long tunnels) carry the blood to every part of the body. You could point out to learners that some blood vessels are large and others are very small, and that you can see them in some parts of the body, for example as blue lines at the wrist.

Answers
Learner's own answers.

4 Vocabulary: Parts of the body (10–20 minutes)

- Ask the class to look at the picture of the skeleton.
- Tell them to read the labels around the picture and point to that part on their own body.
- Then ask them to read and listen to the recording. Play the audio at least twice. Then hand out copies of **Photocopiable 42** and help learners to make their own skeletons.

CROSS-CURRICULAR LINK

Science

You could ask the class to count the number of ribs they have, the number of bones that make up their arms and legs, or the number of vertebrae that make up the backbone.

You could also ask learners to find out some interesting 'bone and muscle facts'. Give them some questions in the form of a quiz and have them work in groups and find the answers. For example, you could ask:

- *Which is the strongest / the longest bone in out body?* (the femur)
- *Which is the smallest bone?* (the stapes – one of the ear bones)
- *Which bone isn't connected with any other bone?* (the hyoid – a bone in our throat that holds the tongue in its place)
- *Which is the biggest joint?* (the knee, because three bones connect there)
- *How many muscles do we have?* (600)
- *Which is the largest muscle?* (the gluteus)
- *Which is the smallest muscle?* (the muscles in our inner ear)
- *Which is the strongest muscle?* (the masseter – in our jaw)
- *Which muscle works the hardest?* (the heart)

Audioscript: Track 62
See Learner's Book page 129

⟩ **Digital Classroom:** Use the activity 'The body' to revise vocabulary for parts of the body. The i button will explain how to use the activity.

5 Let's do it! (10–20 minutes)

- Focus on the instructions. Read them with the class as you model the actions.
- Ask learners to read the instructions again and to feel their pulse.
- Learners will need help finding their pulse. Some may be able to find it on their wrist: direct them to lay their second and third finger (not thumb) of one hand against the inside of the wrist of the other hand below the thumb. Some learners will it easier to find a pulse on the neck: direct them to place two fingers on the neck below the ear. Failing both methods, they could simply count their heartbeats with one hand on their chest.
- You will need a stopwatch (or watch/clock with a second hand). Make sure all learners have found a beat then say 'Go' and 'Stop' to time 15 seconds.
- Ask learners to write down the number of heartbeats they feel. Then they do the jumping jacks.
- They take their pulse again and compare the results.

⟩ **Critical thinking opportunity:** Discuss the results of the experiment. Encourage learners to compare their heartbeat before and after exercise, i.e. it beats more quickly after exercise.

CROSS-CURRICULAR LINK

PE

You may wish to invite the PE teacher to the class and have them explain how exercise changes the number of heartbeats and the breathing. The teacher could explain to learners how to improve their stamina, for example by doing aerobic exercise, and the importance of warming up before doing exercise and of cooling down and stretching properly after exercise.

Workbook

Learners do Activities 1–5 on pages 92–93.

> **Digital Classroom:** Use the slideshow and activity sheet 'Look inside a snake, a mouse and you!' to revise internal body parts and compare the human body with the bodies of a snake and a mouse. The i button will explain how to use the slideshow and activity sheet.

Plenary ideas

Consolidation (10–20 minutes)

*   As a class, make a chart with the names of the learners on a large sheet of paper, which records the number of beats they felt when taking their pulse.

*   Divide the class into two groups. They take it in turns to give a definition, for example: *They protect your heart and lungs*, and say the corresponding

body part: *The ribs*. The group that cannot come up with the correct answer misses a turn.

> **Assessment ideas:** Ask learners to get their KWL charts **(Photocopiable 3)** and read the questions they wrote in the *W (Would like to know)* column. Have they found answers to any of the questions? Ask learners to write the new information in the *L (Learned)* column.

Homework ideas

*   Learners look for information about how to look after our bones. They write a few lines about this to share with the class on the following day.

*   **Home–school link:** Learners tell their family about the bones and muscles in their bodies.

8.2 Health: Staying healthy

LEARNING PLAN		
Learning objectives	**Learning intentions**	**Success criteria**
3Ld.02, 3Ld.03	• **Listening:** Listen to conversations about buying fruit; listen to conversations about feeling unwell.	• Learners can listen and understand conversations about buying fruit and feeling unwell.
3Sor.02	• **Speaking:** Speak about healthy habits; speak about vitamins and fruit; speak about health problems; act out conversations.	• Learners can speak about healthy habits.
3Wca.03	• **Writing:** Write missing words in gap text.	• Learners can speak about minor injuries and aches and first aid.
3Ug.07, 3Us.02	• **Language focus:** demonstrative pronouns: *this/that; these/those. Shall I …?*	
	• **Vocabulary:** *healthy, strong, feel ill, hurt oneself, hurt, head, tummy, ear, throat, finger, thumb, hit, knee, elbow, arm, plaster, ice pack, pill, bill. Fruits: kiwi, kumquat, kebab, banana, mango, pear, pineapple*	• Learners can role play going shopping. • Learners can role play reporting and responding to injuries and aches.

21st-century skills

Critical thinking opportunity: Suggest possible reasons for problems.

Creative thinking: Act out the roles of various characters in games and drama; actively participate in investigative, exploratory and open-ended tasks.

Communication: Use simple techniques to start, maintain and close conversations of various lengths.

Materials: Learner's Book pages 130–131; Workbook pages 94–95; large sheets of paper; large sheet of poster paper; red, orange, yellow, green, blue, purple markers or pencils; **Photocopiable 3**

Starter ideas

Healthy food (5–10 minutes)

*   Remind learners of the importance of doing exercise regularly, as discussed in Lesson 8.1. Ask them what other things help to keep their body healthy and strong. Elicit ideas, for example eating healthy food, drinking plenty of water, having plenty of sleep, etc.

*   Ask learners what they like eating and drinking, and what they usually eat and drink every day or during the week. How healthy is the food they eat? Do they eat vegetables and fruit? What is their favourite fruit? And their favourite vegetable? Elicit ideas. Provide words for vegetables and fruit as necessary.

Main teaching ideas

1   Fruit is good for you! (10–15 minutes)

*   Read about the vitamins in fruit with the class. Then ask learners to work in groups and name a fruit that is each colour of the rainbow.

    > **Differentiation ideas:** Some learners may not know the names in English for certain fruits, so accept some use of L1 and give the equivalents in English. More confident learners could come up with more than one fruit for each colour.

*   On a large sheet of poster paper, draw a rainbow with red, orange, yellow, green, blue and purple sections. Ask groups to come to the board and write their fruit names in the corresponding colour section.

CROSS-CURRICULAR LINK

Health and nutrition

Ask the class what comes to mind when they hear the word *vitamin*. Elicit ideas and encourage learners to explain what vitamins are, i.e. they are found in the foods we eat; they are necessary for our body to function in a healthy way: they help us to grow, see well, they form our bones, muscles, skin and organs, and they help us to fight infection.

Ask learners to work in groups to find out more about vitamins – e.g. the main vitamin groups, what each group does and where each vitamin is found, etc. You could encourage them to visit age-appropriate websites such as Healthy Kids. Give each group a large sheet of paper and have them make a table with their findings, e.g. Vitamin group: *Vitamin A*; What it does: *Keeps eyes, skin, teeth and bones healthy*; Where it is found: *Yellow and orange foods.*

Answers
Learner's own answers.

---

2   Listen, write and talk (5–10 minutes)

*   Focus on the pictures and ask the class to name the fruits they see. Ask: *Do you like them?*

*   Tell the class they are going to listen to a sister and brother buying fruit in a market. The class listen and fill in the missing words of the conversation.

*   Play the recording once and ask learners to just listen. Then play it again and have learners complete the conversation.

*   Check answers as a class.

    > **Differentiation ideas:** You could ask more confident groups to predict what words are missing before listening to the conversation. Once they have completed the conversation, less confident learners could work in groups of three and role play the conversation for additional reading aloud practice.

Audioscript: Track 63

Learner's Book page 130

Brother:	Excuse me. What is this?
Fruit seller:	This is a kiwi. It's green inside and very good.
Brother:	And what are these?
Fruit seller:	These are kumquats. They're like little oranges. You can eat the skin.
Sister:	What's that? (*pointing to customer walking away, drinking a juice drink*)

Fruit seller:	That is a fresh juice drink and those *(pointing at fruit kebabs)* are fresh fruit kebabs. You can drink your fruit or you can eat it.
Sister:	*(pointing at fruit kebabs)* I want one of those, please.
Brother:	And I want a box of these.
Fruit seller:	Here you are – one fresh fruit kebab and a box of kumquats.
Sister and brother:	Thank you!

Answers

Brother: Excuse _me_. What is this?

Fruit seller: _This_ is a kiwi. It's green inside and very good.

Brother: And what are _these_?

Fruit seller: These _are_ kumquats. They're like little oranges. You can eat the skin.

Sister: What's _that_?

Fruit seller: That _is_ a fresh juice drink and _those_ are fresh fruit kebabs. You can drink your fruit or you can eat it.

Sister: I want one of those, _please_.

Brother: And I want a box of _these_.

Fruit seller: Here you are – one fresh fruit kebab and a box of kumquats.

Sister and brother: Thank you!

Language detective: *this* and *these* (5–10 minutes)

- Focus on the explanation of *this* and *these* and supply more examples.
- Ask learners to give examples of their own.
- Then ask the class: *We use **these** and **this** for things that are near us. What do we use for things that are not near?* (*that* and *those*) Elicit the answer and have learners complete the rule.
- Then ask them to give some examples.

3 Listen: What's the matter? (15–25 minutes)

- Ask the class if they have been ill or have hurt themselves recently. What happened? Elicit ideas and help with vocabulary.

- Tell the class they are going to listen to some children. Focus on the pictures. Ask: *What do you think they are going to talk about?* Elicit some ideas.
- Play the audio at least twice.
- Allow plenty of time for learners to discuss the questions. Ask: *What words helped you to find the answers?*

> **Differentiation ideas:** You may consider asking less confident learners to work in pairs. You can also share the transcript with them after they have tried to answer the questions, so that they can check the answers and discuss any new vocabulary.

> **Critical thinking opportunity:** Ask the class if they would have helped in the same way. Do they have other ideas? Discuss suitable ways of treating each complaint. Learners may have other suggestions, and local remedies may be different from those suggested here.

CROSS-CURRICULAR LINK

Health

Ask learners why it is necessary to clean a wound. You may elicit the word *germ*. Ask learners to look for information about how the body heals a wound and what we should do to treat it. You could visit age-appropriate websites such as Curious Kids. You could also invite a nurse or a doctor to give the class basic notions of first aid.

Audioscript: Track 64

Learner's Book page 131

1

Nurse:	Hello, Kenji. What's the matter?
Kenji:	I've cut my finger.
Nurse:	Oh dear. Have you washed it well? Or shall I wash it for you?
Kenji:	Yes, I've washed it well.
Nurse:	Shall I bring you a plaster?
Kenji:	Yes, please.

2

Nurse:	Hello, Matt. What's the matter?
Matt:	I fell over in the playground. My knee hurts!
Nurse:	Yes, I see. That's not good. Shall I bring you an ice pack?
Matt:	Oh thank you.

3

Child:	Hi, Mira. Are you ok? What's the matter?
Mira:	My head hurts.
Child:	Did you hit your head?
Mira:	No, no, I was reading a book.
Child:	Would you like a glass of water?
Mira:	No, thanks.
Child:	Shall I get the teacher, then?
Mira:	OK.

Answers

Kenji has cut his finger. Matt has fallen over and his knee hurts. Mira's head hurts.

1   (Kenji) The other person asks, 'Shall I bring you a plaster?'
2   (Matt) The other person asks, 'Shall I bring you an ice pack?'
3   (Mira) The other person asks, 'Would you like a glass of water?' and 'Shall I get the teacher, then?'

> **Digital Classroom:** Use the activity 'It hurts' to practise the conversations about being unwell or hurting ourselves in this lesson. The i button will explain how to use the activity.

4   Act it out! (25–30 minutes)

* Tell the class to work in pairs. They pretend that one of them is not well and the other tries to help.

* Tell learners to use the clues in the pictures.

* They act out the conversation.

> **Differentiation ideas:** More confident learners could add things like expressions of sympathy, words of thanks or dramatic descriptions of injuries if they want to elaborate. With less confident groups, you may wish to brainstorm these expressions and have them write their dialogue before acting it out. Supply additional vocabulary as necessary. Remind learners to use suitable body language and intonation to make their acting more realistic.

> **Assessment ideas:** Circulate, paying attention to pronunciation and intonation. If conditions permit, you may record groups as they act out. When they have finished, they can watch themselves performing the conversation and think how they could have improved their performance.

Workbook

Learners do Activities 1, 2 and 3 on pages 94–95.

Plenary ideas

Consolidation (10–15 minutes)

> **Assessment ideas:** Ask learners to get their KWL charts again (**Photocopiable 3**) and read the questions they wrote in the *W (Would like to know)* column. Have they found answers to any of them? Ask learners to write the new information in the *L (Learned)* column.

* Ask the class what information they have found the most interesting in this lesson. What would they like to learn more about?

Homework ideas

* Learners choose an accident that can happen in the street, at home or in the school. They make a mini-poster with pictures and some sentences offering a solution or advice.

* **Home–school link:** Learners tell their family about what they have learned in this lesson. They can ask them for other ways to treat the ailments in the lesson. If there are doctors or nurses among parents, you may wish to invite them to talk to the children about healthy eating habits and first aid.

8.3 Talk about it: Healthy habits

LEARNING PLAN

Learning objectives	Learning intentions	Success criteria
3Ld.04	• **Listening:** Listen to and understand information texts; listen to and understand conversations; listen for specific information.	• Learners can listen to and understand information texts and conversations.
3Sc.06, 3Sc.07, 3So.01	• **Speaking:** Choose and discuss food; discuss sleeping habits and favourite activities; discuss plans and activities for the coming week; role play conversations.	• Learners can choose and discuss different foods, sleeping habits and favourite activities.
3Rd.02, 3Rd.03	• **Reading:** Read information texts about healthy habits: exercise, nutrition and hygiene; read and understand conversations; read and understand new vocabulary.	• Learners can role play conversations about future plans.
3Wca.04, 3Wca.05	• **Writing:** Write tips for taking care of your teeth; write missing words in gap text; write about activity plans for next week; use correct spelling and punctuation; use correct grammar.	• Learners can read about health and fitness.
3Ug.07	• **Language focus:** future: *will; will* for promises	
	• **Vocabulary:** *roots, leaves, seeds, protein healthy, strong, keep clean, grow, mix, balance, asleep, rest, germs, tiny, wash away, brush, toothbrush, toothpaste, sugar, sweets*	

21st-century skills

Critical thinking opportunity: Work out time using a timeline; discuss cause and effect.

Creative thinking: Act out the roles of various characters in games and drama; actively participate in investigative, exploratory and open-ended tasks.

Learning to learn: Participate sensibly and positively in learning activities in class.

Materials: Learner's Book pages 132–133; Workbook pages 96–97; large sheet of poster paper; thick marker pen; sticky tack or glue; sheets of paper; writing and drawing materials; **Photocopiable 3, 43**

LANGUAGE BACKGROUND

Future *will*

The future with ***will*** is often used when we are announcing a decision, for example:

I will go to the gym three days next week.

I will have green salad and fish, please.

I won't stay up so late at night.

We can also use *will* for promises, for example:

I will eat more fruit and vegetables.

I won't eat so much fast food.

Common misconceptions

Misconception	How to identify	How to overcome
Learners quite often have agreement issues with demonstrative pronouns and nouns that they find difficult to identify as singular or plural, for example clothes, shoes, holiday(s), information, food. For example: *I think these information will help you.* *I like this shoes very much.*	Write an incorrect sentence on the board. Circle the noun and ask: *Is this plural or singular?* Elicit the answer. Offer more examples with problematic nouns. Establish which are singular and which are plural.	Before deciding which demonstrative to use, ask learners to identify the noun. Is it singular or plural? Then they choose the correct demonstrative.
Learners sometimes use the present simple instead of the future when making promises, for example: *I come tomorrow evening on seven o'clock.* *I come to the concert at 9 p.m. or 8 p.m.*	Write a few incorrect sentences on the board and ask the class, for example, *Are you making a promise?* Elicit answers.	Revise with the class the use of *will* for promises. Explain that we never use the present simple for promises. Remind learners to ask themselves if they are making a promise before deciding what tense to use.

Starter ideas

First aid (10–20 minutes)

- If learners have done the homework activity, ask them to share their mini-poster and advice with the class. Collect all the mini-posters and make a first aid poster. You can also ask learners to scan and upload their posters to the class blog.

- Ask learners to get their KWL charts (**Photocopiable 3**) and remind them of what they have discussed so far about healthy habits.

- Ask the class how often they brush their teeth and wash their hands, how many hours they sleep and if they go to bed early or late. How many hours of sleep do they get? How important is it to wash their teeth and hands? Why? Elicit ideas.

Main teaching ideas

1 Think about it. What can we do to stay healthy and strong? (5–10 minutes)

- Ask the class: *What can we do to stay healthy and strong?* Learners discuss their answers.

- Remind the class of the importance of eating fruit. What else is necessary to be healthy and strong?

- Make a class list of ideas. You can either write the list on the board or bring a large sheet of paper and write the ideas there.

Answers
Learner's own answers.

---

2 Listen and talk (10–20 minutes)

- Tell the class that they are going to listen and read about staying healthy.

- Play the audio and ask learners to follow in the text their books.

- Ask learners to discuss the question at the end in pairs. Then ask them to name one other vegetable that is a root, leaf, fruit or seed. Allow a few minutes for this.

> **Critical thinking opportunity:** Ask learners to compare the information they read about with the list they made on the board. Was there anything missing? Can they complete the table with new information?

Health and nutrition

Remind the class of what they learned about vitamins in Lesson 8.2. Revisit the table with the vitamin groups.

Ask the class why protein is so important for our bodies. Ask them what 'protein' means. You may have them look for an explanation and information about proteins on suitable websites such as Science Kids or Healthy Kids.

You could ask the class to make a table with the different types of vegetables: root, leaf, fruit or seed, and write examples for each using the Picture dictionary (Learner's Book page 163) for help. Display the table alongside the fruit rainbow they made in Lesson 2.

Audioscript: Track 65

Learner's Book page 132

Our bodies need food and water to grow and stay healthy.

We need food containing protein to make our muscles strong – foods like eggs, beans, fish, meat and cheese.

Vegetables are also important for our health.

The vitamins and minerals in vegetables help our bodies to make new healthy cells and strong bones.

All vegetables are parts of plants. Some vegetables are roots, like carrots.

Some are leaves, like lettuce. Some are fruits, like tomatoes. Some are seeds, like peas. Different vegetables give us different vitamins, so it is important to eat a variety.

Talk with a partner. Which of the vegetables above have you eaten in the last week?

Together, name one other vegetable that is a root, leaf, fruit or seed.

Answers
Learner's own answers.

3 Talk: A healthy lunch (10–20 minutes)

- Ask learners to look at the menu and think what they would like to have for lunch.

- Tell them that they are going to listen to some children talking about lunch choices.

- Play the recording. Ask: *What does Malika choose to have? What do the other children suggest?* Elicit answers.

- Turn to the Language focus box and read the explanation of the use of *will* – it can be used for decisions or promises. Give a few examples and ask learners to give a few of their own. Also explain the difference between when we use *will* (for decisions or promises) and *could* (for possibility).

- Then divide learners into groups to discuss what they will eat.

- Remind them that their lunch should include some protein and at least one vegetable.

- Focus on the illustration. Tell learners to use some of the food words in the conversation.

› **Differentiation ideas:** More confident learners may improvise and add more items to the menu. Remind them to have a balance of protein and vegetables. You could give less confident learners a copy of the transcript and use it as a model to write their sentences beforehand.

Audioscript: Track 66

Learner's Book page 132

Child 1: Malika, what will you have for lunch?

Malika: I think I will have chicken soup.

Child 1: What's the protein?

Malika: Chicken is a protein.

Child 2: Are there vegetables in chicken soup?

Malika: Um. I don't know.

Child 2: You could have some carrots.

Child 1: Or you could have a salad.

Malika: That's a good idea. I will have chicken soup and a salad!

Answers
Learner's own answers.

4 Listen, sing and write (15–30 minutes)

- Remind the class of the things that help us to stay healthy and strong. Ask: *Why is it important to keep clean?* Tell them to listen and read the text to find out.

- Play the recording up to the song. Then ask learners what they have learned.

- Ask: *What is a germ? What can we do to fight germs?*

- Then play the next part of the audio – 'The Alphabet Song'. As a class, have learners sing the song while they pretend to wash their hands.

- Tell the class to do this every time they wash their hands, to make sure they have done it properly.

- Play the last part of the recording while learners read about brushing their teeth. Ask them to write some tips in pairs.

- Then they share their tips with the class.

CROSS-CURRICULAR LINK

Health

Ask learners to visit suitable web pages like Kid's Health or find information in books about looking after their teeth. What happens if we don't brush our teeth and keep them clean? What foods are good for our teeth? What foods are *not* good for them?

Ask learners to work in groups and make a poster about how to look after their teeth. Have them add pictures to make it more interesting.

Audioscript: Track 67

Learner's Book page 133

Wash your hands and brush your teeth!

Germs are tiny living things which can make us ill if they get inside us. Our hands touch lots of things which have germs on them, but we can't see the germs. Fortunately, we can wash away the germs with soap and water. Always wash your hands before you eat and after you use the toilet.

Here's a tip: sing 'The Alphabet Song' as you wash your hands. By the end, your hands will be clean. Let's try it!

A, B, C, D, E, F, G

H, I, J, K, L, M, N, O, P

Q, R, S, T, U, V

W, X, Y and Z.

Now I've sung my ABCs

Next time won't you sing with me?

Looking after your teeth is another way to stay healthy.

When should you brush your teeth? Write some tips.

Answers
Learner's own answers.

> **Digital Classroom:** Use the activity 'Before or after?' to revise *before* and *after*. The i button will explain how to use the activity.

5 Read and talk (10–15 minutes)

- Ask the class how they think exercise is good for our health. What exercise can they do indoors and outdoors? Elicit ideas.

- Focus on the text. Read it as a class and have learners answer the question – *What are your favourite ways to get exercise?*

- Focus on the importance of sleep. Read and ask learners how many hours they usually sleep every night. What time do they get up?

> **Critical thinking opportunity:** Ask learners to look at the timeline. How do they work out the number of hours they sleep? Elicit answers.

Answers
Learner's own answers.

---

6 Listen and talk (10–20 minutes)

- Tell the class that they are going to role play a conversation between a child and a mum. First, they listen to the conversation and fill in the missing words.

- Play the recording again and check the answers.

- Have learners work in pairs and role play the conversation.

- Then ask them to switch parts and have a new conversation, using the words in the box.

Audioscript: Track 68

Learner's Book page 133

Mum: Remember to brush your teeth.

Child: I will.

Mum: Don't forget to wash your face.

Child: I won't.

Mum: Don't stay up too late.

Child: I won't!

Child: Mum, will you come and turn out the light?

Mum: Yes, I will.

Child: Goodnight, Mum.

Mum: Goodnight, dear.

Answers

won't; will; learner's own answers

Language focus: *will + not = won't* (5–10 minutes)

- Remind learners of the use of *will* for decisions.

- Focus on the negative form – *won't* – and have learners give a few examples.

- Hand out copies of **Photocopiable 43** and ask learners to write their own sentences for future plans.

Workbook

Learners do Activities 1–3 on pages 96–97.

Plenary ideas

Consolidation (15–20 minutes)

- Ask learners: *What will you do to stay healthy and strong next week?* Encourage them to think of what exercise they will do and what time they will go to bed. Elicit ideas.

> **Assessment ideas:** Ask learners to get their KWL charts (**Photocopiable 3**) and read the questions they wrote in the *W (Would like to know)* column. Have they found answers to any of them? Ask learners to write the new information in the *L (Learned)* column.

- Ask the class what information they have found the most interesting or useful in this lesson. What would they like to learn more about?

Homework ideas

- Ask learners to write down what they will do to stay healthy and strong next week. They can also write what the family will do to improve their healthy habits.

- **Home–school link:** Learners talk with their family about staying healthy. What healthy habits does their family have? What promises can they make to improve this?

8.4 Write about it: A happy, healthy week

Learning objectives	Learning intentions	Success criteria
3Ld.04	• **Listening:** Listen for detail; listen and match.	• Learners can listen and understand the details of conversations.
3Sc.07, 3So.01	• **Speaking:** Discuss a pie chart; discuss information; brainstorm ideas.	
3Rd.02	• **Reading:** Read and understand instructions.	• Learners can discuss a pie chart.
3Wca.02, 3Wca.03, 3Wor.01, 3Wor.02	• **Writing:** Write a plan for having a happy, healthy week; use correct spelling and punctuation; use grammar correctly; join sentences using simple connectors.	• Learners can read and understand instructions.
3Ug.07	• **Language focus:** *will* for decisions and promises	• Learners can write a plan for having a happy, healthy week.
	• **Vocabulary:** Revision of Unit 8	

21st-century skills

Critical thinking opportunity: Work with graphic organisers.

Communication: Take turns appropriately in a conversation; interrupt others politely.

Values: Be kind and helpful.

Materials: Learner's Book pages 134–135; Workbook pages 98–99; pictures of people doing different activities (for example, travelling, doing sports, tidying a bedroom, etc.); a calendar (or wall chart); Sample answer for Unit 8; **Photocopiable 1, 44; Differentiated worksheets 8A, B and C**

Starter ideas

My plans for the week (5–10 minutes)

- Show pictures of people doing different activities and ask the class what the people are doing, for example travelling, doing sports, tidying a room, etc. Elicit answers from learners.

- Show a calendar and revise the days of the week. Ask the class a few questions about the things they do on different days.

- Ask: *What will you do next week? Do you have any plans?* Elicit ideas.

Main teaching ideas

1   Listen and point (5–10 minutes)

- **Values:** Ask learners how they feel when people are kind and helpful to them. Elicit ideas.

- Ask if they are kind and helpful to others. In what ways? How do they feel? Elicit answers.

- Focus on the exercise and the pictures. Ask learners to describe them. How are these children kind and helpful? Elicit opinions.

- Tell the class that they are going to listen to these children and point to the matching picture as they hear them described.

- Play the recording twice and elicit the answers.

> **Differentiation ideas:** With less confident groups, you might play the recording once through, so that learners familiarise themselves with the content. Then stop after each child speaks and ask the class which picture matches their words. More confident

learners could write short notes about what each child did, for example: *The first girl helps the little girl to find the classroom.*

Audioscript: Track 69

Learner's Book page 134

Girl 1: I saw a little girl in the hall last week who was crying because she was lost. I helped her find her classroom. Now we're friends. Whenever we see each other, we wave.

Boy 1: I went to the market with my grandma and I carried the bags home. They were very heavy! Luckily, I am very strong.

Girl 2: Once I got a bad mark on my test and I felt bad. My friend played games with me and cheered me up.

Answers
Girl 1: image a; Boy 1: image c; Girl 2: image b

---

2 Talk about ways to stay healthy and strong (10–15 minutes)

- Remind the class of all of the different ways they can take good care of themselves. Elicit ideas (for example, exercising, healthy eating, washing, sleeping well, etc.).

- Ask the class to look at the pie chart and talk with a partner about it. They say two things about each section of the pie chart using the examples in the book as a model.

› **Differentiation ideas:** More confident learners may produce more complex sentences, for example: *Doing exercise three times a week makes you strong. Eating fruit of different colours gives you plenty of vitamins.* Less confident learners may write their sentences before attempting to say them. They could also review previous units to help them think of examples.

Answers
Learner's own answers.

---

3 Write: Make a plan for having a happy, healthy week!, and Language detective (30–45 minutes)

- Tell the class that they are going to make a plan for having a healthy, happy week.

- First they will brainstorm ideas, and then write a list of four things they will do next week. The next week, they will check their writing and try to tick off all the items on the list.

- **Step 1:** Ask learners to brainstorm ideas with a partner or in a group. Tell groups to think about what they will do next week to be healthy. They can use the questions to help them come up with ideas.

- Focus on the example in the Learner's Book. In this example, two children – Brian and Teresa – have already filled in the mind map with their intentions and promises.

- Have learners read the example mind map and then ask them to say what Brian and Teresa have promised, using full sentences.

- Tell the class to read the example sentences and explain why *will* is used (i.e. because Brian and Teresa are making promises). Revise the use of the future tense to make promises and to speak about future intentions. Give a few examples, such as *I will go to the gym three times next week. On Monday, I'll help my neighbour do the gardening.*

- Tell learners to use the sentences in the book as a model.

- Give each learner a copy of **Photocopiable 44** and have them write their ideas in the mind map. Ask them to add details.

- Focus on the Language tip. Remind learners of the short forms of *will.* Ask: *If **she'll** / **he'll** are the short forms of **she will** / **he will**, what are the full forms of **they'll** / **we'll** / **I'll**?* Elicit the answers and have learners write them in their book.

- **Step 2:** Tell learners to write a tick box plan for their happy healthy week. They choose four favourite ideas from the mind map and write four promises of things they will do.

- Tell learners to look at the beginning of Brian's list and use it as a model. Remind them to use the words *I will* and *I'll*. Also remind them that the days of the week in English begin with capital letters.

- Allow plenty of time for learners to choose, write and rewrite as necessary.

- **Step 3:** When they have finished, tell learners to read and revise their writing. Explain that it is a good idea to read the sentences aloud, to check if they sound right and decide if they want to add or take away any words. Then have them check that they have written the four promises, used *will* correctly and written the days of the week with an initial capital letter.

- **Step 4:** Ask learners to get their Writer's checklist (**Photocopiable 1**) and use it to check their work. Focus on the checklist and read it with the class. Then have learners check and correct spelling and punctuation using the checklist.

- Remind the class to use their list next week and tick off each promise when they have done it. Highlight the importance of being honest in their responses.

- See **Sample answer for Unit 8** for an example answer to this writing task.

Answers

Learners plan, write and check their ideas for a happy healthy week.

Language detective: they will, we will, I will

> **Workbook**
>
> Learners do Activities 1–5 on pages 98–99.

> **Digital Classroom:** Use the grammar presentation 'Will and won't' to revise *will*. The i button will explain how to use the grammar presentation.

Plenary ideas

Consolidation (5–10 minutes)

> **Differentiation ideas:** As a class, discuss with learners what they found the most difficult to do in this lesson. Ask: *How can you overcome the difficulties?* Can the class offer advice? Elicit ideas. Ask learners to write down ideas and reflections in their learning log.

Homework ideas

- Learners write the family promise plan. They write the four family promises they have agreed on.

- **Home–school link:** Learners share their promises with their family. They discuss a family promise plan, and agree on four things they promise to do as a family.

- Hand out copies of **Differentiated worksheets 8A, B and C** depending on each learner's ability, and ask them to complete the activities at home.

8.5 Read and respond: Taste, smell and your brain

LEARNING PLAN

Learning objectives	Learning intentions	Success criteria
3Ld.04, 3Lo.01	• **Listening:** Listen and understand an informative text; listen and understand opinions.	• Learners can read and understand an informative text about our tongue, nose and brain.
3Sc.01, 3So.01, 3Sor.02	• **Speaking:** Speak about the senses; discuss a text about our tongue, nose and brain; give opinions; discuss similarities and differences; initiate and maintain a conversation; use correct pronunciation and intonation.	• Learners can understand the meaning of words from context.
3Rd.01	• **Reading:** Read and understand an informative text about our tongue, nose and brain; understand the meaning of words from context.	• Learners can discuss a text about our tongue, nose and brain.
3Wca.04, 3Wca.05	• **Writing:** Write notes; write sentences; use correct spelling and grammar.	• Learners can discuss similarities and differences.
	• **Vocabulary:** *survive, taste, smell, tongue, taste buds, flavour, bitter, sour, salty, sweet, umami, lips, chew, cell, brain*	• Learners can carry out an experiment.

21st-century skills

Critical thinking opportunity: Carry out experiments and draw conclusions; compare information and find similarities and differences.

Learning to learn: Take basic notes about key information while reading and listening; summarise information on a selected topic when doing a project.

Values: Accept and respect differences.

Materials: Learner's Book pages 136–137; Workbook pages 100–101; dictionaries; large sheets of paper; drawing materials, bowls of sugar, salt and lemon juice; a pack of cotton buds; equal-sized cubes of various fruits/vegetables, e.g. watermelon, strawberry, pear, banana, tomato, kiwi; toothpicks; **Photocopiable 3**

Starter ideas

Promises (10–15 minutes)

- If learners have done the homework activity, ask volunteers to share their family promises with the class.

- Remind the class of their promises. Have they fulfilled any of them by this time? Invite learners to tell the class if they have.

Main teaching ideas

1 Explore, read and listen (15–30 minutes)

- Ask learners what was the first thing they saw when they woke up in the morning. Ask: *What did you hear? And see? What did you smell? And touch? And taste*? Elicit answers.

- Ask: *Which parts of the body help you see, smell, taste, touch and hear? Why are our senses necessary? Can we use more than one sense at a time?* Elicit answers.

  > Critical thinking opportunity: Focus on the illustrated text in the Learner's Book. Ask: *What is the first thing you looked at?* Elicit answers. Did all of the learners look at the same things?

  > Assessment ideas: Ask learners what they think the text is going to be about. How do they know? What helped them? Discuss the pictures, the headings and the subheadings.

- Ask learners to explore the pages. Where do they start reading on a page like this? Elicit answers.

- Allow learners to explore the text for a few minutes, and then tell them to listen and read.

- Play the recording while they read.

> **Audioscript: Track 70**
>
> See Learner's Book pages 136–138

2 Values: Different ways of learning (10–20 minutes)

- When learners have finished reading, ask them to work in groups and discuss the questions in the Learner's Book.

- Ask them to make notes of their answers.

- When all groups have finished, ask them to appoint a spokesperson and share summaries of their discussion with the class. Did they all have the same experiences?

- Highlight the fact that we cannot expect people to have the same experiences we have and the importance of respecting those differences. Point out that we should not consider someone 'weird' because they have experiences that are somewhat or very different from ours.

- Have groups share summaries of their discussion with the class.

> **Differentiation ideas:** With less confident groups, it may be useful to have them write their conclusions in full before attempting to share them with the rest of the class. They can also have more than one spokesperson and share the responsibility of communicating their experiences. You could also invite them to make a mini-poster and write a summary of the answers.

Answers

Learner's own answers.

3 Fact finder (10–15 minutes)

- Ask the class to work with a partner or in a small group. Ask them to re-read the text.

- Have them read the questions and help each other find the answers.

- When they have finished, have them share the answers as a class.

Answers

a sour
b over 10,000 taste buds
c Children have more taste buds and are therefore more sensitive to some tastes.
d people, food, money, diseases

> **Digital Classroom:** Use the activity 'Taste and smell' to reinforce comprehension of the text. The i button will explain how to use the activity.

4 Vocabulary (15–25 minutes)

- Ask learners to find each of the words in the text. Then they match the definitions with the correct vocabulary words.

> **Differentiation ideas:** You could invite more confident learners to explain what each of the words mean. Less confident learners may find this somewhat difficult to do in English but still want to do it. Allow for some use of L1 and echo in English. Have them repeat after you.

> **Assessment ideas:** This text is very rich in vocabulary. You could ask the class to work in groups and choose five or six new words. Ask groups to tell the class which words they have

chosen, to make sure each group works with a different set of words. Groups work out the meaning of the new words. They write a definition (a sentence and a picture or diagram if necessary) on a large sheet of paper. They can check meaning using a dictionary. When they have finished, ask groups to explain what they did to work out the meaning of the new vocabulary. Put all the mini-posters up on a large sheet of poster paper for all groups to read.

Answers
a combines, b odour, c adults, d chew, e danger

5 Try this! (30–45 minutes)

- Explain to the class that people often have a much better sense of smell than they think. The more we practise smelling things and identifying different smells, the better we get. Then tell the class that they are going to try the Hands-on experiment on Learner's Book page 139.

- Bring bowls of different strong-smelling foods into the class, such as a ripe banana, laundry soap, vinegar, orange juice, scented flowers, etc. Also have some open jars.

- Divide the class into pairs. Ask Learner A from each pair to choose one of the foods and put some into a jar, while Learner B from their pair closes their eyes. Learner A goes back to their partner and holds the jar near them. Learner B uses their sense of smell to locate the jar (make sure they keep their eyes closed) and then identifies what is in the jar by smelling it.

- Swap roles so that every learner has a chance to smell and locate the jars.

- Once everyone has had a go, ask the class: *Which odours are the easiest and the hardest to find?* You could carry out a class survey to see if learners agree which is the easiest/hardest.

- Once they have finished the experiment, you can tell learners to avoid placing unclean objects or objects that that have been contaminated by touching surfaces or handled by other people in their mouth.

> **Workbook**
>
> Learners do Activities 1–4 on pages 100–101.

Plenary ideas

Consolidation (15–20 minutes)

- When all the class has finished the experiment, compare the results.

⟩ **Assessment ideas:** Ask learners to get their KWL charts (**Photocopiable 3**) and to read the questions they wrote in the *W (Would like to know)* column. Have they found answers to any of them? Ask learners to write the new information in the *L (Learned)* column.

- Ask the class what information they have found the most interesting or useful in this lesson. What would they like to learn more about?

Homework ideas

- **Home–school link:** Learners do the experiments with their family.

- Learners write the results of the experiments they have done with their family.

8.6 Project challenge

LEARNING PLAN

Learning objectives	Learning intentions	Success criteria
3Sc.04, 3Sc.05, 3Sc.06	• **Speaking:** Discuss a project; discuss steps of a project; organise work; present their project to the class.	• Learners can read and understand instructions.
3Rd.02	• **Reading:** Read and understand instructions.	• Learners can give instructions.
3Wca.04, 3Wca.05	• **Writing:** Write sentences; write a quiz; write instructions; use correct grammar and spelling; use correct punctuation.	• Learners can plan a project.
		• Learners can write instructions.
	• **Language focus:** Unit 8 review	
	• **Vocabulary:** Unit 8 review	• Learners can write a quiz.

21st-century skills

Creative thinking: Design new items based on a model.

Communication: Share thoughts with others to help further develop ideas and solve problems.

Learning to learn: Listen and respond positively to feedback; understand why a correction was given; learn from mistakes and feedback.

Materials: Learner's Book pages 140–141; Workbook pages 102–103; Project A: writing supplies, sheets of paper, reference books; Project B: writing supplies, sheets of paper, drawing supplies, one file card for each learner; **Photocopiable 3, 45**; End of Unit 8 test

Starter ideas

Looking back (15–25 minutes)

> **Assessment ideas:** Ask the class to choose the lesson they liked most in this unit, and ask them to explain why. Ask: *What was the most difficult thing in this unit? Do you feel that you have done well? What would you say is your strongest point? And your weakest point?*

• Ask learners to get their KWL charts (**Photocopiable 3**). Revisit what learners have contributed in the different columns. Ask them to think how they can use the information they have learned in this unit. As a class, have learners discuss how they can use the information in everyday life. You may do this discussion as a Think-Pair-Share activity in which learners first reflect individually, then discuss their ideas with a partner and finally share their ideas with the class.

Main teaching ideas

Learners choose an end-of-unit project to work on. Look at the examples in the pictures and help learners to choose. Provide materials.

Project A: Write a quiz about our amazing body (60–90 minutes)

- In groups, learners do some research and find out about the bones in our body. They can search using the internet or look up information in reference books.

- They write quiz questions and give three answer choices for each question. Ask them to use the sample questions as a model. Then they write the answers in an Answer key and add interesting details.

- Each group gives the quiz to the rest of the class to solve.

- When the groups have finished, go over the answers together.

Project B: Write a book called 'Let's move!' (60–90 minutes)

- Learners work in groups to write a book or a digital PowerPoint presentation.

- Each group member thinks of an exercise or a race. They can also make up steps to a dance and choose some music.

- They write instructions and draw pictures to explain the exercise or race. They can refer back to the jumping jacks instructions on Learner's Book page 129 as a model.

- **Writing tip:** To help learners edit their instructions for clarity, suggest the following: when they have written instructions, give them to a partner. The partner will read them and try to do the exercise. If the partner doesn't understand the instructions, they make changes so that instructions are clearer.

- If learners are making a PowerPoint, they can video-record group members doing the exercise, race or dance, and include the video in the PowerPoint.

- Groups then share their book/PowerPoint with the class. They teach the races, exercises and dances, and try them out together.

> **Assessment ideas:** When learners have finished their projects, give them a copy of **Photocopiable 45** and read the information as a class. Ask them to work independently and think about their work on their project. They reflect and answer the questions. Ask them to tick off the aims they have achieved. Insist on the importance of giving honest answers.

> **Workbook**
> Learners do the Check your progress quiz on pages 102–103.

Plenary ideas

Reflect on your learning (5–10 minutes)

- Draw learners' attention to the 'Reflect on your learning' questions in their Learner's Books.

- Learners answer the questions to reflect on their project work.

Consolidation (10–20 minutes)

> **Assessment ideas:** Use a growth mindset exit slip. Give each learner a card with the following title: Challenge – Victory. Ask them to describe the challenge they faced when they started the unit and how they solved it. Ask: *Was it easy to solve? Was it difficult? How difficult was it? What did you do to meet the challenge? Did you succeed, or is there something you are still not happy about?*

Tell learners to draw a connecting line between the two words that describe how the trip from the challenge to overcoming it was, for example a straight line means it was easy, a winding line shows difficulties, etc.

Then they can put their cards up on a notice board. Have the class read the cards. Have they had a similar problem? What did they do? Learners discuss their responses and give each other advice.

Homework ideas

- Learners draw a picture of what they have liked most about this unit.

- **Home–school link:** Learners show their family their project.

8.7 What do you know now?

How can we stay healthy and strong? (30–40 minutes)

*   Learners work in pairs. They work together through all the tasks set in this section.

*   They write the answers in their notebooks. You may ask them to have a special section in their notebooks where they record the answers.

Answers
1–5 Learner's own answers.

Look what I can do! (15 minutes)

*   Review the *I can …* statements on page 142 of the Learner's Book. Learners demonstrate what they can do.

*   Learners colour in the faces to show which things they can do.

*   Encourage them to be honest in their answers.

> **Workbook**
>
> Learners answer the Reflection questions on page 103.

> 9 Robots

Unit plan

Lesson	Approximate number of learning hours	Outline of learning content	Learning objectives	Resources
1 What are robots like?	1.75–3.0	Learn and talk about different types of robot.	3Lo.01 3So.01 3Sor.01 3Rd.01 3Wca.05 3Wc.02 3Ug.09	Learner's Book Lesson 9.1 Workbook Lesson 9.1 ⬇ Photocopiable 46 ⬇ Photocopiable 47 **Digital Classroom:** Video – Robots at work; Activity – Big and little
2 The uses of robots	1.75–2.75	Describe and compare what robots can do.	3Lm.01 3Sc.06 3Sc.07 3Rd.03 3Wca.04 3Wca.05	Learner's Book Lesson 9.2 Workbook Lesson 9.2 **Digital Classroom:** Activity – Robots
3 Robot waiters	1.5–2.5	Practise ordering food from a robot waiter.	3Ld.03 3Ld.04 3Sc.07 3Sor.02 3Rd.02 3Wc.02 3Uv.09	Learner's Book Lesson 9.3 Workbook Lesson 9.3 ⬇ Photocopiable 48 **Digital Classroom:** Grammar presentation – Quantifiers
4 Instructions for robots	1.75–2.5	Write instructions for our personal robots.	3Sc.02 3Sc.04 3Sc.05 3Rd.01 3Wc.01 3Wca.04	Learner's Book Lesson 9.4 Workbook Lesson 9.4 ⬇ Sample answer for Unit 9 ⬇ Photocopiable 1 ⬇ Photocopiable 2 ⬇ Photocopiable 49 **Digital Classroom:** Activity – How to make an omelette
5 Zaydor	1.75–3.0	Read part of a story about a family with robots.	3Sor.01 3Sor.02 3Rd.01 3Ro.01 3.Wc.02 3Uv.07	Learner's Book Lesson 9.5 Workbook Lesson 9.5 **Digital Classroom:** Activity – Robot revolution

(continued)

Lesson	Approximate number of learning hours	Outline of learning content	Learning objectives	Resources
6 Project challenge	1.5–2.25	Design and talk about a robot, write and perform a song.	3Sc.06 3Sc.07 3Rd.02 3Wca.02 3Wca.03	Learner's Book Lesson 9.6 Workbook Lesson 9.6 ⬇ Photocopiable 1 ⬇ Photocopiable 50 ⬇ Photocopiable 51 ⬇ Differentiated worksheets 9A, B and C
7 What do you know now?	0.75–1.0	Self-assessment and reflection.		Learner's Book Lesson 9.7

Cross-unit resources
⬇ Unit 9 Audioscripts
⬇ End of Unit 9 test
⬇ Progress test 3
⬇ Unit 9 Progress report
⬇ Unit 9 Wordlist

BACKGROUND KNOWLEDGE

In Lesson 9.5, learners read a story about E, who is a special robot. Learners are also introduced to the concepts of 'telepresence' and 'immunodeficiency'.

Robots

In this unit, learners read and learn about robots. Czech writer Karel Kapek first used the word 'robot' in 1920.

In 1928, W.H. Richards invented one of the first humanoid robots – called Eric. It could move its hands and head, and was controlled through remote control. George Devol invented the first digitally operated and programmable robot in 1954. It was called the Unimate, and it started the modern robotics industry.

Modern robots have three main characteristics: they have some sort of mechanical construction; they have electrical components to control and power the machinery; and they contain computer programming.

Telepresence

Telepresence is technology that allows someone to feel as if they were present, and to give the appearance that they are present, at a different place to their actual location. The position, movements and voice of the person using the technology can be transmitted, thereby giving the experience of being present at a location different from their actual physical location. Telepresence technology is used in education to connect learners who are unable to go to school because of geography or, in the case of Maddie in the story, health. It is also used in space exploration, dangerous environments, surgery and entertainment.

The immune system

The immune system is made up of special organs, cells and chemicals that fight infection. When our body gets an infection, the immune system can respond in many ways; for example, it can raise the body's temperature. Some people's immune system can over-react, and cause allergies and autoimmune diseases. In some other people, the immune system doesn't work correctly, and causes immunodeficiency – this makes people vulnerable to infections.

TEACHING SKILLS FOCUS

Skills for life: Creativity

Creativity is another key life skill, just like critical thinking. There is no singular definition of creativity because it is a complex concept, and one that can be studied and discussed from many different perspectives. However, it is accepted that creativity involves the ability to see patterns and come up with new and original ideas to solve problems. Being creative does not merely mean being creative in art or music – we all have the potential to be creative under different conditions and in different ways.

Language learning offers a great opportunity for the development of creativity in learners. Language is creative by nature, as we can express ideas in many different ways that provoke different reactions. Language lessons can offer opportunities for learners to engage in creative situations by supporting and valuing different types of creativity, providing interesting and challenging work, using creative strategies and techniques, and encouraging multiple solutions to problems.

Your challenge

The following tips may help you to provide opportunities for learners to develop their creativity:

- Do some unusual activities at the beginning of the lesson to help learners prepare for the lesson and become mentally alert.
- Combine apparently unrelated ideas and have learners make unusual connections.
- Ask learners to think about things they do every day and come up with ideas about how they could do them differently.
- Have learners work together and encourage discussion.
- Arrange the class in different ways depending on space and the type of activity.
- Allow thinking time after questions.

In each unit of the Learner's Book, opportunities to engage in creativity-development activities are highlighted. Look through Unit 9 and highlight opportunities for introducing some of the ideas above.

Reflection

How did the activities work? Did I encounter the difficulties I had anticipated? How did the solutions I had envisaged work? How can I improve them?

9.1 Think about it: What are robots like?

LEARNING PLAN

Learning objectives	Learning intentions	Success criteria
3Lo.01	• **Listening:** Listen to a song; listen to a poem; listen to a conversation about robots; listen to and understand the opinion of speakers; listen for detail.	• Learners can listen to a song/a poem. • Learners can listen to a conversation about robots and understand the opinion of speakers.
3So.01, 3Sor.01	• **Speaking:** Talk about different types of robots; ask and answer questions about robots; describe robots; express preferences and opinions, with reasons; make predictions.	• Learners can talk about different types of robots. • Learners can ask and answer questions about robots.
3Rd.01	• **Reading:** Read a poem; figure out unknown words and expressions.	
3Wca.05, 3Wc.02	• **Writing:** Answer questions, make notes; complete a table.	• Learners can express preference and opinions.
3Ug.09	• **Language focus:** revision of comparative and superlative adjectives, including *the most / the least* + noun; *will* for predictions about the future	• Learners can discuss the implications of technology on the future.
	• **Vocabulary:** *rock, lab, put away, rattle, click, puff, replace, acceptable, malfunction, trip, pick on, bully, exception*	• Learners can compare robots' height and weight.

21st-century skills

Critical thinking opportunity: Consider the implications of technology on the future; give opinions and support reasons; compare and contrast.

Collaboration: Use language to interact with others in the group; be aware of when and how to take turns and when and how to interrupt; be aware of how to clarify ideas.

Learning to learn: Engage with practice activities in class; memorise and repeat key words and phrases.

Materials: Learner's Book pages 143–145; Workbook pages 104–105; dictionaries; large sheet of paper (approximately as long as the height of the tallest learner); drawing materials; rulers; measuring tape; weighing scales; pictures of different robots (not just anthropomorphic ones); photos of famous television and film robots, e.g. Chappie, R2-D2, C-3PO and BB-8 (*Star Wars*), Johnny 5, Wall-E, T-1000 (*Terminator 2*), Transformers, Rosey (*The Jetsons*); sticky notes; **Photocopiable 46, 47**

LANGUAGE BACKGROUND

Comparatives and superlatives

One-syllable adjectives form the comparative and superlative as follows:

- Most adjectives form the comparative and superlative by adding -er, -est:
  late – later – latest

- Adjectives ending in -e, add only -st:
  nice – nicer – nicest

- Adjectives ending in one vowel + one consonant double the consonant:
  big – bigger – biggest   *fat – fatter – fattest*

Two-syllable adjectives form the comparative and superlative as follows:

- Adjectives ending in -y form the comparative and superlative by -ier and -iest:

  happy – happier – happiest
  pretty – prettier – prettiest

- Some two-syllable adjectives form the comparative and superlative with -er and -est, especially adjectives ending in an unstressed vowel:

  simple – simpler – simplest
  quiet – quieter – quietest

- With many two-syllable adjectives, both -er/-est and *more/most* are possible, for example *common*. With other adjectives, including those ending in -ing, -ed, -ful and -less, only *more/most* can be used.

Three-syllable adjectives or adjectives with more syllables form the comparative and superlative only with *more* and *most*.

Starter ideas

Getting started (10–15 minutes)

- Ask the class what image comes to mind when they hear the word 'robot'. Elicit ideas.

- Show a few pictures of different robots (not just the typical anthropomorphic ones) and ask learners what they are. Ask: *What can robots do for us?* Elicit ideas.

- Ask learners what different kinds of robots they can think of. Do any learners have a robot at home?

Answers
Learner's own answers.

> **Digital Classroom:** Use the video 'Robots at work' to introduce the topic of robots. The i button will explain how to use the video.

Sing along! *Rock the robot* (10–15 minutes)

- Tell the class they are going to listen to a song. Give each learner a copy of **Photocopiable 46**: Sing along! *Rock the robot*.

- Play the song at least twice. Ask the class what the song is about. Elicit answers.

- Play the song again and encourage learners to clap along. Then sing the song and encourage learners to join in and mime.

> **Differentiation ideas:** Encourage less confident learners to identify unfamiliar words in the song lyrics and to look up the words in a dictionary. More confident learners can supply example sentences with the new words.

Audioscript: Track 71
Learner's Book page 143

Rock the robot

It rocks in the lab, all day long
Clicking and rattling and singing this song
All the other robots
Want to see
How this robot moves when it sings with me

Rockin' Robot
Clink, clink-ity clink
Rockin' Robot
Clink, clink-ity clink

All the other robots
big and small
Want to dance along
When he plays this song

Rockin' Robot
Clink, clink-ity clink
Rockin' Robot
Clink, clink-ity clink

All the engineers
and the scientists too
Put away their screens
And start shakin' their shoes

Rockin' Robot
Clink, clink-ity clink
Rockin' Robot
Clink, clink-ity clink

It rocks in the lab, all day long
Clicking and rattling and singing this song
All the other robots
Want to see
How this robot moves when it sings with me

Rockin' Robot
Clink, clink-ity clink
Rockin' Robot
Clink, clink-ity clink!

Main teaching ideas

1 Talk about robots (10–15 minutes)

- Ask learners to work in pairs and give each learner a sheet of paper.
- Each learner takes it in turns to close their eyes and imagine a robot. They then describe it to their partner, who draws the robot based on the description.
- Learners look at their partner's drawing and discuss how it is the same and different to their imaginary robot. Remind learners to be sensitive when giving their partner feedback.

Answers
Learners draw robots based on their partners' descriptions.

2 Listen and match to the pictures (5–10 minutes)

- Focus on the pictures. Explain to the class that robots come in many shapes and sizes, and they do many different things. Tell the class that they are going to listen to a conversation and match the pictures to the type of robot.
- Play the recording once and elicit the answers.

> **Assessment ideas:** Ask learners how difficult they found matching each robot image to the description in the recording. What helped them decide what the correct answers are?

Audioscript: Track 72
Learner's Book page 144

Child: What's this? It's really small.

Adult: It's a robot.

Child: It doesn't look like a robot.

Adult: You're thinking of a robot that looks a like a human.

Child: Yes.

Adult: That's a humanoid robot.

Child: But all robots look like people.

Adult: Well, robots like the one in this picture do. It is 154 centimetres high and it weighs 58 kilograms. There are even bigger humanoid robots like the ones you see in science-fiction films. Humanoid robots can do many things that humans can do, such as cleaning or cooking or helping people in other ways.

Child: That's a robot.

Adult: Yes, but many robots don't look like people at all. One of the biggest robots is the space arm. It is a long, narrow robot. It is about 15 metres long and it weighs over 400 kilograms. Astronauts use it to fix space stations.

Child: That's a robot?

Adult: Yes, and there are also smaller robots like this RoboBee. It's about the size of a bee – very tiny and light. It is 3 centimetres long and weighs 80 milligrams. The RoboBee has got a camera and can fly, so scientists think in the future it will search in very small places.

Answers
1 photo c, 2 photo a, 3 photo b

3 Listen again and complete the table (10–20 minutes)

- With the class, revise measurements for length, height and weight using the Measurements and weights page in the Picture dictionary in their Learner's Book (page 162).

CROSS-CURRICULAR LINK

Maths

Ask learners to get their rulers and look at how it is divided. Ask: *How long is it?* Elicit answers, e.g. 30 centimetres long. Ask them to take a couple of pencils of different lengths and measure them. Ask: *How long are they?*

Bring a measuring tape and measure how tall learners are. On a large sheet of paper, write their names and draw a line to show their heights.

Bring a weighing scale and ask learners to weigh a book. Ask: *How heavy is it? And a notebook? Is it lighter or heavier?* Ask learners to work out the difference, e.g. the book is 300 grams heavier than the notebook.

Tell the class they are going to listen to the recording again. They complete the table by writing the measurements as they hear them.

> **Assessment ideas:** Allow a few minutes for learners to look at the table. Then ask what measurements they need to use, i.e. metres and centimetres for length and height, grams for weight.

- Play the recording twice. Learners write down the information. You could copy the table on the board and ask volunteers to fill in the information.

> **Differentiation ideas:** Encourage more confident learners to say what they have written as a full sentence, for example: *The humanoid robot is 154 cm high and it weighs 58 kg.* Less confident learners may write the sentences before attempting to say them.

- When learners have finished, ask them to read and answer the questions.

> **Differentiation ideas:** With less confident groups, it may be necessary to revise comparative and superlative adjectives (see 'Language background' section above). Show pictures of animals of different sizes and weights, for example a blue whale, a shark and a clown fish, and ask: *Which is the heaviest animal? Which is bigger, the whale or the shark? Which is the smallest?* You can do the same with pictures of buildings of different heights, for example: *Which building is the tallest – the Eiffel tower, the Petronas or the Burj Khalifa? Which is the shortest?*

Answers

	humanoid robot	RoboBee	space arm
Length or height	154 cm	3 cm	15 m
Weight	58 kg	80 mg	400 kg
One thing it does	Can do many things that humans can do, such as cleaning or cooking or helping people in other ways	Has got a camera and can fly	Fixes space stations

a the space arm, **b** the RoboBee, **c** the space arm, **d** the RoboBee

4 Discuss with your partner (5–15 minutes)

- Ask learners to work in pairs and discuss the questions. Encourage them to give their opinions using the example phrasing '*I like … better because …*' and '*I think … because …*'.

- Learners could write down their answers as they discuss them with their partners.

- When they have finished, ask each pair to share their opinions with the class.

> **Assessment ideas:** Circulate, listening to learners' interactions and checking the correct use of comparative and superlative forms.

Answers
Learner's own answers.

5 Vocabulary: Sizes (10–15 minutes)

- Focus on the words on the image of the robot. Explain that each word on the left has an opposite word on the right. Ask learners to match each of the size words to their opposites.

- When they have finished, check answers as a class.

> **Differentiation ideas:** You could ask less confident learners to write sentences using the opposites. More confident learners could think of more words and their opposites, and add these to the list on the image.

- Hand out copies of **Photocopiable 47** and ask learners to complete the sentences.

Answers
big – small, huge – tiny, wide – narrow, long – short, heavy – light

> **Digital Classroom:** Use the activity 'Big and little' to revise size adjectives. The i button will explain how to use the activity.

6 Read and listen to the poem (20–30 minutes)

- Show photos of famous robots, such as Chappie, R2D2, 3PO and BB8 (*Star Wars*), Johnny 5, Wall-E, T-1000 (*Terminator 2*), Optimus Prime or any of the Transformers, and Rosey (*The Jetsons*). Ask learners: *What are they like? Are they good or evil robots? How do you know?* Elicit ideas.

- Explain again that a humanoid robot is a robot that is designed to look like a human. Ask learners: *Do humanoid robots have personalities like people?* Elicit ideas.

- Tell the class that they are going to read a poem about a special robot. Ask learners to read along as they listen.

- Play the recording once. Ask learners to underline new vocabulary. Can they guess the meaning from the context? Ask learners to work in pairs and come up with an explanation of the new vocabulary.

- Play the recording again and have learners mime the actions as they listen and say the poem.

- Ask the class to describe what the robot in the poem does or doesn't do. Would they like to have a robot that does all of these chores?

> **Critical thinking opportunity:** Focus on the last two lines of the poem and ask learners what they mean. Who do they think does all of the things the robot refuses to do? Elicit ideas.

Audioscript: Track 73

See Learner's Book page 145.

7 Think about the robots of the future (15–20 minutes)

- Revise the use of the future simple. Also remind the class of the promises they made in Unit 8. What did they promise to do? How many of them have they ticked off?

- Ask volunteers to read the promise, for example: *I will go to bed earlier every night for a week.* Ask: *Did you do it?* Elicit the answer.

- Explain that we also use the future simple when we are making predictions. Focus on the activity and ask learners to think about the robots of the future. Ask them to write three things they think robots will do in the future. Learners should begin their sentences as shown in the activity: *In the future, robots will … .*

- When they have finished, ask learners to share their sentences with the class.

Answers
Learner's own answers.

Workbook

Learners do Activities 1–4 on pages 104–105.

Plenary ideas

Consolidation (10–20 minutes)

- Ask the class to make more predictions about the future. What do they think will happen in 10, 20 and 50 years' time? What will the world be like in 100 years? Have learners make predictions using 'will'.

> **Assessment ideas:** Ask learners what they have found the most interesting in this lesson. Give them sticky notes and ask them to write one thing they have found very interesting, one thing they didn't know before and one thing they already knew. Collect all of the notes and put them up on a noticeboard.

Homework ideas

- Learners write a poem about their robot and how it misbehaves. They use the poem in this lesson as a model.

- **Home–school link:** Learners tell their family about the robots they have learned about in this lesson.

9.2 Technology: The uses of robots

LEARNING PLAN

Learning objectives	Learning intentions	Success criteria
3Lm.01	• **Listening:** Listen for detail.	• Learners can read and understand a text about robots.
3Sc.06, 3Sc.07	• **Speaking:** Ask and answer questions; express preference and opinions, with reasons; make predictions; discuss what robots can and can't do.	• Learners can discuss what robots can and can't do.
3Rd.03	• **Reading:** Read about advances in technology; read and understand vocabulary from context.	• Learners can express preferences and give reasons.
3Wca.04, 3Wca.05	• **Writing:** Write notes; write sentences; answer questions; use correct grammar and spelling.	• Learners can make predictions.
	• **Language focus:** direct objects	
	• **Vocabulary:** *sample, explore, rescue, factory, operation*	

21st-century skills

Critical thinking opportunity: Compare different types of information (for example, looking for similarities and differences); make predictions and estimations from given information.

Collaboration: Listen attentively while other learners are contributing; respectfully wait for their turn to speak.

Learning to learn: Participate sensibly and positively in learning activities in class.

Materials: Learner's Book pages 146–147; Workbook pages 106–107; bindings to make a poem book (optional); card to make a cover for the poem book (optional); dictionaries; file cards

LANGUAGE BACKGROUND

Direct objects

In English, a direct object may be a noun, pronoun, a noun phrase or a compound noun that shows who or what receives the action of a verb. It answers the question *Who?* or *What?* For example:

• *I had to return **the jacket** to the shop. It was too big for my brother.* What did I have to return to the shop? The jacket. This is what is being returned.

• *Marisa's parents took **her** to Paris on holiday.* Who did they take to Paris? Marisa. She is the one taken to Paris.

Direct objects can be replaced with an object pronoun in English. For example:

• *I bought a jacket from a shop. I had to return **the jacket** to the shop.* This sentence can be changed to:

• *I bought a jacket from the shop. I had to return **it** to the shop.* 'The jacket' is replaced with the object pronoun 'it'.

Starter ideas

Poetry time! (15–25 minutes)

- Divide the class into groups and ask learners to recite the poem 'My robot's misbehaving' from the previous lesson.

- If learners have written a poem for homework, ask them to read it to the class.

- You can have learners upload the poems to the class blog. Alternatively, you can help them to make a book of robot poems. They could bind the poems together and make a cover for the book.

Main teaching ideas

1 Talk about robots (5–10 minutes)

- Ask the class what they think robots can do. What would they like robots to do for them? Elicit answers from the class.

- Ask learners to look at the pictures and guess what each of the robots does.

Answers
Learner's own answers.

2 What can these robots do? (5–15 minutes)

- Tell the class that they are going to listen and read about the robots in the pictures.

- Ask the class to read the titles. Then ask learners to listen and match each title to the correct paragraph.

- Play the recording. Learners choose the titles. Play the recording again to check answers as a class.

> **Critical thinking opportunity:** Ask the class what information in the paragraphs helped them decide.

> **Differentiation ideas:** Less confident groups may need to listen and read the text twice. It may also be useful to play the recording, stopping after each paragraph to give learners time to decide. More confident learners may just listen once and decide. Then they can read the text. While less confident learners are listening or reading again, you could ask more confident learners to work in pairs and write four questions about the text. They swap questions with another pair and answer them.

> **Assessment ideas:** You could ask a few comprehension questions to check understanding of the text.

Audioscript: Track 74

See Learner's Book page 146.

Answers
Paragraph 1: Robots can go where we can't survive.
Paragraph 2: Robots can go where it's dangerous for us.
Paragraph 3: Robots can do jobs that people find boring.
Paragraph 4: Robots can help with delicate operations.

3 Talk about robots and humans (10–15 minutes)

- Ask learners to read the text for Activity 2 again, which describes what robots can do.

- Then divide the class into pairs. Ask them to discuss what robots can do that humans cannot do. Learners can write some notes as they discuss their responses to the question.

- Encourage them to use the sentence starters in the activity.

> **Critical thinking opportunity:** After a few minutes, ask pairs to share their ideas with the class. Do they all have the same ideas? Encourage the class to discuss the differences.

Answers
Learner's own answers. Suggestions include: Robots can go deep in the ocean. Some robots can go into dangerous places, like burning buildings or buildings that have fallen down. Other robots can go into very small spaces. Robots can hold tiny tools and lights, which can reach places that a doctor's hands cannot reach.

4 Find the blue words in the texts that match these definitions (15–20 minutes)

- Tell learners to read the texts again and look for the words in blue. Learners write the blue words.

- Ask learners to read the definitions and match each of them to one of the blue words. Check answers as a class.

- Ask learners to re-read and underline other words in the texts that may be new or confusing. Learners can then look these up in a dictionary.

Answers
to look someone or something – *search*
trying to fix a person's body – *operation*
things we use to fix things – *tools*
places where we make things like cars, machines, products we use – *factories*
to save people in danger – *rescue*
small quantities of things to study – *samples*
to visit and find your way in a new place – *explore*

5 What do robots do? Complete the sentences with objects from the text (15–20 minutes)

- Ask the class to look at the sentence halves; explain that the sentences are missing the objects. Learners read the text again to find which object is missing in each sentence half and write them in. Check answers as a class.

> **Assessment ideas:** Remind learners of the information they learned about robots in Lesson 9.1. Ask them to write at least two more sentences about robots using the ones in the exercise as a model, for example: *My robot does my homework. My robot doesn't make my bed.* Ask them to identify the direct objects in their sentences.

Answers
1 Robots take <u>photos</u>.
2 Robots explore <u>planets</u>.
3 Robots rescue <u>people in danger</u>.
4 Robots do <u>operations</u>.
5 Robot arms hold <u>tiny tools</u>.

6 Talk about robot jobs in the future (10–15 minutes)

- Ask the class: *What do you think robots will be able to do in the future?*

- Have learners work in pairs and discuss their responses. Direct them to use the sentence openers in the Learner's Book.

- After a few minutes, have pairs share their ideas with the class and discuss any differences.

Answers
Learner's own answers.

Workbook

Learners do Activities 1–3 on pages 106–107.

> **Digital Classroom:** Use the activity 'Robots' to extend the topic of what robots can do. The i button will explain how to use the activity.

Plenary ideas

Consolidation (15–30 minutes)

> **Critical thinking opportunity:** Ask the class: *Will robots replace teachers in the future? Would you like to have a robot teacher? Why?* Have an open class discussion of the pros and cons of having robots replacing teachers.

> **Assessment ideas:** Give each learner a file card and ask them to imagine they are the teachers and they are writing a test. Ask them to write one question for the test based on what they have learned in this lesson. Make it clear that they must know the answer! When they have finished, put up the cards on the noticeboard, and ask learners to read and answer them individually. How many right answers did they get?

Homework ideas

- Learners design their own robot, draw a picture and write a short text about it.

- **Home–school link:** Learners tell their family what they have learned about robots. They ask them what they think robots will do in the future, and share their own ideas.

9.3 Talk about it: Robot waiters

LEARNING PLAN

Learning objectives	Learning intentions	Success criteria
3Ld.03, 3Ld.04	• **Listening:** Listen and understand conversations; listen for detail.	• Learners can listen to and understand conversations.
3Sc.07, 3Sor.02	• **Speaking:** Role play ordering food; discuss a menu; talk about food; describe what is happening in a picture.	• Learners can talk about what robots can do.
3Rd.02	• **Reading:** Read and understand instructions; read a menu.	• Learners can describe what is happening in a picture.
3Wc.02	• **Writing:** Write a menu; write sentences.	• Learners can write a menu.
3Uv.09	• **Language focus:** countable and uncountable nouns	
	• **Vocabulary:** *Can I…?, Do you have any …?, Let me check, Would you like …?, Is that everything?, Thank you for your order.*	• Learners can role play ordering food.

21st-century skills

Critical thinking opportunity: Consider implications of technology on everyday life.

Creative thinking: Take part in a role play.

Communication: Take turns appropriately in a conversation; interrupt others politely.

Materials: Learner's Book pages 148–149; Workbook pages 108–109; **Photocopiable 48**

LANGUAGE BACKGROUND

Countable and uncountable nouns

In English, as in other languages, some nouns are countable and some are uncountable.

Countable nouns are those that name objects, people, animals, etc. They can be counted by the unit using numbers and the article *a/an*. They have singular and plural forms, and can be used with certain determiners, such as *some, many, few, a few, fewer, a lot of, lots of, plenty of, these, those*. For example, *a table, a few magazines, three lions, an island, some people, a lot of children*.

Uncountable nouns are those that name materials, liquids, qualities and other things that we see as masses and not as separate objects. We do not use numbers or *a/an* with these nouns and they do not have plural forms. They can be used with certain determiners, such as *the, some, much, most, little, a little, less, a lot of, lots of, plenty of, this, that*. For example, *the/some water, a little money, less patience, plenty of space, most information, lots of sugar*.

Some names for food are uncountable and singular, while others are countable and usually plural. For example, *fruit, rice, spaghetti, gnocchi* and other pasta foods, *sugar, salt*, etc., are considered uncountable. Other foods can be regarded as a collection of separate elements and are therefore countable, for example *vegetables, beans, grapes, oats, lentils*.

Common misconceptions

Misconception	How to identify	How to overcome
Learners quite often have issues with uncountable nouns that they find difficult to identify as singular, for example *furniture, music, homework, seafood, information, equipment, work, music, advice.*	Write an incorrect sentence on the board. Circle the noun and ask: *Is this plural or singular?* Elicit the answer. Offer more examples with problematic nouns.	It may be useful to compare with similar nouns in the learners' language as the misconception sometimes originates there. In many languages these nouns are countable. Compare both languages and establish that in English they refer to a group of things – they represent a single person, place, thing or idea, so they are singular and require a singular verb. Make a poster with these problematic nouns as they appear in lessons. Learners can check with the list.
Learners quite often have issues with uncountable nouns that look plural because they end with a 's' but are in fact singular, for example *news, athletics, dominoes, scissors.*	Write an incorrect sentence on the board. Circle the noun and ask: *Is this plural or singular?* Elicit the answer. Offer more examples with problematic nouns.	Establish that in English, these nouns are always singular despite ending in 's'. Make a poster with these problematic nouns as they appear in lessons. Learners can check with the list.

Starter ideas

Robot gallery (10–15 minutes)

- If learners did the homework activity from the previous lesson, ask them to show the pictures of the robots they designed and read their descriptions.

- Display the pictures and have the class vote for the most useful, funniest, craziest, etc., robot.

- You could take photos of the pictures and upload them to the class blog. Alternatively, display the pictures in a common area of the school for other classes to see.

Main teaching ideas

1 Talk about the picture (5–10 minutes)

- Ask learners to look at the picture and describe what they see. What do they think it is? (a robot waiter) Do they think it is possible to have robots working as waiters? Have they ever seen a robot waiter in a restaurant? Would they like to go to a restaurant with robot waiters?

- Discuss the picture as a class.

Answers

Learner's own answers.

---

2 Listen and circle true or false (5–10 minutes)

- Read the sentences as a class. Explain that some of the sentences are true and some are false.

- Tell the class that they are going to listen to a recording about robot waiters. They listen and decide if each of the sentences is true or false.

- Play the recording at least twice. Then check answers as a class.

Audioscript: Track 75

See Learner's Book page 148.

Robots are already a big part of the food industry. Robots make food in factories. In many restaurants, robots help to make food in the kitchen. In many restaurants in China, robots are now waiters.

The robots aren't all the same. In some restaurants, you order your food on a tablet and a robot waiter brings you your food. These robots can't talk or listen. But in other restaurants, the robot waiters are more advanced. They can actually talk, listen, take your order and bring you your food. You can also pay the robots with your credit card.

Answers
a true, b true, c false, d true, e true

Language detective (10–15 minutes)

- Focus on the explanation of countable and uncountable nouns, and the examples. Give some more examples and extend the explanation if necessary, for instance to outline what determiners we can and can't use.

- Elicit examples from learners.

> **Digital Classroom:** Use the grammar presentation 'Quantifiers' to revise quantifiers with countable and uncountable nouns. The i button will explain how to use the grammar presentation.

3 Say which words are countable and uncountable (10–20 minutes)

- Focus on the words and explain that some are countable nouns and some are uncountable.

- Ask learners to classify them. When they have finished, ask each learner to pair up with a partner and compare their tables. Have them discuss any differences.

- Copy the table on the board and ask learners to fill it in. Then elicit more examples of each group, for example materials, and add them to the table.

Answers
Countable nouns: sandwiches, grapes, chips, pizzas, biscuits.
Uncountable nouns: juice, chocolate, soup, bread, water, milk, pasta

4 Talk: Practise asking for foods (10–20 minutes)

- Look at the pictures and ask learners to identify the foods.

- Divide the class into pairs or small groups. Explain that they are going to role play ordering food in a restaurant, using the sentence and question openers to ask for foods. Learners can take it in turns to be the waiter.

> **Differentiation ideas:** With less confident groups, you may wish to model the activity with volunteers. Learners can also write their lines before acting out. More confident learners may add more food items and include more exchanges, for example the waiter may come back and ask: *Is everything all right, sir/madam? Could you bring me some more (water), please?*

Answers
Learners practise conversations asking for foods.

5 Look at this menu from a robot restaurant (5–15 minutes)

- Ask the class to look at the menu. Tell them that they are going to listen to three children ordering food. They listen and tick the items as they hear them.

- Play the recording twice. Then elicit answers from the class.

> **Differentiation ideas:** As an extension task and to give extra practice on countable and uncountable nouns, you may ask less confident learners to listen again and note down the food items the children ordered. Then ask questions, such as: *Did they have any soup? How much water did they have?* More confident learners can make a summary of the dialogue.

Audioscript: Track 76

See Learner's Book page 149.

Robot: Beep. Can I take your order?

Child: Yes. Do you have any soup?

Robot: Beep. Let me check … beep … beep. We don't have much soup. Would you like some salad?

Child:	No, thank you. Can we have pasta and some bread?
Robot:	Pasta and bread ... beep ... Would you like any chips with that?
Child:	No, thank you.
Robot:	Beep ... A little water?
Child:	Yes, some water, please.
Robot:	Any biscuits for dessert?
Child:	No biscuits, thanks ... but do you have any ice cream?
Robot:	Beep ... yes ... we have a lot of ice cream: chocolate, vanilla, strawberry, mango ...
Child:	Some chocolate ice cream, please.
Robot:	Is that everything?
Child:	Yes, thank you.
Robot:	Beep ... Thank you for your order. Beep ... beep ...

Answers

Learners tick the expressions as they hear them.

6 Act it out! (10–20 minutes)

*   Divide the class into pairs and ask learners to role play ordering a meal from a robot waiter.

*   Ask learners to write their own menu and then use the expressions to order.

*   Once pairs have practised their exchanges, choose some to act it out for the class.

> **Differentiation ideas:** Less confident learners may use the menu in Activity 5. They can also write the dialogue in full before acting it out. Having a written script might help them be more confident. Encourage more confident learners to add more foods to their menus and to use more complex vocabulary in their exchanges.

> **Assessment ideas:** You could ask pairs to record themselves, or you may record them while working. When they have finished the activity, they can watch the recording and discuss how they could improve their performance, what could have been done differently or the mistakes they may have made. If they wish, they can role play the situation again with improvements.

Answers

Learners act out ordering from the menu.

7 Talk (10–15 minutes)

*   Focus on the activity. Ask learners to work in pairs or small groups and make a list of the technology they use every day.

*   Tell them to look at the Technology section of the Picture dictionary, on page 170 of the Learner's Book, for more ideas.

> **Critical thinking opportunity:** You may extend the conversation by asking learners to discuss how much time they spend using the technology and how frequently they use it. Could they do the same things without that technology? Has this technology helped them in any way? How? When they have finished, ask them to share their impressions with the class. Do they all perceive technology in the same way? Are there any differences?

Answers

Learner's own answers.

Workbook

Learners do Activities 1–4 on pages 108–109.

Plenary ideas

Consolidation (10–15 minutes)

*   Hand out copies of **Photocopiable 48** and ask learners to write about their robot restaurant.

> **Assessment ideas:** Do this activity as Think-Pair-Share. Ask the class to think of one thing that has stuck with them today. What information do they think they will remember or use in the coming weeks/months? How will they apply the new knowledge in their daily lives? Allow some minutes for personal reflection, then have learners pair up with a partner and discuss their ideas. Share responses as a class. Learners can then write their ideas in their learning log.

Homework ideas

*   Learners design their own waiter robot and write a few lines about what it can do.

*   **Home–school link:** Learners can role play the restaurant situation with their family.

9.4 Write about it: Instructions for robots

LEARNING PLAN

Learning objectives	Learning intentions	Success criteria
3Sc.02, 3Sc.04, 3Sc.05	• **Speaking:** Discuss tasks robots can do; give instructions; describe what robots can do; use sequencing words to order instructions; listen to and understand instructions.	• Learners can read and understand instructions.
3Rd.01	• **Reading:** Read and understand instructions.	• Learners can listen to and understand instructions.
3Wc.01, 3Wca.04	• **Writing:** Draw and write about your own robot; write instructions for robots; use sequencing words correctly.	• Learners can write instructions for robots.
	• **Language focus:** sequencing words: *first, next, then, finally*	• Learners can use sequencing words correctly.
		• Learners can give and carry out instructions.

21st-century skills

Critical thinking opportunity: Explain why things happened.

Collaboration: Acknowledge the usefulness of the different views of others in achieving the task.

Materials: Learner's Book pages 150–151; Workbook pages 110–111; sheets of paper; Sample answer for Unit 9; Photocopiable 1, 2, 49

Starter ideas

Robots galore (15–25 minutes)

- If learners have done the homework activity from the previous lesson, ask them to show their pictures and explain what their robots can do. Display the pictures around the class. You could also take photos of the pictures and upload them to the class blog.

- Divide the class into groups and give each group a sheet of paper. Each group chooses five words from Unit 9 Lessons 1–3 and writes three definitions for each – where only one definition is correct. When groups have finished, ask them to read the words and the definitions. The rest of the class guesses which is the correct definition. The group with the most correct guesses is the winner.

Main teaching ideas

1 Talk and write (5–10 minutes)

- Ask learners to imagine that they have their own personal robot. They are going to write about what their robot can do.

- In pairs, ask learners to brainstorm a list of tasks they would ask their personal robot to do.

- Tell them to make notes using the examples in the Learner's Book as a model.

Answers

Learner's own answers. For example, take clean clothes from the laundry basket.

2 Read Ali's instructions (15–20 minutes)

- Explain that robots follow the instructions we give them, so it is essential that we give robots very precise instructions. Robots cannot decide if something is missing from the instructions or if the instructions are wrong, because they are machines and not humans.

- Ask learners to pretend that you (the teacher) are a robot and to give you the instructions for making a sandwich. You follow the instructions – it is quite likely that instructions will be too general, and this will give you the opportunity to do crazy things! You may wish to watch a video on YouTube where children program their teacher to be a robot.

- Ask learners to look at the instructions that Ali has created for his personal robot. Ask: *Has he included all of the steps?* You may ask learners to work in pairs. One of them reads the instructions and the other carries them out.

> Critical thinking opportunity: Ask learners what problems the 'robot' had in carrying out the instructions. What was missing? What mistakes did the 'robot' make? Encourage learners to say how they would need to improve the instructions.

- Draw learners' attention to the words at the beginning of each entry and explain that they shows the ordering of the instructions – 'First', 'Then', 'Next' and 'Finally'.

Workbook

Learners do Activities 1 and 2 on page 110.

---

3 Write, and Language focus (45–60 minutes)

- Tell learners that they are going to write instructions for their own personal robot to follow, to do one of the tasks they have listed.

- **Step 1:** Ask learners to look again at the list of tasks they wrote for their personal robot and to choose one. Then ask them to think about the different instructions that their robot will need to follow to do the task. Ask learners to write notes for these instructions.

  Tell learners to remember to use words like *First, Next, Then* and *Finally* to make the order of the instructions very clear.

When they have finished, ask learners to read their notes over carefully and make any changes or additions.

- **Step 2:** Tell learners that they are now going to choose a name for their robot and draw a picture of it. Learners work independently and write their instructions in full using their notes. Explain that they need to make each instruction as clear and simple as possible, and check they are in the correct order.

- **Language focus:** Focus on the sequencing words. Ask learners to use them to order the instructions. Ask learners to read Ali's example and see how he uses these words. You may also give an example yourself and ask learners to give their own.

- **Step 3:** When they have finished, ask learners to read the sentences aloud. They use the bulleted questions in the Learner's Book to check that their instructions are clear and accurate.

- **Step 4:** Focus on the checklist and read it with the class. Ask learners to use it and their Writer's checklist (**Photocopiable 1**) to check their work.

  Distribute copies of **Photocopiable 2**. Have learners exchange their work with a partner and review their partner's work, using the Peer editing checklist.

  When learners have finished their revisions, tell them to write the final draft of their instructions on **Photocopiable 49**.

- See the **Sample answer for Unit 9** for an example answer to this writing task.

Answers

Learners plan, write and check their robot instructions.

> Digital Classroom: Use the activity 'How to make an omelette' to reinforce process and instructions. The i button will explain how to use the activity.

4 Role play (10–20 minutes)

- When learners have finished checking their instructions, divide the class into pairs.

- They read out the instructions and the partner acts them out as if they were the robot. Ask them to assess if the instructions work. Can the robot complete the task? If not, what is missing?

- Learners make any necessary adjustments and try again until the instructions are accurate enough.

> **Assessment ideas:** You could ask learners to record themselves while they are doing the role play. Then they watch the recording and evaluate how well the instructions worked and what they need to adjust, if anything at all.

Workbook

Learners do Activity 3 on page 111.

Plenary ideas

Consolidation (10–20 minutes)

> **Assessment ideas:** Learners may take turns reading their instructions to the class. The class carries out the instructions and then comments on how accurate they were. Did they have any difficulty carrying them out? Would they improve the instructions in some way?

Homework ideas

- Learners write about what their family would like their personal robot to do for them.

- **Home–school link:** Learners read the instructions to their family and have them act them out as though they were the robots. They can also ask family members to imagine they had a personal robot too. What would their robot do for them?

9.5 Read and respond: Zaydor

LEARNING PLAN

Learning objectives	Learning intentions	Success criteria
3Sor.01, 3Sor.02	• **Speaking:** Discuss characters; discuss what happens in a story; talk about how technology can help people who are sick; discuss and plan a story.	• Learners can read and understand a story about a robot.
3Rd.01, 3Ro.01	• **Reading:** Read a story about a robot that is badly behaved; understand the meaning of unknown words and expressions.	• Learners can talk about how technology can help people who are sick.
3.Wc.02	• **Writing:** Write short sentences to describe the characters in the story.	• Learners can understand the meaning of unknown words and expressions.
3Uv.07	• **Language focus:** Common adverbs of sequence	• Learners can write notes.
	• **Vocabulary:** *puff, replace, acceptable, malfunction, trip, pick on, bully, exception*	

21st-century skills

Critical thinking opportunity: Make predictions and estimations from given information; describe consequences of different potential actions of characters in a story.

Values: Consider why some people do bad things.

Materials: Learner's Book pages 152–155; Workbook pages 112–113; file cards or large sticky notes; dictionaries

Starter ideas

Robot stories (10–15 minutes)

- Ask the class if they have read any stories about robots. What kind of stories were they – were they sad, funny, exciting? Elicit answers from the class and invite volunteers to tell the class about them.

- If they have not read any stories about robots, you could look for extracts or summaries of age-appropriate stories and share them with the class. You could also find some examples on suitable websites such as Fatherly, BBC Learning English or Puzzling Posts. Ask learners which stories they would like to read and why.

Main teaching ideas

1 Read and listen (10–30 minutes)

- Tell the class that they are going to read part of a story about a particular kind of robot who goes to school.

- Focus on the introductory lines. Ask learners to point to Sammy, Zayne and Damon in the pictures.

- Then ask the class to listen to and read the story.

- Play the recording. Learners listen and follow in their books.

  > Differentiation ideas: With less confident learners, you may wish to stop the recording at certain points and ask a few comprehension questions, such as: *Where does Zayne go? What is Zaydor doing in the classroom? What does Sammy do?* More confident learners could write one or two sentences to summarise each of these sections.

CROSS-CURRICULAR LINK

Health

In the story, Zayne has a problem with his health so he can't be in school. You could sensitively discuss times when people might not be able to go to school or work because of illness. Discuss ways learners can try to stay healthy: washing their hands frequently, eating healthily and exercising regularly.

Audioscript: Track 77

See Learner's Book pages 152–154.

Answers
Learner's own answers.

---

2 Match the words to the meanings (10–15 minutes)

- Ask learners to find the words and expressions in blue in the text.

- Then ask them to read each sentence that has a blue word in, and have them match each word or expression to its meaning.

- When they have finished, check answers as a class.

- There may be other words that are unfamiliar to learners. Ask them to re-read the text and underline them. With a partner, have them discuss their meaning and then check answers as a class.

Answers
puff: to breathe quickly and heavily
replace: to be or do something instead of another
acceptable: all right
malfunction: not working correctly
trip: to fall over something
pick on: to tease or treat someone badly
bully: a person who behaves badly towards smaller or disadvantaged people
exception: not the rule

---

3 Write about characters (10–20 minutes)

- Explain to the class that the text gives lots of clues about the different characters. Ask learners to re-read the extract to find out about each of the characters, and make notes about the information they read.

- When they have finished, learners compare notes with a partner and discuss any differences.

- After a few minutes, draw the table from the Learner's Book on the board and ask volunteers to fill in the information. Have they all come up with the same information? Encourage learners to explain where in the text they found the information.

Answers
Learner's own answers.

> **Digital Classroom:** Use the activity 'Robot revolution' to reinforce comprehension of the text. The i button will explain how to use the activity.

4 Talk: Retell the story (10–15 minutes)

- Remind the class of the sequencing words they used in Lesson 9.4.
- Ask learners to work in pairs. They retell the *Zaydor* story using their own words and the sequencing words.

> **Assessment ideas:** Circulate, listening to learners' interactions and focusing on the use of the sequencers. Make notes of mistakes for remedial work.

> **Differentiation ideas:** Less confident learners may re-read the story once again before attempting the retelling. They could also make a few notes to help them remember.

Answers
Learner's own answers.

5 Values: Understanding people (10–20 minutes)

- Ask the class what Sammy finds out. How does Sammy help Zayne? Why is Zaydor's behaviour excellent at the end?
- Ask learners to talk about these questions with their partner.
- Tell the class that sometimes it's important to understand why people do bad things. Explain that Zayne was making Zaydor do bad things because he was feeling lonely, bored and scared in hospital. When Sammy understood this, he could help Zayne and Zaydor to do good things.
- In pairs, ask learners to discuss what they might say or do when they are feeling lonely, bored or scared.
- Sensitively discuss why people might do bad things, and how you might help them change their behaviour. For example, you could ask: *Why might someone be a bully? Do you think a bully is a happy person? How can you help them change their behaviour?*

Answers
Learner's own answers.

CROSS-CURRICULAR LINK

Science and technology
Discuss with the class how technology helps people with their health, and how it may help them in the future, for example digital apps that monitor blood pressure or sugar levels, wearable technology such as watches with sensors, etc. You may also direct learners to suitable websites such as MIT news, where they can learn about new robots that can help patients at home, assist surgeries, do chores in hospitals, etc.

6 Predict: Read the end of the story (20–45 minutes)

- Ask the class to read the last two paragraphs of the text. What do they think will happen next? Elicit a few ideas with the class.
- Ask learners to work in pairs and make a list of things that could happen afterwards. Have them pick the funniest and write the second part of this story; for example, Zaydor actually malfunctions after accidentally drinking orange juice.

> **Differentiation ideas:** Allow pairs to choose how they are going to work on the story, for example they can write it, draw a comic strip with speech bubbles, look for pictures and create a slideshow, or write a script and act it out afterwards.

> **Assessment ideas:** When they have finished, ask pairs to check their spelling, punctuation and use of sequencers. They can exchange their story with another pair and offer feedback. When they get their story back, they read the feedback and make changes if necessary.

- Finally, pairs can read or present their story to the class. They can then vote for the funniest. You could upload the winning story to the class blog.

Answers
Learner's own answers.

> **Workbook**
>
> Learners do Activities 1–6 on pages 112–113.

Plenary ideas

Consolidation (15–20 minutes)

> **Assessment ideas: Exit tickets:** Give each learner a file card or a large sticky note, and ask them to write:

* one thing they have learned in this lesson

* one thing they can use in another context, for example another subject class, at home, etc.

* one question they still have in mind.

When they have finished, ask them to share their ideas with the class. Can other learners give an answer to their lingering question?

Homework ideas

* Ask learners to look for information about a technology that can help people who are unwell. They can look up information in books or newspapers or on the internet, and write a few lines. They can also add a picture.

* **Home–school link:** Learners tell the story to their family and ask them how they think the story will continue. Then they can read their story ending to their family.

9.6 Project challenge

LEARNING PLAN

Learning objectives	Learning intentions	Success criteria
3Sc.06, 3Sc.07	• **Speaking:** Discuss a project; discuss steps of a project; organise work; present their project to the class; explain what a robot is used for.	• Learners can read and understand instructions.
3Rd.02	• **Reading:** Read and understand instructions.	• Learners can give instructions.
3Wca.02, 3Wca.03	• **Writing:** Write sentences; use correct grammar and spelling; use correct punctuation; write a song.	• Learners can plan a project.
	• **Language focus:** Unit 9 review	• Learners can build a robot and explain what they can use it for.
	• **Vocabulary:** Unit 9 review	• Learners can write a new robot song.

21st-century skills

Creative thinking: Design new items based on a model.

Collaboration: Respect the importance of doing a fair share of group work; keep to the instructions to complete the task; invite others to give their opinions during the task.

Communication: Share ideas with a peer in order to improve the quality of their work.

Materials: Learner's Book pages 156–157; Workbook pages 114–115; Project A: modelling materials such as Lego™ blocks, building materials, small boxes in different sizes or plastic bottles, glue, staples, plastic wheels, plastic eyes, aluminium foil, acrylic paint, brushes; Project B: drawing materials, sheets of paper, recording of *Rock the robot* (audio track 71); **Photocopiable 1, 50, 51**; End of Unit test 9; Progress test 3; **Differentiated worksheets 9A, B and C**

Starter ideas

Looking back (15–20 minutes)

- Ask the class to choose a lesson from this unit they liked a lot. Ask them to explain why they liked it and to make a short summary.

- As a class, sing *Rock the robot* from Lesson 9.1 (audio track 71 on Learner's Book page 143) and invite learners to recite the poem of the misbehaving robot (on Learner's Book page 145).

> **Assessment ideas:** Divide the class into two teams and play Definition Bingo to revise new vocabulary and useful phrases. This game will give you the opportunity to assess how much vocabulary learners remember from previous lessons. Definition Bingo is played like normal Bingo, but using definitions instead of words. Choose words from this unit that you would like to revise. Write definitions for these words on slips of paper and put them in a box or a bag. Write the words on the board. Learners draw a six-square grid, choose six words from the list and write them in their grid. Pull the slips of paper out of the box one at a time and read the definition. Learners cross out the corresponding word. The first one to complete a line or the whole card calls out *Bingo*!

Main teaching ideas

Learners choose an end-of-unit project to work on. Look at the examples in the pictures and help learners to choose. Provide materials.

Project A: Design a robot for a specific purpose (60–90 minutes)

- Ask learners to work with a partner to design their own robot. Distribute copies of **Photocopiable 50**.

- Tell pairs to think about a person or a situation where a robot could make life much better. Have them make notes of their ideas. Then ask them to define what their robot will do and how it will do it. Encourage them to include different features.

- Ask pairs to discuss and agree on how their robot will look and then draw a picture or make a model of it. If they decide to make a model, supply materials. You could also show them suitable websites from which they can get ideas, such as Makeblock, Research Parent or Pinterest.

- When they have finished, ask learners to present their robot to the class. They should explain what it can do and why. Learners could write a few notes to help them during the presentation.

- **Writing tip:** Before presenting their project, ask learners to practise talking about their robot with their partner. They can record themselves doing this, then watch the recording and help each other fix any mistakes.

> **Assessment ideas:** You may wish to video-record groups as they work, so that they can then use copies of the recordings to assess what they have done and how they have worked. The copies can then be shared with the family and filed in their portfolios.

Project B: Write a robot song and dance (60–90 minutes)

- Ask learners to work with a partner. They are going to make their own song, or change the song from the unit opener. They can use the background music if they want to change the opener song – you may wish to play the song again so that they remember the tune.

- In pairs, ask learners to write out the words to the song and decide the actions they need to include with the song.

- When learners have finished writing the song, ask them to get their Writer's checklist (**Photocopiable 1**) and use it to check their work.

- When they have finished, they practise the song with their partner and make new actions to go with the words.

- Finally, pairs teach their robot song and the actions to the class.

> **Assessment ideas:** You may wish to video-record groups as they work, so that they can then use copies of the recordings to assess what they have done and how they have worked. The copies can then be shared with the family and filed in their portfolios.

> **Assessment ideas:** When learners have finished their projects, give them a copy of **Photocopiable 51** and read the information as a class. Ask them to work independently and think about their work on their project. They reflect and answer the questions. Ask them to tick off the aims they have achieved. Insist on the importance of giving honest answers.

> **Workbook**
>
> Learners do the Check your progress quiz on pages 114–115.

Plenary ideas

Reflect on your learning (5–10 minutes)

- Draw learners' attention to the 'Reflect on your learning' questions on page 157 of the Learner's Book.

- Learners answer the questions to reflect on their project work.

Consolidation (10–15 minutes)

- Ask learners to reflect on and discuss what they liked most about this unit, and encourage them to explain why. This may also be a good opportunity for them to think about what aspects of the unit they have found most difficult and why.

- You may wish to keep a record of their comments to see how they progress over time.

> **Assessment ideas: Portfolio opportunity:** If you have been filing learners' work for Unit 9, you may find it useful to put all the work of this unit together. You could ask learners to make a cover for their Unit 9 work, decorating it with an image that represents what they have learned.

Homework ideas

- Learners draw a picture of what they have liked most about this unit.

- **Home–school link:** Learners show their family their projects.

- Hand out copies of **Differentiated worksheets 9A, B and C** depending on each learner's ability, and ask them to complete the activities at home.

9.7 What do you know now?

How can robots help us? (30–40 minutes)

- Learners work in pairs. They work together through all the tasks set in this section.

- They write the answers in their notebooks. You may ask them to have a special section in their notebooks where they record the answers.

- Whenever their opinion is requested, encourage them to be honest in their answers.

Answers

1–4 Learner's own answers.

Look what I can do! (15 minutes)

- Review the five *I can …* statements on page 158 of the Learner's Book. Learners demonstrate what they can do.

- Learners colour in the faces to show which things they can do.

- Encourage them to be honest in their answers.

> **Workbook**
>
> Learners answer the Reflection questions on page 115.

Check your progress 3

Starter ideas

Revision of vocabulary

- **Materials:** two chairs

- Play a game to revise the verbs and language of instructions of Units 7–9

- **Charades:** Place two chairs at the front of the class with the back to the board. Divide the class into two teams. One player from each team comes to the front, and sits facing their team with their back to the board.

  Write a word from Units 7–9 on the board. The learners in each team mime the word – they cannot speak, spell the word in the air or use sign language. The two learners sitting at the front try to guess the word that their peers are miming. The first one to guess correctly scores a point for their team. That player changes places with another learner in their team. The other team has to keep the same player in the seat until he or she is first to answer correctly. The team with the most points is the winner.

Main teaching ideas

Colour the rainbow (for 2–4 players)

- **Materials:** buttons, paper clips, coins, etc., for each player; crayons or coloured pencils; a piece of paper per player (for learners to cut out nine squares of paper); a copy of **Photocopiable 52**, the Rainbow score card, for each player

- **How to play:** Learners play in pairs or groups of four. Each learner cuts out nine squares of paper and writes '1' on three of the squares, '2' on three of the squares and '3' on the three remaining squares. They then put all the number cards face down on the table. Each learner places their game marker on any space of the circle game track. With the class, read through the rules of the game. Model and explain if necessary. Learners will travel around the circle several times. Each time a player lands on a new colour, he or she colours in that arc of the rainbow on their Rainbow score card. If they land on the same space twice, they can't repeat what they said last time. They have to come up with something different. The first player to colour in all five colours of the rainbow is the winner.

1 Tic-tac-toe code

- **How to play:** Remind the class of the codes they read about in Unit 7. Tell the class to work in pairs. Focus on how to write 'boot' in the new code (see Learner's Book page 160). Then focus on the codes. In order to write a letter, learners have to find the letter in the pictures. They draw the part of the picture that has that letter in it. If there is a dot, they have to draw the dot, too. Then they write a message to their partner in tic-tac-toe code. When they have finished, learners could challenge other pairs to decode their messages.

2 Exercise game

- **Materials:** pieces of paper; a bag for each pair

- **How to play:** Remind learners of the parts of the body they learned about in Unit 8. Have learners work in pairs. Each learner writes the name of a part of the body on a piece of paper. They put the pieces of paper in a bag, and take it in turns to pull a piece of paper from the bag. They make up an exercise for that part of the body, and then teach their exercise to the class.

3 Robot power

- **Use of English:** future with *will*

- **How to play:** Remind learners of what they learned about robots in Unit 9. Ask learners to think about the different kinds of robots, and write three sentences about things robots can do. Then they write three sentences about what they think robots will do in the future. When they have finished, ask learners to share their sentences with the class.

4 Rebus spelling puzzle

- **How to play:** Ask learners to decode the message in the Learner's Book (page 160). Have them follow the instructions. To figure out the secret message, learners spell the picture words and subtract the letters. The remaining letters will spell a word. What's the message? (Well done!)

Acknowledgements

The authors and publishers acknowledge the following sources of copyright material and are grateful for the permissions granted. While every effort has been made, it has not always been possible to identify the sources of all the material used, or to trace all copyright holders. If any omissions are brought to our notice, we will be happy to include the appropriate acknowledgements on reprinting.

Excerpts from the Approaches to learning and teaching series, courtesy of Cambridge University Press and Cambridge Assessment International Education: cambridge.org/approachestolearning

Unit 1: 'Rope Rhyme' from *Honey, I Love* by Eloise Greenfield, illustarted by Jan Spivey Gilchrist. Text copyright © 1978 by Eloise Greenfield, used by permission of HarperCollins Publishers USA; **Unit 2:** (song) *Families All Over The World* by Pam Donkin, © 2006 Pam Donkin. Used with permission. All rights reserved; **Unit 4:** 'Grayish, Greenish' by David M. Schwartz and Yael Schy from *Where in the wild? Camouflaged creatures concealed* by David M. Schwarz and Yael Schy, text copyright 2007 by David M. Schwarz and Yael Schy. Used by permission of Tricycle Press, an imprint of Random House LLC; **Unit 5:** (song) 'Imagination' by The Singing Lizard, used with the permission; 'The Engineer' copyright © 2014 by Stephanie Calmenson. Reprinted by permission of Writers House LLC acting as agent for the author; 'Jenny, Lenny and Jumperoo' by Kathryn Harper; **Unit 6:** (song) 'Fossils' by Wee Sing and Learn Dinosaurs by Pamela Conn Beall and Susan Hagen Nipp © 2001. Used by permission; 'Unfortunately' by Bobbi Katz. Copyright 1986, renewed 2001, used with the author's permission; Paintings "Darwin (Science and Religion)" 2009, "Shevchenko" (2009) by Oleg Shupliak, used with kind permission; **Unit 7:** Excerpt from *Have You Ever Done That?* by Julie Larios. Text copyright © 2001 by Julie Larios. Published by Font Street Books, an imprint of Boyd Mill Press & Kane, a division of Astra Publishing House. Reprinted with permission; **Unit 9:** 'My Robot's Misbehaving' by Kenn Nesbitt from *My Hippo has the Hiccups* copyright © 2009 by Kenn Nesbitt. Used with the permission of Sourcebooks.

Thanks to the following for permission to reproduce images:

Cover image by Pablo Gallego (Beehive Illustration); Photocopiable 32 Snowshill/Getty Images; Worksheet 3 Meet Poddar/Shutterstock

Index of photocopiables

The following photocopiables can be downloaded from Cambridge GO.

1   Writer's checklist (multiuse)

2   Peer editing checklist (multiuse)

3   K-W-L chart (multiuse)

4   Sing along! *Working together* (Unit 1, Lesson 1)

5   Make a chatterbox (Unit 1, Lesson 2)

6   Writing lesson template (Unit 1, Lesson 4)

7   Unit 1 reflection and self-assessment (Unit 1, Lesson 6)

8   Sing along! *Families all over the world* (Unit 2, Lesson 1)

9   Linked paper hearts (Unit 2, Lesson 1)

10   Writing lesson template (Unit 2, Lesson 4)

11   *This is my brother's …* (Unit 2, Lesson 5)

12   Pop-up birthday card template (Unit 2, Lesson 6)

13   Unit 2 reflection and self-assessment (Unit 2, Lesson 6)

14   Unit 2 Birthday graph (Unit 2, Lesson 7)

15   Sing along! *Song of the Shifting Sand* (Unit 3, Lesson 1)

16   *Rattlesnake, Mouse and Clever Coyote* cut-out puppets (Unit 3, Lesson 5)

17   Make a weather chart (Unit 3, Lesson 6, Project B)

18   Unit 3 reflection and self-assessment (Unit 3, Lesson 6)

19   Making bar graphs (Check your progress 1, Activity 4)

20   Sing along! *Clouds* (Unit 4, Lesson 1)

21   Triangle challenge (Unit 4, Lesson 1)

22   Writing lesson template (Unit 4, Lesson 4)

23   Camouflage animals (Unit 4, Lesson 6)

24   *It can help me …* (Unit 4, Lesson 6)

25   Unit 4 reflection and self-assessment (Unit 4, Lesson 6)

26   Sing along! *Imagination* (Unit 5, Lesson 1)

27   Who invented …? (Unit 5, Lesson 2)

28   Make a helicopter (Unit 5, Lesson 3)

29   Writing lesson template (Unit 5, Lesson 4)

30   Unit 5 reflection and self-assessment (Unit 5, Lesson 6)

31   Sing along! *Fossils* (Unit 6, Lesson 1)

32   Number chart (Unit 6, Lesson 1)

33   Dinosaur hunter (Unit 6, Lesson 2)

34   Writing lesson template (Unit 6, Lesson 4)

35   Unit 6 reflection and self-assessment (Unit 6, Lesson 6)

36   Sing along! *This is the song that never ends* (Unit 7, Lesson 1)

37   Writing lesson template (Unit 7, Lesson 4)

38   Write in invisible ink (Unit 7, Lesson 4)

39   Make your own code (Unit 7, Lesson 6)

40   Unit 7 reflection and self-assessment (Unit 7, Lesson 6)

41   Sing along! *Bones and muscles* (Unit 8, Lesson 1)

42   Make a skeleton (Unit 8, Lesson 1)

43   *I will …* (Unit 8, Lesson 3)

44   Writing lesson template (Unit 8, Lesson 4)

45   Unit 8 reflection and self-assessment (Unit 8, Lesson 6)

46   Sing along! *Rock the robot* (Unit 9, Lesson 1)

47   Find the heaviest, lightest, longest, smallest … (Unit 9, Lesson 1)

Photocopiable 1: Writer's checklist

Aim: To encourage correct use of punctuation and learner autonomy.
Learners use the checklist after completing written work that contains direct speech.
They can use it to check their own work or their partner's work.

Preparation time: 5 minutes

Completion time: 10 minutes

Language focus: Correct punctuation – capital letters, full stops, question marks and exclamation marks

Materials: One copy of Photocopiable 1 for each learner

Procedure:

- When learners have completed a writing task in class, give each learner a copy of Photocopiable 1.

- Ask learners to read their written work and use the checklist to check their work for correct punctuation. Then they make any corrections necessary.

Name _____ Date _____

Photocopiable 1: Writer's checklist

☐ The first word of a sentence begins with a capital letter.

This is a book.

☐ The word *I* is always written with a capital I.

I am a student.

☐ The name of a person, city, country or school begins with a capital letter.

Tanya   Mr Kim   Athens   Korea   International School

☐ The days of the week and the names of the months begin with a capital letter.

Monday   Tuesday   January   February

☐ Most sentences end with a full stop

My name is Tony.

☐ A question ends with a question mark.

What's your name?

☐ A sentence that shows surprise or excitement ends with an exclamation mark.

My name is Tony too!

Photocopiable 2: Peer editing checklist

Aim: To encourage correct use of punctuation and learner autonomy.
Learners use the checklist to check their partner's work after completing written work.

Preparation time: 5 minutes

Completion time: 10 minutes

Language focus: Correct punctuation and grammar.

Materials: One copy of Photocopiable 2 for each learner

Procedure:

- When learners have completed a Lesson 4 writing task or a Lesson 6 writing project, pair them with a partner and give each learner a copy of Photocopiable 2.

- Ask learners to read their partner's written work. They use the checklist to check their partner's work for clarity as well as correct punctuation and grammar.

- Remind learners to be kind and positive when speaking to their partner about their work.

Name _____ Date _____

Photocopiable 2: Peer editing checklist

Writer: _____

Peer editor: _____

Check your partner's writing for these things.

Circle any mistakes.

Tick each box when you are done.

☐   The first word of each sentence begins with a capital letter.

☐   Each sentence ends with a full stop, question mark or exclamation mark.

☐   The writer followed the directions for this writing activity. (If not, talk to the writer.)

☐   I can understand what the writer is saying. (If not, talk to the writer.)

☐   I checked for missing words.

☐   I checked the grammar.

☐   The handwriting is clear and easy to read. (If not, talk to the writer.)

Photocopiable 3: K-W-L chart

Aim: For learners to fill in with information on what they already know prior to the session, what they want to know and finally, what they have learned by the end of the session.

Preparation time: 5 minutes

Completion time: 15 minutes

Language focus: (not applicable)

Materials: One copy of Photocopiable 3 for each learner

Procedure:

- This chart can be used in two sessions. At the beginning of a lesson or unit, learners can think about the knowledge they have on a particular topic and what they would like to learn about this topic. At the end of the lesson or unit, learners can return to the chart to review their entries in the first two columns and then complete the third column with facts they have learned.

- At the beginning of the session, encourage learners to fill in the 'Know' column with things they already know about the topic

- Then ask learners to fill in the 'Want to know' column – ask them to write down some questions that they would like to know the answers to.

- As a class, fill in the 'Learned' column during the plenary at the end of the session. When filling in this column, ask learners to see if any of their questions in the 'Want to know' column have been answered in the session.

Name _____ **Date** _____

Photocopiable 3: K-W-L chart

Topic _____

	K-W-L chart		
Know	Want to know	Learned	

Photocopiable 4: Sing along! *Working together*

Aim: Learners sing along with a song from the Learner's Book (Unit 1, Lesson 1)

Preparation time: 5 minutes

Completion time: 15 minutes

Language focus: Various (singing a song about cooperation and collaboration)

Materials: One copy of Photocopiable 4 for each learner

Procedure:

- Encourage learners to think about cooperation and collaboration, and how working together helps to develop friendship, loyalty and responsibility.

- Tell the class they are going to listen to a song. Distribute the Photocopiable.

- Play the song at least twice. Ask the class what it is about. Elicit answers.

- Play the song again and encourage learners to clap along. You could also add gestures to it, e.g. join hands for *Working together / Helping each other,* mimic *laughing together,* touch your head for *share ideas,* etc.

- Sing the song and encourage learners to join in.

Name _____ **Date** _____

Photocopiable 4: Sing along! *Working together*

Working together, getting better and better

Helping each other as we go along.

Learning together, laughing together,

Planning and building – together we're strong.

We can tidy the room, put on a play,

Build a space station, plan a parade.

We can make the world better, share ideas on the way.

Working, building, learning ... let's start today!

Working together, getting better and better

Helping each other as we go along.

Learning together, laughing together,

Planning and building – together we're strong.

Photocopiable 5: Make a chatterbox

Aim: Learners make and play with a chatterbox as a fun way to give and follow instructions (Unit 1, Lesson 2)

Preparation time: 5 minutes

Completion time: 60–90 minutes

Language focus: Instructions/imperatives

Materials: One copy of Photocopiable 5 for each learner; a pre-made chatterbox to show the class; scissors; writing materials; colouring pencils

Procedure:

- Show the class a chatterbox that you have made earlier as an example. Explain that a chatterbox has lots of different options and instructions for you to follow.

- Read out some example instructions you have written on your chatterbox, and ask the class to do what you say. For example: *Stand on one leg and touch your nose.* Explain that learners will make their own chatterbox and write their own instructions inside.

- Hand out the template and walk through the directions quickly.

- Ask the class if anyone already knows how to make a chatterbox. If so, encourage them to demonstrate for the class. If not, encourage learners to read and follow the directions for themselves. Walk around and offer help as needed, but try to give tips and suggestions rather than instructions.

- Encourage learners to think carefully about the instructions they will write on their chatterbox – they should be fun and challenging (and of course, should be written in English).

- Allow learners some time to play with their chatterboxes in pairs and groups. You might want to use them as warmers or as a fun way to end a lesson.

Name _____ **Date** _____

Photocopiable 5: Make a chatterbox

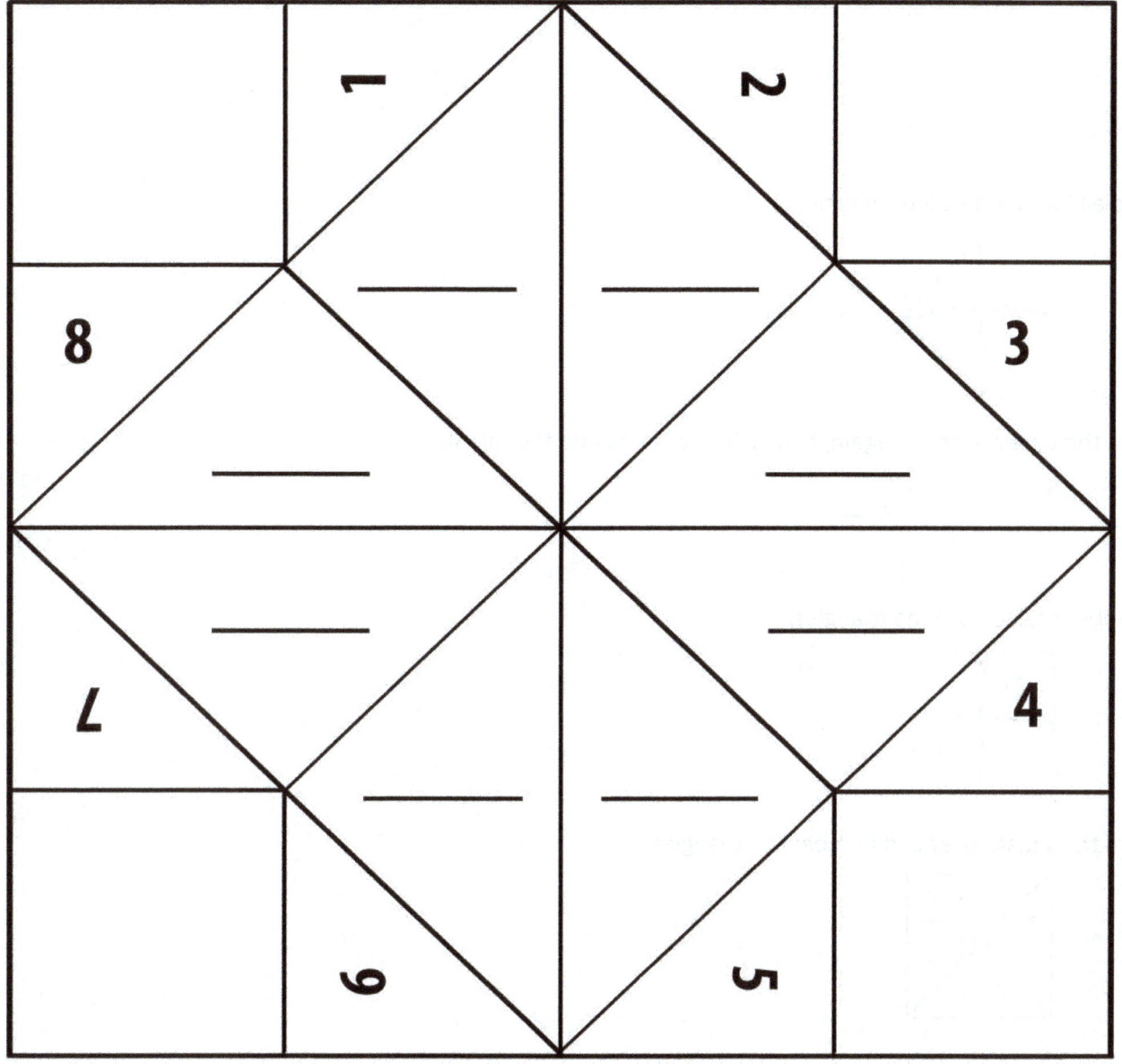

Directions

1   Cut the paper into a square.

2   Fold the paper corner to corner and open.
    Then fold the other corner to the other corner and open.

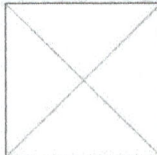

3   Fold all four corners into the middle.

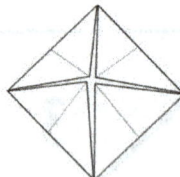

4   Turn the paper over and again, fold all four corners into the middle.

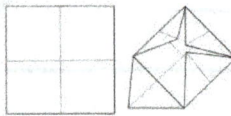

5   Number or decorate the triangles.

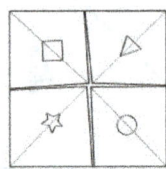

6   Turn the square over and number the triangles.

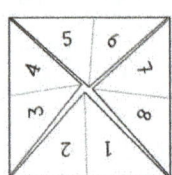

7   Write instructions on the inside of each triangle.

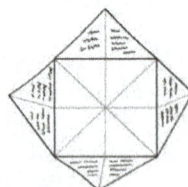

Photocopiable 6: Writing lesson template

> **Aim:** Learners use this as support to complete an activity in the Learner's Book (Unit 1, Lesson 4). They write a paragraph about what they and their partner like doing.
>
> **Preparation time:** 5 minutes
>
> **Completion time:** 60–90 minutes
>
> **Language focus:** *like* + gerund
>
> **Materials:** One copy of Photocopiable 6 for each learner; writing materials

Procedure:

- Tell the class to imagine that they are going to act in a play. They have to decide if they want to be a mammal or a bird. Which mammal or bird would they like to play? Encourage them to explain their choice.

- **Step 1:** Distribute Photocopiable 6. Tell the class that there are many things they can do in a play besides acting. Focus on the table and read the options.

- Divide the class into pairs. Ask learners to think about things they like doing and things they don't like doing. Give examples about yourself, for example *I like singing but I don't like acting.*

- Have learners mark their own answers to the questions in the table. Then they ask their partner the questions and record those answers in the table.

- **Step 2:** Tell learners that they are now going to write some sentences about themselves and their partner using the answers in the table.

- Focus on the highlighted words in the model provided on Learner's Book page 19. Explain the rules of using 'and' and 'or', and give some more examples. Ask learners to give some more examples as well, such as: *I like playing with my friends and reading. I don't like eating soup or getting up early.*

- Learners work independently and write sentences using the information in their table.

- **Step 3:** When they have finished, help learners review the 'Read and revise' questions in the Learner's Book. Ask learners to think of the answers while they are reading their text aloud.

- **Step 4:** Read the 'Check and correct' checklist provided in the Learner Book's with the class. Ask learners if they can think of anything to add to the list, for example checking correct spelling of all words, using *-ing* after *like / don't like*, using *and* and *or* correctly, etc.

- You could give each learner a copy of the Writer's checklist (Photocopiable 1) and Peer editing checklist (Photocopiable 2) and ask them to assess their or their partner's work.

Name _____ Date _____

Photocopiable 6: Writing lesson template

Do you like ...	acting?	making costumes?	singing?	dancing?
My answers	☐ yes ☐ no	☐ yes ☐ no	☐ yes ☐ no	☐ yes ☐ no
My partner's answers	☐ yes ☐ no	☐ yes ☐ no	☐ yes ☐ no	☐ yes ☐ no

Write sentences about what you and your partner like doing.

_____

_____

_____

_____

_____

_____

_____

_____

_____

Photocopiable 7: Unit 1 reflection and self-assessment

Aim: Learners use the checklists as support to reflect on their project work (Unit 1, Lesson 6)

Preparation time: 5 minutes

Completion time: 15 minutes

Language focus: Various

Materials: One copy of Photocopiable 7 for each learner, writing materials

Procedure:

- When learners have finished work on their project, read and discuss the 'Reflect on your learning' questions on Learner Book's page 25 with the class.

- Distribute Photocopiable 7. Ask students to place a tick in front of the project they worked on, Project A or Project B. Explain that they will read and respond to the three items in that column, circling the emoticon that matches their answer.

- Ask learners to independently reflect on their work on the project as they respond to the three statements. Explain the importance of giving honest answers.

- Read the two questions under the chart together. Pause to let learners mark their answers. If you wish, invite volunteers to share their answers.

Name _____ Date _____

End of Unit 1 test

Vocabulary 1

Look at the picture. Choose the correct word for each sentence.
Write the word in the space.

| standing | climbing | kicking | ~~bouncing~~ | measuring | carrying |

Example:

0   A boy is _____*bouncing*_____ a grey ball.

_____

1   A boy is _____ a tree.   [1]

2   Two girls are _____ a table.   [1]

3   A boy is _____ a box.   [1]

4   A small child is _____ on a chair.   [1]

5   A girl is _____ a white and black ball.   [1]

Vocabulary 2

Draw a circle around the correct word.

Example:

0   Don't be (*grumpy*) / *fair* when you lose a match!

---

6   Do you know the *match / rules* of this game?   [1]

7   Can you *win / score* a goal?   [1]

8   Be a good *losing / loser*!   [1]

9   What's the *score / draw* now?   [1]

10   We are on the *winning / winner* team!   [1]

Grammar 1

Write *is*, *Is*, *are* or *Are* in the spaces.

Example:

0   Where _____*is*_____ Harry sitting?

---

11   What _____ Dani and Yolanda doing?   [1]

12   _____ writing a poem easy?   [1]

13   Where _____ they playing football today?   [1]

14   We _____ eating ice cream.   [1]

15   _____ she reading about animals?   [1]

Grammar 2

Choose the correct word for each sentence. Write the correct words in the spaces.

| Where | must | like | ~~How~~ | Who | or |

Example:

0 _____How_____ does the dragon move?

---

16 Is that game easy _____ hard?   [1]

17 _____ has got the ball now?   [1]

18 You _____ not sit on this chair!   [1]

19 _____ are the children going now?   [1]

20 Do you _____ dancing?   [1]

Name _____ **Date** _____

Progress test 1

Vocabulary 1

Draw a circle around the correct word.

Example:

0   Two girls are *skipping /*(*hitting*) a small ball.

---

1   The man is *jumping / standing* on a ladder.   [1]

2   The woman is *carrying / measuring* a box.   [1]

3   Two boys are *stepping / kicking* blue balls.   [1]

4   A boy is *stepping / bouncing* a white ball.   [1]

5   A girl is *holding / skipping* a rope.   [1]

Vocabulary 2

Match the opposites.

Example:

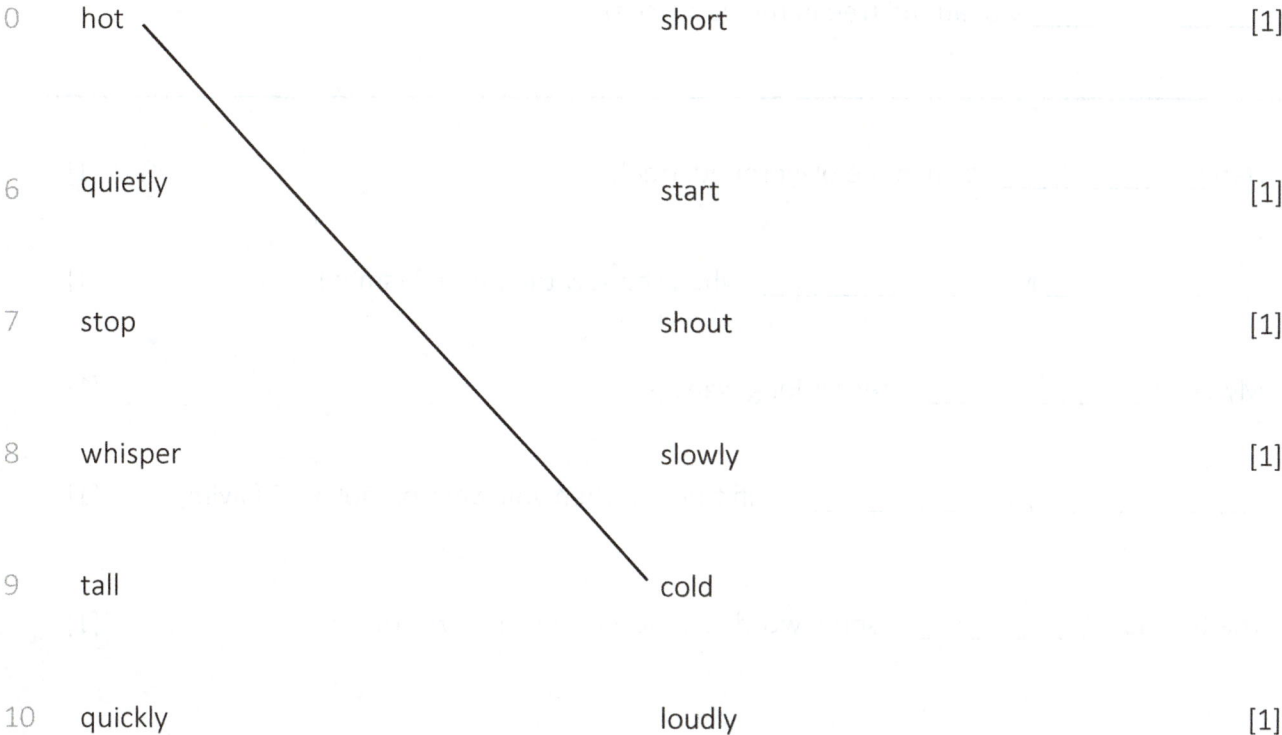

0	hot	short	[1]
6	quietly	start	[1]
7	stop	shout	[1]
8	whisper	slowly	[1]
9	tall	cold	
10	quickly	loudly	[1]

Grammar 1

Complete the sentences using the past simple.

Example:

0   I _____*saw*_____ a beautiful tree in the park. (see)

---

11   Hari _____ cold in the playground. (feel)   [1]

12   _____ Mira _____ when she saw the photo? (smile)   [1]

13   My uncle _____ after his long walk. (rest)   [1]

14   _____ you _____ in the sea when you were on holiday? (swim)   [1]

15   The teacher _____ some words on the whiteboard. (write)   [1]

Grammar 2

Read the text. Choose the right words from the next page and write them on the lines.

My sister's party

Bettina is (0) _____*my*_____ best friend. She is (16) _____ Germany.

She had a big party for her birthday yesterday.

(17) _____, we played games. Then we had some food.

I ate a lot of cake (18) _____ chocolate cake is my favourite! Bettina

(19) _____ very happy at the party. We all gave (20) _____ presents.

Example:

0	me	mine	my	

16	of	from	to	[1]
17	Next	Finally	First	[1]
18	because	or	by	[1]
19	was	were	is	[1]
20	him	her	them	[1]

Reading 1

Read the story. Write some words from the story to complete the sentences.
You can use one, two or three words.

Artur's happy memory

My name's Artur. My family and I have a small house with a garden. I have only one cousin.
His name's Otto. He's a really kind person and he likes helping people.

I remember one day when I was five years old. Otto came round to visit but I wasn't happy.
I wanted to climb the tree in the garden, but I couldn't. I tried and tried, but the tree
was too big. So I was really cross.

Otto smiled when he saw me and said, 'Don't be upset, I know how you can get up into the tree!
Do you really want to do it?'

'Yes, I do!' I shouted.

'OK,' said Otto, 'I have a good idea! Can you stand on my shoulders if I hold your legs?'

'Yes, I can!' I shouted.

So Otto helped me to get into the tree and sit on a branch. Then he climbed into the tree
with me, and sat on a branch too.

When my parents saw us both in the tree, they laughed and took a photo.

Otto said, 'You will soon grow big and tall like me and you will climb lots of trees!'

Example:

0   Artur lives in a ___*small house*___ with his family.

---

21   Otto is Artur's _____.   [1]

22   Otto _____ because he is very kind.   [1]

23   Artur was cross because he couldn't _____ in his garden.   [1]

24   But Artur could _____ Otto's shoulders and then he
      could sit on a branch.   [1]

25   Artur's _____ laughed and took a photo when
      they saw Artur and Otto in the tree.   [1]

Reading 2

Read to find the answers to the questions.

The thorny devil lizard
Thorny devil lizards live in deserts in Australia. They can't get water to drink with their mouths. They use their feet and their skin instead!
There isn't much water in the desert, but the sand is a little bit wet in the evening and in the morning. Thorny devil lizards can stand in the wettest sand and put some of the wet sand on their backs, too. The water goes through the lizards' feet and skin to their mouths and then the lizards can drink.
Some other animals can hold water in their skins, but they can't move water through their skin to their mouths. So the thorny devil lizard is very special!

Example:

0   Where do thorny devil lizards live?

_____ *in deserts in Australia* _____

---

26   Can thorny devil lizards get water to drink with their mouths?

_____   [1]

27   What parts of their bodies do they get water with?

_____   [1]

28   When is the sand wet in the desert?

_____   [1]

29   Where do thorny devil lizards put sand?

_____   [1]

30   Can other animals move water through their skin to their mouths?

_____   [1]

Writing

Answer the questions about yourself. Write sentences.

Example:

0   What do you like doing?

_____*I like playing with my friends and eating ice cream.*_____

_____

31   Which is your favourite month?

_____

_____   [1]

32   What are you wearing today?

_____

_____   [1]

33   What do you know about plants in deserts?

_____

_____   [1]

34   Who is your favourite character in a book?

_____

_____   [1]

35   What couldn't you do when you were a baby?

_____

_____   [1]

Writing

Answer the questions about yourself. Write sentences.

Example:

What do you like doing?

_____

_____

What is your favourite sport?

[1]

What are you wearing today?

Where did you go last night?

What is your favourite place in your home?

[1]

What couldn't you do when you were a baby?

[1]